Praise for *Sanskrit Non-Translatables*

"This book takes the battle for Sanskrit into the territory of the English-speaking public. It makes a convincing case that English is deficient in its ability to express the profound meanings of the shastras for which Sanskrit words are necessary. By following the authors' advice, English will become enriched with key Sanskrit terms that are non-translatable. As English has assimilated non-translatable terms from virtually all major world languages, and takes pride in doing so, there is no reason why it should hesitate to do so for Sanskrit, a Classical language very much alive today. I congratulate the authors for their innovative thinking and bold initiative."

– Swami Govindadev Giri,
Trustee and Treasurer, Shri Ram Janmbhoomi Teerth Kshetra

"As an avid student of Rajiv Malhotra's combative intellectual journey, I was anticipating this book. In the characteristic Indian Dharma Rakshak Parampara - defending Indian civilization over millennia by both shastra and shaastra - in the lineage of shaastra exegetes such as Yaska, Adi Shankara, Guru Gorakhnath, Ramanujacarya, Hemacandracarya, Gyaneshwar, the Sikh Gurus, Sri Aurobindo and Swami Vivekananda, Rajiv Malhotra is a one-man army to take on Western thought. After the 19th century honeymoon with Sanskrit-Hindu intellectual heritage, Western thought has had the political agenda of subverting Hinduism and Hindu culture by the Macaulayised assault on its texts and thoughts. Like a seasoned strategist, Malhotra began from the outer circle and has moved into the conceptual *garbhagrha* of the Western methodology with this book, *Sanskrit Non-Translatables*. This comes after his earlier works articulating the Hindu Civilization as the alternative (*Being Different*), exposing the adversary's agenda of fracturing this alternative (*Breaking India*), counterpoising it with Hinduism's deep conceptual integrity (*Indra's Net*), dispossessing the adversary of the 'weapon' they had tried to appropriate (*The Battle for Sanskrit*) and now the heart of the matter – the counterattack on the studied subversion of the conceptual frame of Hindu civilizational thought by 'Christianising' the core categories through motivated interpretive translations. This book takes fifty-four indisputably foundational concepts, arranges them in a fourfold typology that moves from *terra firma* to *terra cognita* to the cosmos, and contests the irrationality, the untenability and the 'design' of their widely employed English equivalents. The demolition of this conceptual subversion sets free the autonomy of the Indian thought and mind. With its well-thought out prefatory essays, this is a book that every English-educated Indian must read to further 'decolonise' his mind and stand up to the hegemony of Western thought."

– Dr. Kapil Kapoor,
Chairman, Indian Institute of Advanced Study, Shimla

"Rajiv Malhotra carries his battle for Sanskrit a step further in this book. Short of having Sanskrit itself as the language of pan-Indian intellectual discourse, we must insist that as long as English continues to play this role, Sanskrit words should be used in English on account of their unique semantic valence so that a whole culture and an entire worldview is not lost in translation."

– Prof. Arvind Sharma,
McGill University

"*Sanskrit Non-Translatables* by Rajiv Malhotra and Satyanarayana Dasa Babaji is an important book that provides lucid explanations of the central concepts of Sanatana Dharma, and brings attention to the many errors and distortions that have been introduced by the use of English words that do not quite do justice to the Sanskrit originals. It makes a powerful case for what it calls the Sanskritization of the English language by introducing key Sanskrit loanwords into English vocabulary and keeping them untranslated. This is a bold and innovative approach that deserves to be pursued in parallel with teaching Sanskrit itself. It is nothing short of spreading Vedic sanskriti into the English-speaking world by penetrating their minds with powerful Sanskrit terms."

– Dr. Subhash Kak,
author of *Matter and Mind, The Gods Within,* and other books

"This is an indispensable book addressing the difficult situation today – that Sanskrit terms pregnant with meaning cannot be translated into any foreign language; yet we have to make them understandable to people of other cultures who want to learn Sanskrit from the point of view of *jigisha* rather than *jijnasa.* The authors have worked hard to collect relevant material from various sources to prove that the English translations of many Sanskrit terms are false and misleading."

– Dr. Korada Subrahmanyam,
author of *Theory of Language: Oriental & Occidental,* and other books

"This book is an eye-opener and argues a highly original and audacious thesis to enrich the English language by adding Sanskrit words that have no English equivalent. These unique words bring profound meanings discovered by the ancient rishi-s. For English language speakers, it will not only enhance their vocabulary but also introduce them to entirely new concepts for understanding of reality."

– Dr. Vijay Bhatkar,
Chancellor, Nalanda University

Sanskrit Non-Translatables

Sanskrit Non-Translatables

The Importance of Sanskritizing English

Rajiv Malhotra and Satyanarayana Dasa Babaji

Foreword by
Nityananda Misra

AMARYLLIS

AMARYLLIS

An imprint of Manjul Publishing House Pvt. Ltd.
• C-16, Sector 3, Noida, Uttar Pradesh 201301, India
Website: www.manjulindia.com
Registered Office:
• 2nd Floor, Usha Preet Complex, 42 Malviya Nagar, Bhopal 462 003 – India
Distribution Centres
Ahmedabad, Bengaluru, Chennai, Kochi, Kolkata,
Hyderabad, Mumbai, New Delhi, Pune

This paperback edition first published in 2024

ISBN 978-93-5543-373-2

Rajiv Malhotra and Satyanarayana Dasa Babaji assert the moral right to be identified as the authors of this work.

Cover design: Divya Sharma, Infinity Foundation

Printed and bound in India by Repro India Ltd.

Contents

Foreword

Anuvada, which literally means 'saying again' or 'restating' ('*anuvadanam anuvadah*'), is the Sanskrit word for translation. An *anuvada* can be from Sanskrit into Sanskrit, from Sanskrit into Indian languages or from Sanskrit into other languages like English. Owing to the highly mathematical and flexible nature of Sanskrit, it is possible to have a perfectly equivalent *anuvada* from Sanskrit into Sanskrit. The second sutra of Patanjali's *Yoga-Sutra* reads, '*yogah chitta-vritti-nirodhah*', and the *anuvada* in Sanskrit could be '*chittasya vrittinam nirodhanam yogah*'. In languages originating from (or borrowing heavily from) Sanskrit, Sanskrit words can be used as they occur in the original and the *anuvada* can still be quite effective. For example, in Hindi, the *anuvada* of the above sutra could be '*chitta ki vrittiyon ka nirodha yoga hai*'. When it comes to languages that do not share the same history and culture as Sanskrit, a great part of the meaning is lost in translation. In English, the *anuvada* of the above sutra could be: 'Union (yoga) is the suppression of the modifications of the unconscious mind'. To a reader who knows both Sanskrit and English, this *anuvada* will be nowhere close in spirit or meaning to the original Sanskrit sutra. A Hindi speaker reading the above Hindi translation will understand the intent of Patanjali far better than an English speaker reading the English translation. This is because the words *yoga*, *chitta*, *vritti*, and *nirodha* are used in a similar sense in Hindi as they are used in the sutra.

In this much-needed and pertinent book, Rajiv Malhotra and Satyanarayana Dasa Babaji detail fifty-four Sanskrit words from nine themes with their common English translations and highlight what the English translations fail to capture. The authors make a compelling case for using Sanskrit words as is in English translations. Rajiv Malhotra had introduced this concept in his book *Being Different: An Indian Challenge to Western Universalism*, and has highlighted the need for Sanskritization of English for a long time. Satyanarayana Dasa Babaji is a traditionally trained Sanskrit scholar who has translated important texts like the *Bhagavad Gita* and the *Sandarbha* works of Srila Jiva Goswami into English. They offer insightful views into etymologies and ranges of meanings of important Sanskrit words and how their common English translations fail to capture the essence of the original words.

Consider the example of the word *maya,* which is commonly translated into English as 'illusion'. The authors point out that besides *maya* being a 'wondrous Shakti of Bhagavan', in some traditions, it is the cause of illusion and not illusion per se in the Advaita Vedanta tradition. Having learned the concept of *maya* in my childhood from both Hindi and Sanskrit sources, I am aware that another meaning of *maya* is *kripa* (loosely translated as 'compassion'), as attested by the *Anekartha-sangraha* of Acharya Hemachandra (medieval Jain scholar and polymath) and as cited in the work *Bhakti-Sudha* by Karapatri Swami (a guru in the Advaita Vedanta tradition). Thus, 'illusion' or 'deception' is only one of the many meanings of the word *maya* (Acharya Hemachandra lists four meanings in the *Anekartha-sangraha*) and translating *maya* as 'illusion' reduces a word with many shades of meaning to a single narrow meaning. The authors draw our attention to a plethora of other such mistranslations. For example, *advaya-jnana* is more appropriately translated as 'non-dual consciousness' and not 'monistic consciousness'.

While discussing the non-translatable terms, the authors also throw light on many significant concepts in Hinduism. The discussion on Om clarifies several misconceptions about the word that have recently been made popular by a prominent Hindu guru. The discussion on the *mahabhutas* shows how words like 'space', 'fire', and 'air/wind' fail to capture the essence and profound meanings of the words *akasha, agni,* and *vayu*. When we say 'space', we do not get an idea of *shabda* (loose translation, 'sound') but the concept of *akasha* in Hindu philosophy is inextricably linked with the concept of *shabda,* as the definition of *akasha* in the *Tarkasangraha* (a seventeenth century treatise on logic and reasoning by Annambhatta) clarifies: "*shabda-gunakam akasham*".

The important differences between the Indic concept of *svarga* and *naraka* and the Abrahamic concepts of heaven and hell are discussed in detail by the authors. While discussing *ahimsa*, Rajiv Malhotra and Satyanarayana Dasa Babaji incisively point out that opposite meaning (or *virodha*) is only one of the six senses of the prefix '*a*' (from '*na*'). This is known to students of Sanskrit grammar but presenting such fine nuances to laypersons is what the book succeeds at. The chapter on *Kavya* is a refreshing end to the book with discussions on words like *kama, bhava, prema,* and *ananda*. As per the *Nitivakyamrita* (a work on ethics and ethical values by the Jain scholar Somadeva Suri), *kama* is that which grants gratification abounding in bodily sentiment to all indriya-s ("*abhimanika-rasanuviddha yatah sarvendriya-pritih*"). This is a very broad concept which can never be captured by a narrow word like 'lust', as the authors convincingly prove.

Sanskrit Non-Translatables, with its lucid language, will be easy for laypersons to comprehend. The exhibits and tables will serve as useful mnemonics for the readers. The book will immensely benefit the readers and writers of the third category of the *anuvada* mentioned before—from Sanskrit to languages like English.

We know for a fact that translations of important texts from one language to another can never be wholly effective or completely true and faithful to the original. To truly understand and appreciate Shakespeare, one has to read Shakespeare in the original Elizabethan

English. With both concepts and fifty-four examples, *Sanskrit Non-Translatables: The Importance of Sanskritizing English* vividly shows how the 'lost in translation' effect is amplified manifold when translating from a highly structured, refined, rich, and potent language like Sanskrit to a language like English. Readers of the book will realize how translations of Sanskrit texts into Hindi or other Indian languages, which retain much of the original Sanskrit vocabulary, are far more effective than translations into English. The translation of the *Valmiki Ramayana* into English by Robert Goldman (professor of Sanskrit at the University of California, Berkeley) is no doubt good, but the Hindi translation published by Gita Press is undoubtedly better. For a reader who understands Hindi, the latter should be the first preference.

This must-read book will reach many readers across the globe. My sincere hope is that it inspires many of them to learn Sanskrit and read the texts of Hinduism in the original Sanskrit with Sanskrit commentaries, the best *anuvada* possible.

Nityananda Misra, author of
Mahaviri: Hanuman-Chalisa Demystified and other books
Mumbai, 2020

Preface

Satyanarayana Dasa Babaji

The Ancient Indian Psyche

The thinkers of ancient India, the rishi-s and muni-s, had a deep understanding of the fact that the universe functions on some basic principles of rhythms of the cosmos known as ritam, and to maximize well-being, humans must exist in harmony with it. To this end, human life was organized at two levels: individual and social. Further, at the individual level, human life was considered in four parts: brahmacharya, grihastha, vanaprastha, and samnyasa. Considering a life span of one hundred years, twenty-five years were allocated to each stage of life. In order to be in harmony with ritam, an individual, as well as a society, must strive for the four pursuits known as purushartha-s: dharma, artha, kama, and moksha.

Each individual possesses unique characteristics, known as his/her prakriti or nature. According to ideal dharmic social thought, an individual functioned in society in line with his prakriti and was provided with appropriate education. At the collective level, society was organized into four broad categories called varna-s: brahmana (teacher/educator), kshatriya (warrior/king/queen), vaishya (manager/business sector), and shudra (service sector). The varna was not birth-based but was dependent on the individual's acquired prakriti. Every society, which functions as an organized unit, comprises these four unavoidable categories for its sustenance, propagation and prosperity. While these categories have emerged unconsciously all over the world, ancient Indian thinkers recognized it and provided a theory supporting the four varna-s to consciously organize society. Indian society was based on this template and functioned peacefully for thousands of years, scaled paramount heights and attained much glory.

Historically, many great personalities appeared to rectify the situation whenever balance was disturbed. Bhagavan Shri Krishna himself proclaims that He is the propagator of the varna system (*Gita* 4.13), and He appears to restore dharma whenever it is challenged by adharma (*Gita* 4.7).

This ancient system, however, started crumbling when Indian society was invaded by Western forces, primarily with Alexander around 324 BCE. Thereafter, it experienced a downward spiral though its resilience was not completely eliminated. Even when India came under foreign rule, around 1192 CE, and later, under the prolonged rule of the Mughals, its education system was not tampered with and the varna-s survived. The fatal blow came in 1854, when the Indian education system was callously destroyed by the British. It was replaced by the Western education structure to produce clerks to help them control the vast empire. Unfortunately, Western education has no such insight into human life, leave alone the cosmic ritam. Tragically, even post India's independence in 1947, no efforts were made to reclaim the millennia-old heritage. Instead, what continues to this day are the borrowed education system and the constitution of the West, which are a complete mismatch for the Indian psyche.

The Modern Indian Psyche

Modern-educated Indians are a confused lot. Not only have they lost faith in their own traditional values, they are also unable to embrace a Western lifestyle in totality. Most educated Indians portray a Western demeanor, yet in their private lives they practise several beliefs that emanate from ancient tradition, especially at times of birth, death, marriage and festivals. However, they are untrained in their ancient beliefs because nothing in the modern education system fosters them. They may know of and practise certain traditions but have forgotten and surrendered the true meaning and perform them out of a sense of ritual. The lack of sufficient knowledge about one's own sanskriti, and training under the Western education system, has resulted in Indians developing an inferiority complex with regards to their rich sanskriti and dharma. Many derive pleasure in deriding the ancient sanskriti, revealing the unfortunate situation and reality of the modern Indian psyche. Furthermore, dharmic terminology has been inadequately translated into English. Terms such as atma, moksha, dharma, and prakriti are profound concepts in themselves; they are not mere words that can be translated into a single English word. The terms have to be understood and applied as they are; when translated naively into English, the terms lose their original deeper meaning, which has further led to devaluation of Indian sanskriti. To compound matters, a massive effort has been made by missionaries to digest Indian sanskriti into Christianity. The modern Indian psyche thus has to bear a great misfortune in losing its civilizational heritage.

The Torch Bearer

Several Indians are aware that Indian sanskriti is in peril and is being attacked by forces from within and outside. A handful of them are highlighting and being vocal about the danger of it getting lost and are making efforts to revive it. Rajiv Malhotra and Infinity Foundation are leading this resistance and revival. I first heard Rajiv at a WAVES conference in Florida in the US and was taken in by what he spoke. I was teaching a summer course in Hinduism at Rutgers University, and I was eager to meet Rajiv before returning to India.

When I arrived at Rajiv's home, he was working on a manuscript. Even before I sat down, he shot a question at me, "Do you know anything about Jiva Gosvami?" He then casually went on to explain how keen he was to know about *achintya-bheda-abheda siddhanta* propagated by the Indian philosopher Jiva Gosvami (1513-1598). I was instantly taken aback because studying and teaching the works of Jiva Goswami is my domain of expertise and passion; in fact, I founded an entire institute named after him. I had been working on a mammoth project for over two decades of translating and commenting on the magnum opus of Jiva Gosvami titled *Shat Sandarbha*. I never imagined I would make such a deep connection with an Indian living outside India, and one whose intense focus is on Hinduism. Rajiv Malhotra is an Indian intellectual warrior, who is fully absorbed in saving Indian sanskriti and fighting the breaking-India forces. I knew for certain that it was only by the will of Shri Krishna that we met. And although I did not know how, I understood that Rajiv and I had an important mission in common.

I left after our first meeting, excited to share my work and to hear Rajiv's penetrating questions that would go on to refine my thinking with the pinpoint accuracy that he demanded. The first document I shared with him was a paper on achintya-bheda-abheda. He relished the paper, adding that it would be of immense help for his book. He invited me to help him in his work *Being Different: An Indian Challenge to Western Universalism*. I gladly obliged, as I felt life would be breathed back into Mother India. Our friendship cemented and we would meet during my teaching assignments at Rutgers. Over the years, we have recorded several videos on a variety of subjects. Three years ago, the idea of recording Sanskrit non-translatables arose. Rajiv had already introduced this concept in his book, *Being Different*. He proposed that we create fifty-four episodes on Sanskrit non-translatable words. I was very excited with the idea and over the next two years, we made video recordings at his residence in New Jersey, as well as at our center, Jiva Faridabad, in India. Jessica Richmond co-ordinated our recording sessions and organised the required material.

In the midst of the recordings, Rajiv suggested we write a book based of the content of the videos and I immediately agreed. With the fifty-four video episodes and this book, we are taking a big step forward to actualizing Rajiv's mission. Just as Western terminology has entered the Indian psyche, Indian terminology should also enter not only Western, but also the modern Indian's mind. This will be a great step towards reclaiming our sanskriti. I give my blessings that Rajiv Malhotra's vision be realized.

Preface

Rajiv Malhotra

Since twenty-five years, Infinity Foundation has been challenging the prevailing narratives with groundbreaking research and provided original perspectives on dharma and its rightful place in the world. An important book published by the Foundation, *Invading the Sacred: An Analysis of Hinduism Studies in America*, in 2007, took aim at the Freudian psychoanalytic critiques of Hinduism being propagated by a powerful nexus in the Western academia and being spread among Indian intellectuals. The book gave birth to, and incubated, a solid and entrenched opposition that cannot be ignored today. It spurred the Indian diaspora to recognize the pattern of attacks on Hindu dharma under the garb of academia and audaciously 'talk back' to the establishment of Western scholars. This 'reversing the gaze' on Western intellectual elites found its way rapidly to India where it shaped a new generation of self-confident Indians. The term 'Hinduphobia' was adopted by Infinity Foundation to turn the spotlight on to a serious issue and it has now entered the everyday lexicon of serious thinkers worldwide.

Infinity Foundation's next pathbreaking book, *Breaking India: Western Interventions in Dravidian and Dalit Faultlines*, detailed twenty years of my research, talks, and writings on how external forces are trying to destabilize India by deliberately undermining its civilization. The book proved how such efforts are targeted at obfuscating, and ultimately aborting any collective identity of the present-day Indian, based on a positive view of his/her civilization. It exposed the foreign nexuses and applied the term 'sepoys' to refer to their Indian accomplices. The book highlighted that the project to intellectually fragment, or 'break' India targets Hinduism because it is seen as the robust foundation cementing its diversity. Several watchdog movements have sprung into action because of the book, *Breaking India*. It has triggered a domino effect with a plethora of researchers associating themselves with this genre of scholarship to expose more instances of the same syndrome. The theories and vocabulary introduced in the book are now used widely.

The next authoritative work by Infinity Foundation, *Being Different: An Indian Challenge to Western Universalism* addressed the central question: who we as Indians are, and what distinguishes us from others, especially from the West. It presents an original and coherent view of dharma as a family of traditions and unabashedly challenges the West's claim of being the universal lens for studying world cultures. Western Universalism is unfortunately still used as the template for mapping and defining all cultures and therefore, it is vital to be conscious of its distorted interpretations of Indian traditions. *Being Different* has prompted a wide section of Indians to question various simplistic views and interpretations of their traditions, including some that are commonly espoused even by their own guru-s, family and political leaders. It is a beacon for serious intellectuals on how to 'take back' Vedic heritage by understanding it on its own terms.

Indra's Net: Defending Hinduism's Philosophical Unity exposes the widely held thesis in Western academia that Hinduism is a recent invention. This fallacious and ludicrous argument was fabricated during British rule over India in the latter part of the nineteenth century, resulting in dangerous consequences even in post-independent India. The central point of this thesis asserts that Swami Vivekananda, one of the most renowned votaries of Hindu philosophy of the nineteenth century, plagiarized Western secular and Christian ideas and then recast them in Sanskrit terminology to claim their Indian origin. Besides critiquing this thesis, the nexus behind it, and defending Swami Vivekananda's vision, the book puts forward a vision for the future of Hinduism.

The Battle for Sanskrit: Is Sanskrit Political or Sacred, Oppressive or Liberating, Dead or Alive? challenges Sheldon Pollock, arguably the most influential contemporary Sanskrit scholar in Western academia. The consistent theme underlying his entire work is to characterize Sanskrit as the root cause of all of India's current social problems. This thesis attributes to Sanskrit a range of negative issues including social disharmony and lack of innovation. Arguments deeply damaging to the Indian civilization have been formulated by Pollock based on questionable assumptions and interpretations.

The Battle for Sanskrit addresses these issues head-on with a vigorous *purva paksha* or argument of Pollock's Neo-Orientalist school of thought - an influential school that has spawned new adherents and created a lineage of Western scholars and Indian sepoys today. The book led to multiple conferences of Swadeshi Indology and triggered a greater awareness of the deep and insidious goals of Western Indology and the broader academia. *The Battle for Sanskrit* was precipitated by the proposal of an Adi Shankara Chair at Columbia University sponsored by the Sringeri Peetham (one of the four important peetham-s established by the philosopher Adi Shankara), whose Academic Committee was to be headed by Sheldon Pollock. The effect of the book and the awareness it created has discouraged sponsors from pursuing the establishment of such a chair. After the Shankaracharya, head of Sringeri, was personally approached and briefed on the contents of the book, he was convinced not to proceed with the proposed Chair. This created a huge controversy among Non-Resident Indians in the United States who had championed this Chair as a vehicle for popularizing themselves and advancing their own business interests. Infinity Foundation, however, has never shied away from controversy or risks when required for the sake of protecting the wider interest of dharma.

Infinity Foundation has also formulated, funded and implemented numerous major interventions which have affected the civilizational discourse in positive and non-trivial ways.[1] The Foundation became widely acknowledged as the leader in influencing the way scholars are approaching their work on India's civilization, history, archaeology, social sciences, arts, and other fields. Besides intellectuals, its work has deeply influenced people from various walks of life, not just Indians and people of Indian origin, but all those who have an all-abiding interest in these matters.

The Foundation has been producing videos on several subjects that showcase the use and application of a dharma-based lens to study our civilization. This has resulted in a new awakening: to promote the use of our *drishti* (i.e., the ability to look through the dharmic lens). It has adopted the term *kurukshetra* or battlefield, to describe the present-day encounter of civilizations. The Foundation has expanded beyond the mode of pure research, and engages with the general public, providing new insights into the social and political dynamics at work in this kurukshetra.

The Foundation's books have a common approach: to present an analysis of distorted theories and their effects, and to expose the falsities and assumptions, of these theories. The target readership is the serious intellectual in support of the Foundation's aim to develop Intellectual Kshatriyas. These kshatriyas are using the Foundation's core ideas and vocabulary to aid in the thinking, analysis, dissection, and strategic response to the attacks on dharma, thus providing new perspectives. Any coherent body of thought or knowledge system assumes a powerful impact as a thought carrier and a tool of change, in pragmatic and intellectual ways, if it is supported by its own consistent vocabulary. The histories and progress of a civilization can be seen as an evolution of its conceptual framework and vocabulary in understanding itself and the world.

The theory of Sanskrit Non-Translatables is one such powerful framework and has its own vocabulary of terms. It was introduced for the first time in the book, *Being Different*. The theory elucidated that Western scholars and Westernized Indians are accustomed to translating and mapping dharmic concepts and perspectives onto Western frameworks, which is a form of digestion of Vedic civilization into their civilization. *Being Different* argued that this practice is highly problematic. Dharmic traditions are compromised and some elements even atrophy once it becomes acceptable to substitute them with Western equivalents, even though the substitutes do not accurately represent the original Indian idea.

While this problem exists to some extent in all inter-civilizational encounters, it is particularly acute when dharmic concepts in Sanskrit are translated into Western languages. Not only does Sanskrit, like all languages, encode specific and unique cultural experiences and traits, but the very form, sound, and manifestation of the language carries effects that cannot be separated from their conceptual meanings. The non-translatable nature of Sanskrit and its deep meanings are compromised by the cultural digestion of dharma into the West through the inadequate translation of vocabulary. In the course of this digestion, crucial distinctions and understandings are lost, important direct experiences of the rishi-s sidelined, and the most fertile, productive and visionary dimension of dharma eradicated and relegated to antiquity. This loss is often carried out under the guise of modernity.

The current book takes these ideas forward and launches a new movement using Sanskrit Non-Translatables as a device for protecting key ideas from getting distorted, plagiarized, or allowed to become obsolete. The role of Satyanarayana Dasa Babaji has been critical as the subject-matter expert to explicate the nuances of meanings of the important Sanskrit words used to illustrate their non-translatability.

This book is not meant for teaching Sanskrit. It undertakes to explain the inadequate translation of many Sanskrit terms into

English, which is commonplace. It spotlights several Sanskrit terms that are loosely and unthinkingly replaced with English translations and shows how the deep and profound implications of these words get lost.

Though primarily meant for the English speaker/reader, many of these discussions are also relevant to resist the usage of these English terms in native Indian languages.

Chapters 1 and 2 cover the rationale and need for Sanskrit Non-Translatables and ingeminate key ideas on the subject from *Being Different*. The discussion on the origins and unique nature of Sanskrit lays the foundation. The Non-Translatables will play a critical role in the kurukshetra as carriers of deeper ideas and embedded cultural assets, and in the encounters between dharma and adharma.

Chapters 3 through 11 discuss several specific non-translatable terms that are being carelessly translated. For each term discussed, careful and deep thought has gone into explaining why the common translations are inadequate and how they create distortions and confusion. The goal is to lay a strong foundation for readers to start using these Sanskrit words when speaking or writing in English. The aim is to instill confidence that the non-translatable words can be used effectively in everyday engagement in English, enriching the language with new ideas and experiences from the Indian traditions.

To ensure reader friendliness, diacritic marks for Sanskrit pronunciation have only been used in the notes. Most Sanskrit terms have been italicized when they first appear, and this may be repeated in some cases. A Sanskrit term will often be accompanied by a brief phrase in parentheses, providing its approximate and provisional meaning in English. Many Sanskrit terms in the main text are spelled in more than one way depending on the source – for instance, 'Shankara' and 'Sankara'. Purists in Indian scholarship may raise issues with some of these compromises. But our battles are selected carefully and with focus, and this means making practical accommodations.

At certain places in this book where multiple interpretations of the shastra exist within our traditions, the Gaudiya Vaishnava sampradaya's viewpoint is used as the basis for illustrating the non-translatability. This choice is *not* to preclude other traditional views. Satyanarayana Dasa Babaji belongs to that tradition, hence we use that view. However, we invite collaborations with experts from other dharmic traditions so that the full richness of each Sanskrit concept can emerge from various perspectives. The focus is to explain that various Sanskrit terms are not translatable to English words. Using a particular dharmic tradition serves to illustrate this point.

Introduction

Diversity of Civilizations

The distinctiveness of the cultural and spiritual matrix of dharma civilizations is under siege from something insidious: the widespread dismantling, rearrangement, and digestion of dharmic culture into Western frameworks, by disingenuously characterizing the latter as 'universal'.

This process of absorption of dharmic ideas can take place with good intentions and also with the tacit cooperation of individuals immersed in dharma. They sometimes question: Why not assimilate? Aren't we all really 'the same'? What is incorrect about a 'universal' point of view? Isn't the large-scale absorption of Indian ideas, arts, sciences, medicine, business practices and letters something positive? Isn't it wonderful that millions of Americans and Europeans practice and propagate yoga and that Indian cuisine has gone global? Besides, doesn't the West have something to offer India in exchange – such as scientific advances, social justice, business and political know-how? The obvious answer to all these questions would at first be a 'Yes'.

Yet, much of what appears to be an explicit Indian influence on the West is indicative of a process that threatens to deplete the very sources of dharma on which it draws. Talk of global culture and universalism often creates the sunny impression that the fusion of dharmic and Western cultures is always good. This assumption ignores the many distortions and unacknowledged appropriations on the part of the West, as well as the highly destructive influences of fundamentalist Christianity, Marxism, capitalist expansionism and myopic secularism.

Global culture is bridging and blurring boundaries across races, ethnicities, nationalities and faiths. Consumerism is redefining lifestyles and aesthetics by blending universal components. The increased mobility of people, goods and capital is more likely taking us closer to a world of true meritocracy (a phenomenon that Pulitzer Prize winner, Thomas Friedman calls the 'flat world'[2]), and economic and ecological integration is helping dismantle localized obstacles. The youth is especially quick to embrace new kinds of global identities, often at the expense of native traditions.

At the same time, an appreciation of the exotic, colorful and novel aspects of Indian culture appear to be on the rise, owing to the influence of Yoga, Indian cuisine, the film industry, traditional music and dance, and so on. Indian spiritual capital enjoys a pride of place in the global quest for greater well-being, as evidenced by the popularity of Yoga, meditation and Ayurvedic medicine in various forms and by the influence wielded by certain self-help guru-s in popular culture. In fact, Americans invest enormous amounts of money in alternative health and spiritual practices which are of Indian origin, whether or not they realize, or accept, the Indian root.

This leads many to conclude that the essential differences among civilizations no longer matter. Several prominent critics have blamed religious, cultural, racial and national divisions for much of the violence and fragmentation that are destabilizing the world today. They argue that all such distinctions are obsolete and primitive.

The arguments that distinct cultures should coalesce into something universal are expressed in theories that perceive ideal societies as 'post-modern', 'post-racial', 'post-religious' and 'post-nationalistic'. These fashionable constructs seem to announce the arrival of a flat, secularized world that is undifferentiated by specific histories, identities and religious points of view. The anti-modernity movement of the twentieth century was one such construct; its lofty goal of rejecting Western aggression led to colonialism, genocide, two World Wars, Nazism and Communism. Anti-modernity offered little by way of a positive affirmation of differences and little understanding of why it might be valuable and desirable for differences to coexist harmoniously.

What is misleading about the 'flat world' assumption is that while superficial cultural elements do seem to have coalesced into a common global culture, the deeper structures that support the power and privilege of certain groups are stronger than ever before. Globalization is often framed in terms and structures that emerged under Western domination of the world over the past five hundred years or so. These in turn, are founded on the values and beliefs that emerged from the unique historical and religious experiences of the peoples of European origin. When all collective identities are discarded and all boundaries challenged – whether under the rubric of post-modern critique or as a result of a vague sense that 'all are one' and 'we are all fundamentally the same' – the result is not a world free from dominance but one in which the strongest identities along with their versions of history and values prevail.

This asymmetry of power and resources in the production and spread of a dominant narrative leads to abrasive cultural exchanges. It is only recently that China has begun responding to the Western narrative on its own terms. The Islamic world too, powered by oil-generated-wealth, is able to spread its narrative via the Western-controlled channels of knowledge legitimization. Weak cultures and civilizations will end up getting digested and rendered irrelevant in the face of this hegemonic march of history.

The Indian situation in the clash of civilizations is indeed disheartening. The Indian state was weakened to a deep state of atrophy after close to one thousand years of colonial rule and became further diluted after independence in 1947 by way of poor policies and inefficient and corrupt governing structures. It is only recently, after seventy-odd years, that the need and relevance of a truthful civilizational narrative as the basis for nation-building is being considered at the highest levels of governance. Steps, however small, are being taken to build a foundation for an India based on India's self-narratives and its civilizational riches.

Given this reality, it is now up to the Indian peoples and those on the journey of dharma to take control of the civilizational narrative and regain the *adhikara* (authority) to interpret the world on their own terms. The economic prosperity over the last few decades, and the marked absence of crippling poverty has, for the most part, freed Indians to think beyond survival and mere economic progress. The quest for civilizational identity has created a hunger for dharma-based ideas, which now responds to the factually misleading and culturally corrosive narratives of the mainstream.[3]

Threat of Western Universalism

A large section of Westerners and Anglicized Indians assume that the dharmic wisdom embodied in the Sanskrit language can be translated into other languages and imported into other religious and/or scientific paradigms without loss of meaning. For example, *Om* can be Amen, *Shanti* can be Peace, *Ishvara* can be God. We argue to the contrary.

Ancient as it is, Sanskrit remains relevant for its profound creative potential. The richness of the meaning of a word is often deeply embedded within its cultural context, in the history of its evolution over time, and also in the wider context of nuances and implied meanings that accompany its usage. A culture comprises the cumulative collective experience that is unique to its people and is invariably interwoven with their geography and history.

To understand the nuances of a word in its entirety, it is essential to understand the host culture. Language, both reflects and shapes, a culture's thought process owing to its deep structures and categories. The unique experiences of different cultures are not always interchangeable. Many cultural artifacts have no equivalent in other cultures, and to force such artifacts into Western templates results in distortions. This too is a kind of colonization and cultural conquest. Therefore, certain words used to refer to those experiences must remain intact. Over time, if linguistic terms and categories get lost, so does the diversity of cultural experience.

Sanskrit has certain properties which reveal the inherently contextual and unique nature of dharmic philosophy from which it arose. With Sanskrit, there is also another deeper source of non-translatability: Among its primary sounds, there are layers of connections and interrelationships forged by common underlying vibrations. The complete meaning is thus a composite of the collection, not unlike an algebraic formula.

Therefore, great harm is done when a foreign culture, especially a colonial one, imposes its own simplistic, and often incorrect, translations of Sanskrit. Even greater harm is done when the natives of a colonized culture adopt these foreign translations - a process that is often gradual and subtle, and achieved with rewards of upward social mobility offered by the dominant culture.

The dangers of foreign translation are only the first step in the destruction of an entire knowledge system. The discoveries of humanity, passed on through millennia, practiced and fine-tuned over thousands of generations become diluted, dismantled and destroyed within a generation or two. We are witnessing the risk of this happening today with Yoga and Ayurveda, two of Indian civilization's invaluable gifts to mankind. It is not just a question of blindly preserving tradition for its own sake. The practices and the language that describe them are based on very deep theories built on a Vedic understanding of reality, which even challenges the current understandings of science and the narratives of Western modernity and consumer-driven capitalism.

Sanskrit and World Culture

Sanskriti, the Dharma Civilization

Sanskrit is the unifying substrate of dharmic civilization and has profoundly shaped it. Etymologically, Sanskrit means 'elaborated', 'having the samskara of *vyakaranam*', 'refined', 'cultured' and 'civilized', implying wholeness of expression. Employed by the refined and educated as their preferred means of communication, Sanskrit has influenced a distinct cultural system and way of experiencing the world since several millennia. *Sanskriti* is the term for such a culture and civilization (*sanatana-dharma*), one that goes well beyond the borders of modern India to encompass South Asia, much of Southeast Asia and East Asia. Interactions among different regions helped develop and exchange this pan-Asian sanskriti.

Albeit Sanskrit is no longer commonly spoken in Asia, it remains the underpinning of the civilizations of South and Southeast Asia. Thus, even those who don't speak the language may experience its structures and principles as sanskriti. Sanskriti is the lore and repository of human sciences, art, architecture, popular song, classical music, dance, theatre, sculpture, painting, literature, pilgrimage, rituals and religious narratives, all of which embody pan-Indian cultural traits. It also incorporates all branches of natural science and technology, including medicine, botany, mathematics, engineering, architecture, dietetics among others.

A stunning achievement of this repository is one of Sanskrit's most revered scholars Panini's grammar, a meta-language of such clarity, flexibility and rigor, that certain pioneers in computer science are today turning to it for ideas.

It was the scientific and secular aspect of Sanskrit that induced even the Arabs to welcome Indian scholars to Baghdad to engage in scientific discourse and translate their books into Arabic.

Sanskrit Unites the Great Tradition and Little Traditions

Since time immemorial, Sanskrit has been the language of the literati and the chosen medium for their ideas and works of art. It flourished as a living language across many regions before being eclipsed first, by Persian and then, by English after the military and political conquests of India. Sanskrit thus gained strength as the spiritual, artistic, scientific and ritual *lingua franca* across vast regions of Asia and as a useful vehicle of communication among speakers of local languages, much as English is today. Additionally, Sanskrit was interconnected with local languages in a two-way process: the meta-structure of Sanskrit was transmitted top-down into local languages and, simultaneously, there was a bottom-up assimilation of local culture and language into Sanskrit's flexible, open architecture.

Sanskriti flourished with the exchange between these two cultural streams, respectively known as the 'great' tradition and 'little' traditions. While the sophisticated urbane population (known as the 'great tradition' in anthropology) provided sanskriti with refinement and comprehensiveness, cultural contributions from the rural masses (the 'little traditions') gave it popularity, vitality and a diverse outlook. The web of interconnectedness was woven by festivals and rituals. Scholars have used these tracers to understand the reciprocal influence of Sanskrit and local languages. Sanskrit served as a meta-language and framework of categories for the vast range of languages across Asia.

Once information about local or regional cultural traits is recorded and encoded in Sanskrit, it becomes shared as part of sanskriti. Conversely, when elements of sanskriti are localized, they acquire a distinct regional identity and color. The unity within the diversity found in South and Southeast Asia amply reflects this pattern.

Owing to the relationship between Sanskrit and local languages, and to sanskriti's role as the common cultural architecture, it is not necessary to *know* Sanskrit in order to absorb the embedded values and inherent meanings. Similarly, a speaker of a local language would have access to the ideas, values and categories within the cultural matrix of sanskriti.

There is a rich symbiosis between the *shastriya parampara* (i.e., the classical formal knowledge) and *loka parampara,* which is popular and informal oral knowledge. Indeed, the latter is acknowledged beautifully and respectfully in classical texts, such as the *Natyashastra* by sage Bharata Muni and literature on Ayurveda. All these cultures and knowledge systems comprise a continuum.

Many tribal practices and customs permeate the mainstream customs observed in temples. For example, in the temple at Puri, in the eastern state of Odisha, dedicated to Lord Jagannath, the main *murti*-s undoubtedly express regional and popular motifs, and similar syncretism is found in the Meenakshi temple at Madurai, in the southern state of Tamil Nadu. Both Richard Lannoy and the American anthropologist McKim Marriott note that the relation between 'Little Traditions' and the 'Great Tradition' is reciprocal (i.e., they are mutually dependent and exist in harmony with each other).[4] According to Marriott, the reciprocal sponge-like action of give-and-absorb generates a double movement – upward and downward. The former nourished the Great Tradition with the emergent elements of the village folk cultures, while the latter transmitted the universal, generally urban culture.

The Purana-s were a vehicle for spreading sanskriti beyond the elites and served as an ancient form of pop culture with spiritual messages embedded in fables and tales. Prolific writer, Vijay Nath, in his book *Purana-s and Acculturation: A Historico-Anthropological Perspective* explains how the Purana-s integrated various social strata, *jati*-s, dharmic sects and regions of classical India in a manner that was both decentralized and flexible.[5] These elements became a device for social mobility.

As a result of large migrations from the heartland to outlying regions, new forms of cultural exchanges between the migrants and locals transpired. The flow of influence went both ways. One of the most visible from 'below' was the collective or group singing and ritual performances, a feature still in practice in tribal communities. The interaction between sects across a varied landscape of communities and languages involved separate deities, rituals, stories, local shrines and pilgrimage sites (*tirtha*-s), which became part of Puranic stories. The guardian deities of various local professional and artisan groups were recognized in this process. Rituals from the *agama-s* became more prominent, along with specific initiations designed to formalize discipleship with a guru.

In the case of Bhagavan Shiva, his family of deities expanded to include *yaksha*-s as attendants.[6] The Purana-s popularized a larger number of *tirtha*-s and pilgrimages to them. A tirtha in the Purana-s was believed to offer special powers for spiritual purification. Gradually, tirtha-s started to serve as substitutes for Vedic *yajna*-s.[7] Such rituals were not limited to any specific *varna* (social class) and became even more popular than some formal dharmic rites. The local political chiefs and businesses benefited as a result of the increased popularity of their particular tirtha, similar to the contemporary impact of any tourist attraction on the local power structure and economy. It became a matter of pride and importance for a remote community to be visited by pilgrims. Purana-s also facilitated temple building insofar as they were the first texts with rules on temple architecture and planning.[8] Local tribal communities often got assigned important roles as functionaries in the temple, and this helped bind the temple–tribe nexus in remote areas across India.

The numerous local variations show the contextual nature of dharma which has been enriched by the Purana-s.[9] There is a critical difference between this process and Christian inculturation which, in keeping with its inherent history-centrism and exclusivism, is intended as only an interim step in the process of converting the subject to a history-centric worldview. On the other hand, dharmic osmosis across traditions has resulted in local variations being sustained over long periods without pressure to convert people to metropolitan dharmic traditions.

Both classical and popular practices share the all-inclusive epic tradition (the *Ramayana* and the *Mahabharata*), reflecting cultural integration between formal and folk traditions. Lannoy writes:

> The motley bands of professional artists, bards, wandering minstrels, and holy men who have been traveling the roads of India in unending procession since antiquity may be counted as an important element in this 'link language'. So too are the caste and sect gurus who have acquired their charisma through resolution of life's contradictions, the 'play of opposites,' the multiplicity of cultural allegiances. In the final analysis it is a single unifying power which the Indian culture-bearer utilises to draw together the diversity of peoples in this consistently oral society: the power of music. Social fusion is achieved through the universal appeal of melody, rhythm, and cadence. (Lannoy 1971:193)

Pluralism in Hindu society, therefore, is the result of peaceful coexistence among minority groups; it did not come about due to violent conflict aimed at achieving social change. Unfortunately, a certain group of Western and Indian scholars insists on emphasizing conflict, which serves the agenda of vote-bank politics. Under colonial rule, European colonizers imposed their canonized texts and theories on those whom they conquered. Worse still, they completely liquidated indigenous peoples and, with them, their rich and valuable traditions of knowledge. They saw the natives as 'tribals'. Contemporary scholars have superimposed the same structural dichotomy in the vain hope of understanding India through divisive and conflict-ridden categories. There has been a concerted effort to show that learned dharmic traditions are hegemonic and oppressive to the 'real' natives of India. In India, however, the so-called tribals (characterized by rural life and informal knowledge systems) have always coexisted in harmony with formalized dharma systems.

Sanskriti and Pan-Asian Civilization

Across India, the stories of Krishna are adapted into numerous local subcultures. The Devi has a form localized for virtually every Indian village and often for every *jati*. A number of festivals and rituals are adapted by local people in various parts of India, resulting in an astounding diversity of regional and folk traditions becoming anchored in the traditions of Hinduism.

In the pan-Asian context, there were exchanges, mutual influences and transformations among independent cultural traditions. Such exchanges occurred when these cultures encountered each other through exploration, trade, transplantation of knowledge systems, and so forth. These were, for the most part, free from any deliberate or systematic agendas. Over time, there have been attempts to reframe and actively shape the new knowledge in the local context. This is why the *Ramayana* has been adapted and assimilated into many Asian cultures and languages. For instance, there is an Ayodhya in Thailand, and in Bali's 'monkey forest', monkeys are worshipped as a reminder of Hanuman, the deity who resembled a monkey and worshipped and served Shri Rama.

From at least the beginning of the Common Era (CE) until about the thirteenth century, Sanskrit was the primary linguistic and cultural medium for the ruling and administrative circles extending from as far as Purushapura (Peshawar) in Gandhara (Afghanistan and parts of Pakistan) to as far east as Pandurang in Annam (South Vietnam) and Prambanam in Central Java. It influenced much of Asia for over one thousand years. Sanskriti was neither imposed by an imperial power nor sustained by any centrally organized Church ecclesiology. Thus, it has been both the result and cause of a cultural consciousness shared by most South and Southeast Asians regardless of religion, class or gender.

Centuries prior to the Europeanization of the globe, the entire arc – from Central Asia through Afghanistan, India, Sri Lanka, Thailand, Cambodia, Vietnam and all the way to Indonesia – was a crucible of a sophisticated pan-Asian civilization. In *A Cultural History of India*, A.L. Basham notes that "[by] the fifth century CE, Indianised states, that is to say states organised along the traditional lines of Indian political theory and following the Buddhist or Hindu religions, had established themselves in many regions of Burma, Thailand, Indo-China, Malaysia, and Indonesia".[10] Years earlier, the British historian A.J. Toynbee remarked: "India is the central link in a chain of regional civilizations that extends from Japan in the far north-east to Ireland in the far northwest. Between these two extremities the chain sags down southwards in a festoon that dips below the Equator in Indonesia".[11]

However, unlike the violent spread of the Roman civilization which made Latin the European language for centuries, the Sanskritization of Asia was entirely peaceful – without conquest, domination, or subversion of local identities. This is not to say that political disputes and wars of conquest never occurred but, in most instances, the motive was not the imposition of cultural or religious homogeneity.

Arun Bhattacharjee's *Greater India* elaborates further on this point:

> The unique feature of India's contacts and relationship with other countries and peoples of the world is that the cultural expansion was never confused with colonial domination and commercial dynamism, far less economic exploitation. That culture can advance without political motives, that trade can proceed without imperialist designs, settlements can take place without colonial excesses, and that literature, religion and language can be transported without xenophobia, jingoism and race complexes are amply evidenced from the history of India's contact with her neighbors...Thus although a considerable part

> of central and south-eastern Asia became flourishing centers of Indian culture, they were seldom subject to the regime of any Indian king or conquerors and hardly witnessed the horrors and havocs of any Indian military campaign. They were perfectly free, politically and economically, and their people, representing an integration of Indian and indigenous elements, had no links with any Indian state and looked upon India as a holy land rather than a motherland - a land of pilgrimage and not an area of jurisdiction. (Bhattacharjee 1981:1-3)

Asia's brightest students went to centers of learning in India, such as Takshasila and Nalanda. King Baladeva of Indonesia was so supportive of the university in Nalanda that he made a generous donation in 860 CE. That a foreign king thousands of miles away in Southeast Asia would support a university in India underscores the importance of pan-Asian scholarly exchange.

Early Buddhist scriptures were in Pali and other Prakrit (local vernacular) languages, but later ones were composed in what is known as 'hybrid Sanskrit'. There was a trend for using elegant Paninian Sanskrit for both verbal and written communication. The Tibetan script and grammar were developed based on Sanskrit and indeed are virtual mirror images of it.[12] Along with the spread of Buddhism to Tibet came a vast complex of cultural elements: dogmas, philosophical and metaphysical ideas, religious and spiritual practices, forms of social organization and a rich artistic tradition.

Sanskriti has had an obvious influence on Thailand dating from 1500 CE. Sanskrit was used for public, social, cultural and administrative purposes in Thailand and other parts of Southeast Asia. Today, Sanskrit is highly respected as the medium for validating, legitimating and transmitting royal succession and instituting formal rituals. Khmer society, 800-1300 CE (in Cambodia), was highly Indianized, and the later Thai kings embraced Indian religions and based their principles of government on Hindu practices.

China and India had a unique and mutually respectful exchange. Buddhist thought is the most notable and obvious import to China from India. The T'ang Dynasty (618–907 CE) opened the doors to sanskriti from South and Southeast Asia. Indian influence over China reached its zenith in the seventh century when more Chinese monks and royal embassies came to India than in any other period. Nalanda University attracted large numbers of Buddhist monks from across Asia. Chinese scholars at Nalanda studied not only Buddhism but also Vedic philosophy, mathematics, astronomy and medicine. Numerous Indian texts were translated into Chinese and became established in Chinese thought.

Between 950 and 1033 CE, a large number of Chinese pilgrims visited India and absorbed the sanskriti superstructure. They left inscriptions of their visits at sacred sites and constructed stupas at Bodh Gaya in honor of their emperor and empress.[13] Indian guru-s and pandit-s were accorded due respect on their visits to China. The Chinese emperors appointed an official board of translators to translate Indian texts, and Indian scholars were commonly brought to lead these efforts.

Buddhism's spread across Asia is well-acknowledged but beyond mere religion, this pan-Asian civilization also became a fount of knowledge in fields as diverse as language, linguistics, mathematics, astronomy, medicine, botany, martial arts and philosophy. Indian astronomers were consulted in the preparation of official calendars.[14] In the seventh century CE, three astronomical schools known as Gautama, Kashyapa and Kumara flourished in China. It had already adopted the Indian theory of nine planets. Key Sanskrit astronomical, mathematical and medical texts were translated during the T'ang period. Distinctions between Buddhism and Hinduism in doctrines, practices and institutions were blurred and considered relatively unimportant by the receiving cultures. In China, for example, Buddhist missionaries were venerated as much for their brahmanical learning as for their monastic vows. Historians generally refer to this large-scale export of sanskriti as the export of Buddhism, which dilutes the role of dharmic culture in general.

The arts were domains of confluence of Chinese culture and sanskriti and gave rise to the school known as Sino-Indian art. This school became prominent in the Northern Wei period (386–534 CE). There are a number of rock-cut caves at Thunwang, Yun-kang and Longmen with colossal images of Buddha sixty to seventy feet high, as well as frescoes. The inspiration came not only from the images and paintings that were imported from India (from Ajanta and Sarnath, for example) but from the Indian artists who visited China. Indian musicians also travelled to China and even Japan to spread their talent, including some who were sponsored by Chinese emperors. Two principal forms of music - Bodhisattva and Bhairo - were taken from China to Japan by an Indian musician named Bodhi during the T'ang period. Thus, sanskriti preserved the uniqueness of each culture it influenced.

This difference between how both sanskriti and Western civilization spread may be restated in business terms using the analogy of 'push' versus 'pull' marketing. Push marketing comprises intrusive advertising, door-to-door sales calls, tactics of intimidation, pamphlet campaigns, posters to invite prospects, junk mail solicitation (including spam), telemarketing, negative political campaigns and other manipulative strategies. In many instances, these methods are unethical or even outright unlawful. The spread of Christianity, and later of Islam, was achieved largely by such heavy-handed and aggressive means. To this day, Christian organizations, much like multinational enterprises, continue to set targets for conversions for every district of India (among other countries) with budgets calculated in terms of cost per conversion. 'Soul harvesting', as it is officially called by the Vatican and various Protestant evangelicals, is like any multinational drive for market share.

In pull marketing, the product demand drives the transfer without pressure or intimidation from the supplier. The consumer takes the initiative to find and approach the supplier. Common modern examples include searching for a defined need, such as the use of Google, eBay and other sources sought out by the buyer.[15]

In the case of sanskriti, the receiving cultures found assimilation to be highly advantageous and sought out Hindu–Buddhist itihasa, Purana-s, symbols, rituals, doctrines, ideas of governance and aesthetics from the Indian mainland. The best evidence of this is that for more than one thousand years the rulers of China, Tibet, Thailand, Myanmar, Cambodia, Vietnam, Sri Lanka and other nations sent their brightest students to the *vihara-s* (educational institutions) of India.[16]

Sanskrit, Modernity and Post-modernity

Ever since the time of William Jones (1746-1794), renowned for his knowledge on ancient India, Sanskrit scholars have contributed to the creation of linguistics in Western academia. Colonial Indologists considered the European study of Panini's grammar a major breakthrough. Sanskrit scholars in Europe were the initial developers of modern linguistics as an academic discipline.

Ferdinand de Saussure (1857–1913), the West's 'father of structuralism', spent his academic career in Paris studying and teaching the Sanskrit grammar of Panini. Saussure's PhD was on conjugate verbs in Sanskrit and he, in turn, influenced Claude Lévi-Strauss (1908–2009), the eminent anthropologist. Lévi-Strauss was one of many Western thinkers influenced by Saussure's work. After Saussure's death, his students published his class notes posthumously but removed all traces and references to Sanskrit, Panini and Indian texts, replacing them with generic and universal principles that could be applied to modern European languages. The philosophical principles contained therein became known as structuralism, revolutionizing European art, sociology, history, philosophy and psychology. Structuralism was the precursor of post-structuralism, the philosophical core of post-modern thought.[17]

Well into the twentieth century, courses in Sanskrit were a requirement for doctoral candidates in linguistics in most major universities in the West. Only after a period of intensely studying Sanskrit in the academy (and two centuries after its discovery by the West) was the science of linguistics sufficiently Europeanized to become independent of Sanskrit.

The Nobel prize winning American born British poet T.S. Eliot (1888–1965) was one of the few Westerners to understand both the potency of Sanskrit and its relationship to dharma. He studied the language at Harvard, where it was an integral part of the philosophical curriculum. Ultimately, he refrained from embracing either Hinduism or Buddhism as a result of his own cultural upbringing and conditioning. In her book, *T.S. Eliot and Indic Traditions: A Study in Poetry and Belief*, Cleo McNelly Kearns explains that it was the poet's study of the Upanishads and Vedic texts that showed him that breath, sound and silence were at the heart of language. Eliot understood that a mantra's efficacy depends not on its meaning, per se, but on the effect that its correct utterance and accompanying breathing techniques have. While he did not use the term, he could have been speaking of *mantra-Shakti* when he wrote that language works through:

> ...syllable and rhythm, penetrating far below the conscious level of thought and feeling, invigorating every word; sinking to the most primitive and forgotten, returning to the origin and bringing something back, seeking the beginning and the end. It works through meanings, certainly, or not without meanings in the ordinary sense....[18]

The Importance of Protecting Sanskrit

Despite the stark contrast between the predatory nature of the West and the slow cultural spread of Sanskrit-based dharma cultures, they are competing in modern times for global mindshare. The rapacious methods of Western modernity notwithstanding, the impact of Yoga, Ayurveda, meditation and Indian nature-based wellness on global mindshare is enormous. Yet, there has been mindless distortion, billions of dollars spent in creating false narratives and fake movements, and global scale efforts to de-Indianize and de-Sanskritize this knowledge. Despite efforts to de-legitimize the Sanskrit tradition by dogged scholars and their Indian sepoys, the Church and other umbrella organizations antithetic to the Bharatiya traditions, the internet and online channels especially in recent times, have helped counter the narrative in popular consciousness. It is through these informal channels that much of the revival and re-legitimization can happen. Most formal channels such as academia, journals and other top-down structures that legitimize knowledge, are presently too entrenched and prefer maintaining the current status quo on the narratives of Western supremacy and Western worldviews. Much of the riches of the Sanskrit knowledge systems await rediscovery.

The numbers of known and catalogued manuscripts in the Indian knowledge traditions are in the millions and their wealth remains untapped. These legitimate riches derive from the Sanskrit traditions and are part of a global heritage. This is recognized globally by saner elements of modern society, however begrudgingly. This cannot be denied.

The concept of kalpavriksha/kalpataru has a special significance in the sanatana tradition. The kalpataru of Sanskrit is in danger of being destroyed. The destruction of Sanskrit learning centers by Islamic invaders, discovery of Sanskrit by the West, the colonial effects on Sanskrit learning in India, state-sponsored denudation of Sanskrit post-Independence and the distorted digestion of its knowledge systems, has caused severe weakening of the dharma ecosystem in various ways. We can easily record more than one thousand years of attack on Sanskrit. Sanskrit, sanskriti and the associated knowledge systems need nurture and protection. The book, *The Battle for Sanskrit*, was a recent and grave reminder of the continuing subterfuge and a response to the global anti-Sanskrit forces that are part of the kurukshetra.

This book's focus on a Sanskrit non-translatables initiative is a step toward raising awareness and making the case for a change in behavior, and in vocabulary, leading to gradual and deep change in thinking. The practice of Yoga and meditation in their various forms and the use of the methods of Ayurveda - its theories, diagnostic methods and pharmacologies have already impacted human awareness and raised global consciousness in significant, and as yet unfathomable ways. The collective global human mind is slowly getting tuned to appreciate, and possibly embrace, the way of dharma. Sanskrit Non-Translatables is the obvious next step in this journey.

1

The Case For Sanskrit Non-Translatables

The Kurukshetra Today

The global kurukshetra today poses a clear and present danger of Vedic civilizations being taken apart, some elements of it destroyed, and others digested into Western Universalism. The term 'cultural genocide' is appropriate for this condition. Unlike a physical genocide where an entire community is annihilated, in this case culture is obliterated even though the individuals physically survive and live within the predator culture. The Sanskrit Non-Translatables initiative is a strategic reaction to the dangers of a cultural genocide.

The term 'genocide' was invented by Raphael Lemkin (1900-1959), a Polish Jewish jurist, who also actively lobbied to make it an international crime, not limited to the physical destruction of a people and include cultural genocide. His draft for the United Nations law regarding genocides proposed that "*...disintegration of the political and social institutions, of culture, language, national feelings, religion...*" of a people be included in the final law.[19] This clause was vociferously opposed by certain countries because of the fear they would be accused of such genocide. It was removed in the final version of the Convention on the Prevention and Punishment of the Crime of Genocide. In December 1948, the UN General Assembly passed Resolution 260 adopting the law on genocides, but cultural genocide was not included as a crime.[20]

Though we are primarily explaining the mechanics of the Judeo-Christian and Western secular forces of universalism, Islam too poses critical problems, though of a different kind. Muslims in India comprise close to a quarter of the population. The Hindu origins of the Muslims of the subcontinent are expressly denied.

Sanskrit terms were replaced with Persian to develop Urdu. Gradually, Hindi has become increasingly Urdu from the influence of the indigenous film industry where so-called Hindi movies are actually more Urdu than Hindi. Though the thesis of Sanskrit non-translatables is being argued using Western Universalism as the threat, a parallel argument exists for Sanskrit becoming digested into Islamic ideologies.

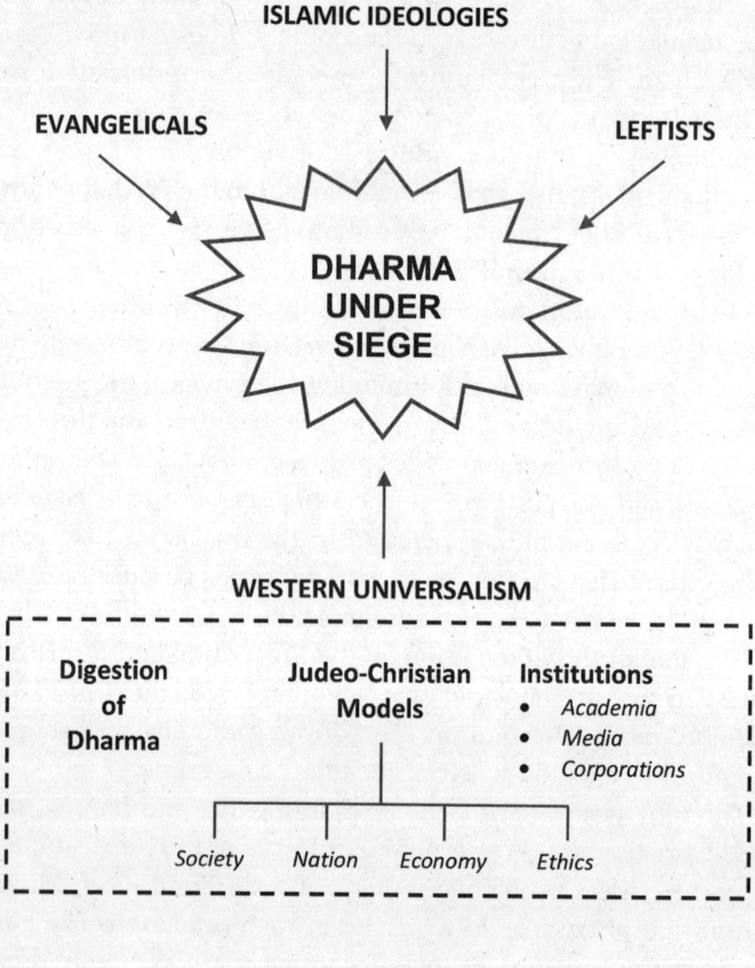

Figure 1: The Kurukshetra

Digestion and Destruction

The appropriation and assimilation of alien cultures is deeply embedded in the Judeo-Christian history of the West. The proselytizing and predatory requirement in the West's cultural psyche is robust and driven by assertions of supremacy based on religious, racial and economic factors. The reasons for this obsession with dominance have to do with the nature of the Judeo-Christian faiths and its anxiety over difference with others. There are four main ways in which this anxiety expresses itself:

1. Destruction of others through outright violence or forced conversions.
2. Isolation of others from the mainstream so that they no longer pose a threat.
3. Inculturation, a form of infiltration of other faiths in order to dilute their difference and eventually digest them.
4. Digestion, the process of chopping up a prey into tiny parts, assimilating the useful portions into the host's body, and rejecting what is not considered useful - such that the entity which got digested ceases to exist as its own self.

Though blatant destruction is not widespread today, the other expressions are commonly prevalent.

Isolation occurs when the dominant West appears to tolerate the difference of the other side but ignores it and tries not to engage with it as an equal. In this way, whole cultures and peoples - alive and with much to offer to global culture - can be dismissed as old-fashioned, quaint or banal, or as offering little more than an opportunity for a museum exhibit. Refusal to engage is the exclusive privilege of the dominant partner in such an encounter. No such luxury is afforded to those who are forced to accept claims of Western Universalism; they must either engage by accepting the terms of the debate established by the West or else continue to be excluded.

An even more insidious way of dealing with the sense of difference is for the dominant side to pretend to adopt the ways and styles of the other – but only in order to disarm and bend it to its will. This strategy, known as 'inculturation', has been rampantly practised in Christian history for conquest and conversion. For centuries, Church theologians and officials have debated and adjudicated hundreds of specific cases of inculturation experiments by enterprising missionaries in Africa, Latin America and Asia. They determined what to allow and what to ban. These rulings have official authority and are important in understanding how Christians expand market share through constant adaptation and self-correction.

The inculturation process works in stages. At first, the native tradition is honored by the missionaries. Some of the natives' practices and symbols are superficially adopted to instill a feeling of pride that their heritage is being appreciated. The short-term intention is to make Christianity seem less alien and hence attractive to the natives. In the long term, however, the indigenous peoples are weaned away from the core of their religious identities and their traditional identities eventually become an innocuous husk; their very meaning transformed into a pale reflection of Christianity. Once the new member is firmly placed in this ambiguous or hybrid religion, has burnt bridges with native traditions, and become dependent on the Church, the proverbial knife is twisted. In the case of Hinduism, Hindu aspects are downplayed, and Christian aspects emphasized. This is done carefully after ensuring that the link with Hinduism is sufficiently softened and the person's dependency on the missionaries is strong. Hinduism is not yet denigrated openly but caste, dowry, female 'abuses' and other examples of 'backwardness' are emphasized as the defining qualities. In the final stage of Hinduphobia, Hinduism is openly attacked, and the person is turned into an aggressive Christian. It is only after analyzing the long-term implications of this transformation that the treachery becomes apparent.

The concept of digestion shares many aspects of the strategies discussed previously and is in part, a consequence of them. The digestion of one culture by another is carried out under the guise of a desire to assimilate, reduce differences, and gradually dilute and sideline the less dominant culture. At the level of popular culture, India and the West may meet as equals but at deeper levels, where the core assumptions of a civilization reside, the playing field is tilted. Cultural appropriation gives a false impression of equalization. The less powerful culture is assimilated into the dominant one in such a way that:

1. The dominant civilization dismembers the weaker one into parts from which it picks and chooses which pieces it wants to appropriate.
2. These appropriated elements get mapped onto the language and social structures of the dominant civilization's own history and paradigms, leaving little, if any, trace of the links to the source tradition.
3. The civilization that was thus digested gets depleted of its cultural and social capital because the appropriated elements are modified to fit the host's own history, and these elements are shown to be disconnected from, and even in conflict with, the source civilization.
4. The depleted civilization enters the proverbial museum as yet another dead culture, ceasing to pose a threat to the dominant one.

After being digested, what is left of a civilization is waste to be excreted and destroyed. The erasure of differences is what makes a culture vulnerable to becoming digested and recast in the image of the host's frameworks and structures. The dominant side superimposes its concepts, aesthetics, language, paradigms, historical template and philosophy, positioning them as the universal worldview. Concurrently, the images, symbols, histories and languages of the weaker culture get absorbed, with inevitable distortion, into the dominant one.

A counterargument to this claim states that the host civilization itself (the West, in this case) undergoes mutation as a result of digesting another civilization. Also, the enhancement of the predator civilization and corresponding depletion of the civilization being preyed upon are interpreted by many historians as the desirable march of world civilization - with the West positioned as the axis and as the engine driving humanity forward. Non-Western civilizations are considered relevant only as sources of Western civilization (as in 'our past'), as theatres in which the West operates ('our civilizing mission') or as threats to Western interest ('our frontiers'). The interests and identities of the cultures that get digested are of little consequence.

Besides the obvious racism inherent in such arguments, there is the collective loss of human diversity and shared accomplishments. In harvesting the fruits of other civilizations, the West has also destroyed their roots, thereby completely eliminating their ability to produce more bountiful harvests. The elements appropriated are terminal, because the residual skeletons of the digested civilizations are incapable of further creative evolution and contributions. Just as the non-West bequeathed gifts that have enriched the world (even though in most cases these have been reclassified as Western history and progress), there is undeniably much more that would have been produced from those sources had they not been digested.

We have seen how a common means by which a dominant party resolves its difference anxiety is through digestion - much as a predator consumes another as food. The following figure illustrates the various processes at work. The digestion is analogous to the food consumed by a host in that what is useful gets assimilated into the host, while that which does not fit the host's structure gets eliminated as waste. Resultantly, the source tradition, similar to the food, ceases to exist, and the host (i.e., the West) gets strengthened. The overall diversity of cultures suffers, because there is greater homogeneity as a result of the loss of the source tradition.

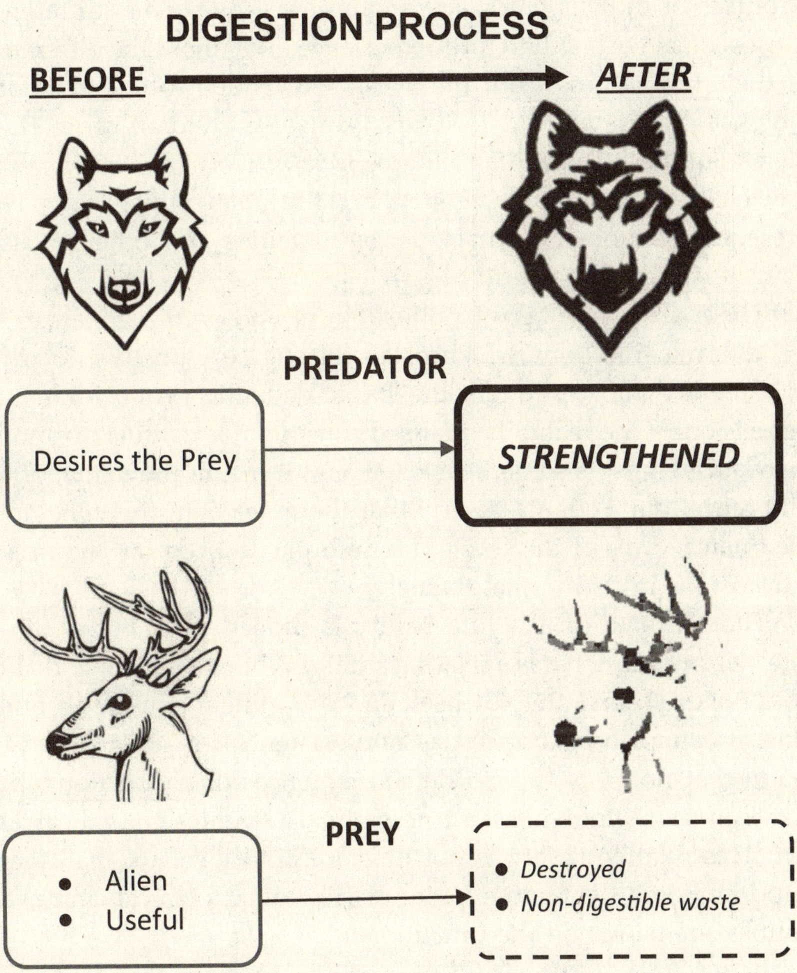

Figure 2: Phenomenon of Digestion

The Problem of Sameness

Our cultural leaders, global *guru*-s and so-called dharmic institutions have provided little in terms of an opposing dialectic. A large populace of Indians has been programmed to fear that difference causes violence and therefore, experience guilt about the difference of their Indian-ness from the West. They hope to end religious violence by gravitating towards 'sameness' and diluting their own identities. The Indian elite especially feel comfortable with the 'clean' Westernized version of Hinduism which sameness presents – devoid of rituals, *agama-s,* deities and other aspects that the West is unable to digest.

There are a number of philosophical and spiritual stances in the dharma traditions which ostensibly agree with this doctrine of sameness. For example, the basic Vedantic proposition that there is only One reality has caused considerable confusion among many. 'Oneness' is sometimes cited as if it meant the denial of all difference, but Vedanta asserts that there are both the 'One' and the 'many forms of the One'. The multiplicity of forms comprises our cosmos in its infinite diversity.

The ultimate or absolute reality is indeed One, but with an internal structure that is a relative reality. While this relative reality does not exist separately by itself and is contingent on the absolute One, it cannot be dismissed as non-existent. It is in this relative realm that not only *karma* (the consequences of past actions) but also *dharma* (the pursuit of a true path) are manifested and carried out. This relative reality is not illusion. Both levels of reality are important, and the relative point of view makes ethical, and even political demands on the practitioner.

It is a misinterpretation of Vedanta to state that since the existence of our world is only relative and not absolute, no worldly outcomes should matter. In truth, no school of dharma calls for the abandonment of the relative world, and every school of dharma encourages responsible action without attachments to the rewards. This is the central theme of the *Bhagavad Gita* in which Krishna educates Arjuna not to escape responsibility in this relative world.

If differences did not exist in the relative reality, there would be no ethics, because dharma and adharma would be viewed as the same. The idea that everything is the same cannot be used to guide our actions in this relative world. Thus, the naive principle of sameness violates dharma teachings which clearly differentiate between *sat* (truth) and *asat* (falsity), *daivika* and *asurika*.[21]

Such misunderstanding of dharma is a common safe haven for those Hindus who suffer from ignorance of dharma, fear of being associated with 'the Hindu Right', or merely the pressure to be politically correct. Such Hindus approach difference as unreal and the problem itself as illusory, hence as something to ignore. In practice, this passive posture leads to the dilution, distortion and eventual digestion of their dharma.

Indians who misunderstand the teachings of Vedanta are inclined to interpret the Christian mission, especially in the form of inculturation or tolerance, as a form of respect for Hinduism and acceptance of its truth. When a Christian adopts the guise of a Hindu and approaches a Hindu community, Hindus tend to see this as an honest acknowledgment of sameness. They respond openly, dropping their guard despite the centuries of duplicity under which they have suffered. Herein lies the real danger - in fooling Hindus into believing there is a level playing field, or that there is no competitive motive at all.

Simply because the Christian evangelist approaches, seeming like a Hindu and using Sanskrit terms, Hindu symbolism and gestures, the Hindu erroneously concludes that he also accepts Krishna, Shiva and Devi as manifestations of the Supreme Being. The Hindu naively assumes that the Christian considers *puja* to be a valid prayer on par with Biblical prayer, that the Christian respects the murti-s as sacred, and that he regards the guru-s as enlightened and not just 'wise teachers'.

The hard reality, however, is that most Christian denominations forbid their followers to validate even Judaism or Islam, much less Hinduism or Buddhism. The assertion of some vaguely Hindu 'sameness' of all religions is a one-way street which perniciously pushes the dharmic traditions towards dilution and assimilation;

indeed, this process may lead to their eventual digestion into the belly of expansive institutionalized religions. Patanjali's *Yoga Sutra*-s, the seminal ancient text of the profound philosophy and psychology on which Yoga is based, is in some quarters, being reduced to a simple form of Western cognitive science.

When Western seekers enter the Indian spiritual arena, they tend to slip into the common misperceptions about Vedanta noted previously and over-prize what are the 'same' in the various religions, conveniently overlooking the very real (and valuable) differences. Also, the Western seeker does not approach this task with a clean slate; there has been past conditioning as a result of his or her collective identity as Jewish, Christian, or secular. This cannot be emphasized enough: The Westerner's mental framework is already wired for certain values, attitudes and categories. Therefore, what is termed 'universal' is in effect largely Western in disguise. We shall see how this leads to contradictions and tensions across various cultures.

Post-modernism, a philosophical trend in Western academics to which both secular Indian intellectuals and spiritually inclined Indians are drawn, has made it fashionable to deconstruct what its adherents call the 'grand narratives' of history, seeing these as little more than the stories of the triumph of Western progress, largely achieved by suppressing or violently overthrowing other groups. More problematically, post-modernists advocate that all identities be dismantled or blurred and view all positively distinctive cultures as being oppressive to weaker, or less assertive ones. Several popular writers have adopted the post-modern stance and assumed that today's America exemplifies a society in which hybrid cultures are blurring identities and making all boundaries obsolete. America, according to this view, is on its way to becoming a society free from difference anxiety, because American society is getting freed of its chauvinistic grand narratives.

The ground reality, however, is different. Beneath the veneer of popular culture, the foundation of the West, especially with respect to its Judeo-Christian roots, remains largely intact. Post-modern scholars would do well to go beyond the analysis of pop culture and abstract patterns and attempt to deconstruct the oppressive Western institutions of government, business and Christianity, where the power structure really resides. American socio-political unity has been achieved and maintained from the beginning through a frontier mentality which has always needed an outsider to annex, and then effectively eliminate.

Post-modern deconstruction facilitates the digestion of dharma into the West by disassembling it into a library of random, unrelated components similar to the way clip art is copy-pasted as useful additions to proprietary frameworks. Some scholars take these components apart so as to de-contextualize them from the rest of the dharma tradition, thereby enabling them to be digested or destroyed selectively. The digestion of Indian civilization by the West is encouraged by arguments that there is no such thing as an Indian civilization, the claim being that Hinduism is an artificial construct developed under British influence.

As discussed previously, dharmic sameness arguments and post-modernism induced escapism are not solutions in the face of cultural genocide. An effective response to complex, multi-phase phenomena like digestion requires considerable strategic maturity.

Poison Pills

A strategic way of dealing with the universalist march of digestion is to introduce elements called 'poison pills' into the dharma narrative that cannot be separated from the Vedic context. Poison pills are those non-negotiable elements or tenets that cannot be digested into the DNA of a predator, because consuming them would lead to the destruction of the predator's constitution. If a predator absorbs such an element, it will mutate so profoundly that it will not survive. The predator, as such, will be dead, even though some new identity may have emerged in its place. These poison pills are intended to be dangerous for consumption by predators. This will safeguard dharma and also provoke the Abrahamic religions to undergo a dramatic change from some of their current defining doctrines and dogmas.

The presence of poison pills in Hinduism will create a conflict within the predatory culture: on the one hand, members of that culture want to appropriate Hindu ideas and practices such as Yoga, meditation, *Advaita* (non-dual philosophies), and so forth. On the other hand, as these contain poison pills (such as karma-reincarnation), they undermine some of the predator's core tenets. This use of poison pills for our defense will work only if we can prevent the subdivision of Hinduism into parts, because once it gets divided and compartmentalized, the predator can pick what he wants and ignore the poison pills. Therefore, the poison pills must remain non-negotiable and integral parts of Hindu dharma. The principle of Integral Unity introduced in the book *Being Different* (detailed in the next section) is vital to its survival.[22] The skillful deployment of this device can equip Hindus for encounters with others, even those who do not see themselves as predators but whose approaches are, perhaps unintentionally, predatory.

Some have raised concerns that the term 'poison pill' has a negative connotation and should be replaced by something that sounds positive. But poison pills need to be understood with the same positivity as Shiva's *trishul* (trident), used for piercing the veil of falsehood, and thereby liberating mankind from the bondage of ignorance. The poisoning is similar to killing the ego, except now it is the collective ego of the West (the predator).

Sanskrit non-translatables must be understood in the context of poison pills. The Sanskrit non-translatables strategy is a means to regain *adhikara*, the right of dharmic peoples to control the interpretation of knowledge in their own framework. This is a fundamental first step required to prevent digestion into a Western Universalism and in the long run, prevent a complete cultural genocide.

Regaining the Adhikara

The metabolism of digestion and the processes enabling cultural genocide have to be understood so that there is hope to counter them. Digestion works in a series of steps and only by understanding the entire process can one understand its ultimate consequences. First, the 'desirable' elements (such as a subset of Yoga) are separated from the rest of the source tradition, thereby rupturing its integral unity. These separated elements then get 'scrubbed' to wash away or cleanse the dharmic contexts in which they are naturally found so as to 'secularize' them. Finally, they get re-contextualized either as Judeo-Christian or as Western science while the dharmic sources get erased or else, denigrated as inferior. As a result, the predator culture boosts its power at the expense of the source that is digested. The adopted practices thus get distorted so as to make them 'digestible'. To illustrate, Swami Vivekananda triggered an avalanche of Hindu influences in the West, but over time, these became digested into various trendy 'Western thought' movements.[23] There are also cognate enterprises such as 'Christian Yoga', 'Non-Dual/Integral Christianity' and 'Integral Judaism', all of which borrow heavily from Hinduism and related healing modalities, usually without attribution.

In an effort to boost their own status, scholars who serve as facilitators of digestion typically map Hindu contributions onto Western frameworks. While many such digestions do enhance humanity's collective knowledge, several others cause serious distortions. In any case, the lack of formal acknowledgement contributes to a tendency to treat the Hindu sources as redundant and irrelevant. This limits the potential for Hinduism to continue to play its part in human consciousness evolution and reduces it to an archaism which is left behind because it is supposedly superseded by 'new' paradigms.

There are those who question why it is bad for Hinduism to get digested in this way. After all, the prey is absorbed into the life of the predator and can actually extend that life and contribute to its 'evolution'. To address this issue, it is useful to contrast Western appropriations from Greece with Western appropriations from India.

The modern conception of the West includes Greece as a subset, making it unnecessary to replace Hellenistic sources with other Western substitutes. Therefore, Hellenistic sources have retained their identity and distinctiveness as part of what is seen as 'our Western past'. When such classical thinkers as Plato and Aristotle are used as source material by modern Western scholars, they invariably receive proper attribution. It must be noted, however, that Hellenistic sources have been incorporated only selectively and their religious elements, which are 'pagan' in nature, have been mummified.

In contrast, for many Western scholars, India remains the alien 'other'. India is too different, too far away and too vast and varied to be included intact as a subset within the West in the way Greece has been. The inclusion of a unified India in the Western self-conception would threaten the very sense of what it means to be 'Western'. Therefore, what India offers must be taken apart so that it can be separately consumed and digested without attribution or preservation of the names of the sources. For this to become possible, the coherence and unity of India must be undermined, so that it is made to appear fragmented and incoherent.

This intellectual breakup of India is akin to a predator tearing apart its prey into morsels that lend themselves to digestion. It would not be feasible for a predator to swallow a large prey whole. Instead, it must be cut into parts, and as each part passes through the predator's digestive system, it must be further broken down systematically, until every last protein and nucleic acid molecule has been processed by enzymes to yield raw material as nutrients for the predator's growth. Ultimately, no trace remains of the prey's own DNA; the raw-material nutrients produced by digestion are reassembled into the predator's cells, under the control of the predator's DNA.

The appropriation and absorption of non-Western sources into the West proceeds in a similar digestive process, so that the West may retain its sense of selfhood while capturing those aspects of India it seeks to own. This is why mainstream Western academics do not teach Bharata, Kapila, Panini, Patanjali, Bhartrahi, Shankara, Kautilya, Kalidasa, Nagarjuna, Aryabhatta and Ramanuja, and other Indian greats on par with Greek thinkers such as Aristotle and Plato. We believe that the classical thinkers of all civilizations ought to be incorporated into curricula based solely on their merit and current relevance.

Just as the individual ego is at the center of one's narrative about oneself, so also is a people's collective ego at the center of its shared narrative. The West's expansive collective self ascribes a teleological role to its own coherence. Since it finds itself coherent and views the other as incoherent, it seeks to digest the source of that perceived incoherence by fragmenting it and selectively mapping some of those fragments onto its own framework. Whatever it discards ends up being ejected as the waste product of the digestion process. This is why the act of bolstering one's own coherence, while aggressively undermining the coherence of others, is undeniably central to the fight for world dominance.

It is unfortunate that Hindu and Buddhist ideas are routinely attributed to Western sources - be they Hellenistic, early Christian or modern. This methodical re-mapping allows contemporary Western thinkers to co-opt the mantle of India's wisdom for their own. To protect, what is called 'Western heritage' from the exposure of its vast indebtedness to Indian civilization, each successive generation promotes the further dilution and erasure of India's pivotal influence. Worse yet, it has become trendy among Western thinkers to reject Indian thought while simultaneously espousing similar ideas clothed in Western vocabulary.

The openness of both Hinduism and Buddhism has helped these traditions spread and flourish across Asia for several centuries. But the export markets in Asia in those centuries were different from the present-day Western ones: Asian recipients welcomed and integrated Hinduism and Buddhism into their own belief systems without feeling threatened. There was no need to distort them in order to make them fit or hide their Indian origin. But today, Hinduism and Buddhism face a fresh challenge when they encounter the Abrahamic religions whose claims depend on an exclusivist history of prophets. To bypass this challenge, Indian guru-s and/or their Western collaborators compromise the dharma to make it digestible for the Western consumer. Many Indian guru-s who have been hoisted as prominent 'global' personalities owe their popularity to the compromises they have made.

The practical impact of this process of digestion is that, if left unchecked, those who are attracted to Yoga (for instance) will find it more easily available as part of Christianity or other Western movements which are savvier at marketing and have a positive 'brand' value. They will miss out on the authentic Hindu teachings. Hinduism will become obsolete and perhaps even extinct. A loss of adhikara leads slowly to digestion, the process of metabolism finally leads to a total cultural genocide.

Following the understanding of the forces at play in this kurukshetra, the processes of digestion and its metabolism leading to an eventual ethnocide, it is important to acknowledge the problem. The forces at play are dangerous and well-funded with a long history of successful operation. Most importantly, they have clear and decisive goals. The regaining of adhikara is the first step toward protecting the fundamentals. The focus needs to be on the following:

1. Identifying and preventing the reframing of ideas.
2. Preserving the context of the evolution of the ideas.
3. Preventing the re-contextualization and re-packaging by those without adhikara.
4. Protecting the experiential basis of Indian knowledge.
5. Preventing the mangling of texts, practices, symbols, artifacts.

Bharatiya sanskriti is the only living civilizational lifestyle which has, as its basis, the Integral Unity of the Cosmos (*jagat*). The sound signified by *Om* is nothing but an acknowledgement of this reality. This deep realization is the source for every dharma-driven practice, tenet, *sampradaya, darshana;* one could extend this to every single artifact of dharma. Sanskrit is the only complete carrier of this lifestyle.

The vocabulary of Sanskrit has evolved alongside the understanding of the cosmos and has latent in it the potential for infinite discovery. The protection of Sanskrit and its vocabulary, the focus of this book, will lead to a deeper exploration of the riches it carries. As seen in the historical past dating to the age of the rishi-s, a deeper awareness of the workings of the cosmos, enabled by Sanskrit will lead to the re-flowering of dharma in a contemporary context. The protection of sanskriti and the commitment to the Integral Unity of the Cosmos will lead to dharma-driven harmony and universalism.[24]

2

The Theory of Sanskrit Non-Translatables

Rationale for Sanskrit Non-Translatables

The previous chapter discussed the basis for the idea and conception of the Sanskrit non-translatables. Along with the discussions on the necessity for this project from the perspective of inter-civilizational discourse, what needs to be understood is why the English language by itself is unable to represent meanings of terms from Sanskrit knowledge systems. A higher dimensional signal, when accessed in a lower dimensional medium will lead to loss of clarity. For example, a video made with the best technology today, when viewed on a 1970s monochrome television with mono audio, cannot hope to do justice to the original content.

What follows are some of the major aspects that underpin Sanskrit words and their meanings compared with the equivalent basis in English. The very foundations between the two are vastly different. The sources of knowledge in the dharmic system include the Veda-s, the four Upaveda-s, Purana-s and other schools of thought that comprise the *ashtadasha vidyasthana*-s, while the English meanings have their basis in Judeo-Christian and Hellenistic thought. The resultant knowledge systems carry this difference, amplified with further metaphysical developments. Mapping words from such vastly different systems results in gross violence to the digested civilization, in this case, the dharmic one.

<table>
<tr><th colspan="2">PROBLEMS WITH TRANSLATIONS
• Constriction of Context
• Distortion of Meaning
• Loss of Authenticity</th></tr>
<tr><th>DHARMIC FRAMEWORK</th><th>WESTERN FRAMEWORK</th></tr>
<tr><td>18 Primary Knowledge Sources
(Ashtadashavidya)
• 4 Veda-s: Rig, Yajur, Sama, Atharva
• 6 Vedanga-s: Shiksha, Vyakarana, Chandas, Nirukta, Jyotisha, Kalpa
• 4 Upaveda-s: Ayurveda, Dhanurveda, Arthashastra, Gandharvaveda
• Mimamsa, Nyaya, Purana-s, Dharmashastra-s</td><td>Materialistic Science</td></tr>
<tr><td>Planes of Meaning:
Adhibhautika, Adhidaivika, Adhyatmika</td><td>Empirical Plane Only</td></tr>
<tr><td>Context:
• Vyutpatti nimittah (etymological),
• Pravritti nimittah (intent)</td><td>Arbitrary Relationship of Words and Meanings</td></tr>
<tr><td>Darshana-s: Yoga, Sankhya, Nyaya, Vaisheshika, Purva Mimamsa, Vedanta</td><td>Hellenistic Thought</td></tr>
<tr><td>Sampradaya, Mata, Marga</td><td>Institutions and Sects</td></tr>
<tr><td>64 Kala-s:
Geeta, Vadya, Nritya, Natya, Alekhya, etc.</td><td>Disconnected Disciplines</td></tr>
<tr><td>Karma, Punarjanma, Varnashrama, Purushartha</td><td>No Karma or Rebirth</td></tr>
<tr><td>Multi-valued Logics</td><td>Law of Excluded Middle</td></tr>
<tr><td>Space-Time are Tertiary Evolutes</td><td>Space-Time Primary</td></tr>
<tr><td>Interconnected Epistemologies and Ontologies</td><td>Judeo-Christian Epistemology</td></tr>
<tr><td>Complex Causation</td><td>Simple Causation</td></tr>
</table>

Figure 3: Rationale for Sanskrit Non-Translatables

In order to understand why Sanskrit is unique, why it has a significant number of non-translatables, and why the civilizations rooted in it differ from others, one must delve deeply into the understanding of sound and language in the Veda-s. Throughout the ages, Indian rishi-s and grammarians have believed that primordial vibrations comprise all reality and that vibrations are at the heart of the cosmos. The reverberations from this cosmic 'pulsing', as discovered, constitute the alphabet of Sanskrit, and does not associate meanings with sounds arbitrarily. Human language and the concepts and objects they represent are the tangible outer manifestation of these vibrations at varying levels of concreteness.

This deep reality from which sound and form emerge was not discovered through individuals akin to Abrahamic prophets (who merely communicate God's messages) or intellectual inquiry, but by direct experience in deep meditation.

A rishi is one who 'sees' and 'hears' the eternal truth. Their extraordinary faculties enable them to directly experience the vibrations of the infinite and the concrete objects to which they correspond. The rishi does not compose vibrations but hears or tunes into them. These vibrations are known as *mantra-s*.

Sanskrit texts can be understood intellectually, but some of them are sequences of vibrations with experiential 'meanings' and can only be known through Yogic practice. Their very nature as sound makes them non-translatable. For example, no ordinary word can fully communicate or elucidate the experience of the heat and pain that fire causes upon being burnt. The word 'burn' offers only a conceptual association for fire, not an experiential one.

Besides a Sanskrit sound being correlated with its deep meaning, such a sound can also produce an effect. The purpose of a Sanskrit mantra lies in the effect it creates.

Sanskrit reflects the dharmic belief in the integral unity of the cosmos and it contributes to the attainment of that unity. The uniqueness of Sanskrit and, in particular, how sound manifests the latent vibrations of all reality, is explored next. The primordial vibrations bring about myriad physical phenomena, including our conceptions of them and their names. The one reality becomes manifested as all the diversity we experience, comprising an integral unity. Consequently, certain important Sanskrit words are non translatable into other languages.

Direct Experiences and Traditions

Many Indian traditions are based on Sanskrit's primordial quality. Some rishi-s have described their experiences in terms of *Shakti*, with its pranic manifestations. Others have explained the cosmos in terms of *Shabda-Brahman*, the vibratory supreme reality. According to the *sphota* theory, *dhvani* (sound) and *artha* (meaning) are, in fact, a hyphenated reality - two sides of the same coin - and undifferentiated in their un-manifest essence. As sound manifests, this pairing of sound-meaning remains, but the distinction appears more prominent until the ordinary (untrained) mind believes that sound and its meaning are independent. This means the apparent independence of sound and meaning are at a lesser quality of consciousness.

The Veda-s personify this primordial vibration as Vak, the Goddess who brings forth the root sounds that create all ideas, rhythmic vibrations and concrete objects. She is the generator of worlds and the material out of which worlds are made. According to dharmic philosophy, there are four levels of *Vak*: un-manifest, subtle potential, mental image and outer expression.

According to the Shiva-Sutra-s, ordinary knowledge comes from phenomenal associations, and this knowledge relates to the outer world. The associations, however, themselves need something to bind them, and the energy that does so is *matrika*. Matrika strings together words and symbols, turning them into language that we can understand.[25]

In Tantra traditions, every object has a phonetic sound, a built-in name. An object can sometimes have more than ten different names, but the central or *bija-mantra* ('seed' vibration), which is the nucleus, focus and spirit of the object, remains unchanged. Therefore, if one is attuned to, and unified with, an object's seed vibration, one achieves a complete understanding. Shabda-Brahman is the primordial sonic consciousness of the cosmos. The *Srimad Bhagavatam* explains the un-manifest Om and how its manifestation brings about the Veda-s and all of creation.

Vedic rishi-s see themselves as microcosmic organisms, an exact counterpart of the macrocosm (cosmos). They obtain knowledge of the latter directly by immediate sensory awareness which has been refined through Yoga. Patanjali's *Yoga-Sutra*-s describe this as *'ritambharaprajna'* (vision, insight).[26]

Indian logic, similar to the Indian approach to nature, advances not only by conceptual assumptions but by adopting multiple modes of perception. Thus, says Lannoy, "Hindus discovered, through direct cognition, the mantra system of musical incantation uniting the laws of phonetics and the physiology of sound waves." (Lannoy 1971:273-74) He regards the marriage of words to music as one of the great philosophical occupations of ancient India.[27]

The West's narrow specializations are based on synthetic unity of the cosmos and are unable to access such rich insights. The closest Western analogy would be the scientist's description of ecological relationships wherein the environment and the organism living in it are viewed as a single unified entity.

Unity of Sound-Meaning-Object

As explained earlier, Sanskrit stems from the discovery of the ultimate essence of each object through an insight mastered by rishi-s. Their intuitive understanding of this integral unity enhanced their taxonomic knowledge of animal and plant life. It also cultivated empathy and innate reverence for such life - in contrast to the adherence to environmental regulations in modern society which are often the result of political or pragmatic mandates.

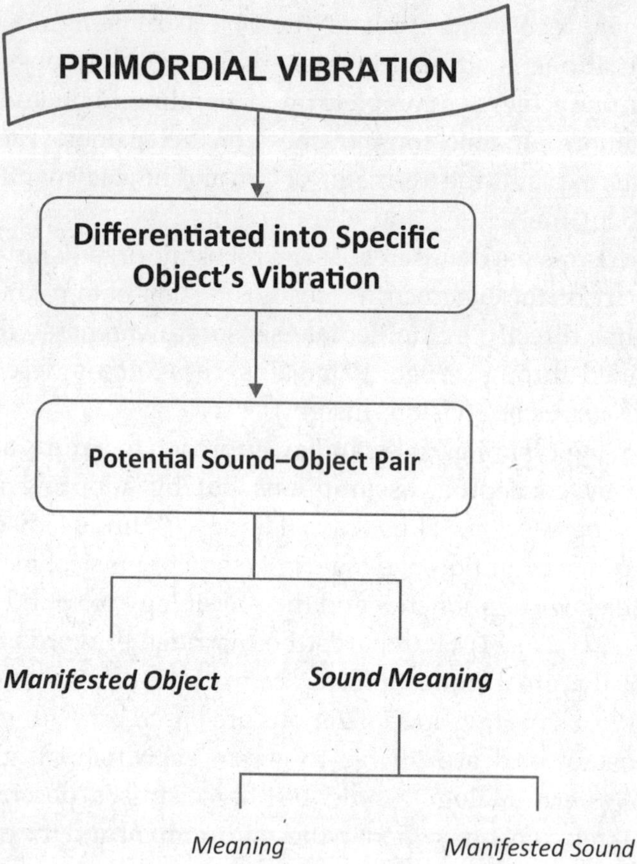

Figure 4: Unity of Sound-Meaning-Object

Figure 4 illustrates how every object starts as a vibration that includes both the object in potential form and the corresponding sound. These vibrations gradually manifest and are experienced as separate sounds. The sound manifests further and becomes the meaning-sound pair. Thus, every object contains a built-in name.

Indian grammarians are also cosmologists who see the patterns of the cosmos (ritam) as homologous with the rules of language. The term *vyakaranam* includes Grammar and analyses speech *vikhary*, with the undifferentiated *Madhyama* (*Sphota*) in the background. The various stages in the evolution of cosmic vibrations from the primordial, unified state to subtle and finally concrete manifestations, correspond to the development of the inner self. Thus, Indian linguistics, psychology and cosmology explain the same reality via their respective disciplines.

Lannoy explains the priority given to this scientific method of discovery over several generations: "The Brahmans impressed upon the minds of every subsequent generation a need to study the influence of sound phenomena on human consciousness by orientating the perceptual centers toward the inner acoustic space of the unseen. These 'ancient physiologists' ascribed an ethical significance to physiological sensitivity". (Lannoy 1971:275)

The Vedic comprehension of yoga is predicated on the words that unite mind and matter.

Mantra

A mantra originates in the subtlest levels of existence - where there is silence. Upon discovering that vibrations manifest as concrete sounds and objects, the rishi-s explored ways to return to the source. Numerous meditation systems utilizing mantras were developed, tested and propagated to take the practitioner to the original state of unity consciousness. Sanskrit, then, is a vehicle for achieving self-realization.

It is important to note that mantras are discovered, much in the same way that Einstein discovered $E=mc^2$. The reality existed prior to its discovery. The same goes for mantra-s, which are *apaurusheya* (impersonal/authorless).

Each mantra is associated with the actual rishi or sage who discovered, tested and verified it. The earliest oral records clearly designate specific rishi-s as the 'seers' of mantra-s. Sri Aurobindo explains the process of discovery:

> To arrive at the Mantra he [the rishi] may start from the colour of a rose, or the power or beauty of a character, or the splendour of an action, or go away from all these into his own secret soul and its most hidden movements. The one thing needful is that he should be able to go beyond the word or image he uses or the form of the thing he sees, not be limited by them, but get into the light of that which they have the power to reveal and flood them with it until they overflow with its suggestions or seem even to lose themselves and disappear into the revelation. At the highest, he himself disappears into sight; the personality of the seer is lost in the eternity of the vision, and the Spirit of all seems alone to be there speaking out sovereignty its own secrets. (Sri Aurobindo 1997:38)

Sanskrit thus provides an experiential path that leads back to the source. It can be used as a device to reverse the trajectory of manifestation, starting with human sounds and going back to the source of creation. For instance, we could discover that from a primordial vibration, which we may refer to as A, there came a root sound, B, which led to a subtle sound, C, which became audible as D. We could reverse the path: start with D (audible sound) to take our consciousness back via C (the subtle sound) and B (the root sound) to reach A (the primordial sound). This is the principle of many systems of Yoga, Tantra and various other sadhana-s.

Transcendental Meditation, as taught by Maharishi Mahesh Yogi (1918-2008), uses a sound called *bija-mantra*, which is at first chanted silently, and slowly replaces all other thoughts. Only the mantra remains. Gradually, the mantra gets softer and dimmer, becoming a faint whisper within. Then that disappears, leaving behind a subtle hint of its presence. The deep silence that remains is hyper-alert self-awareness, and amazing experiences of transcendence occur in this state. Starting with a silent repetition, one has thus retraced a sound to the primordial source. Scientific research seems to support the claim that reading Vedic Sanskrit texts - even without knowledge of their meaning - produces a distinct physiological state.[28]

Hence, mantras are not arbitrary verses, nor are they to be understood only in conceptual terms. Their deepest truth is vibratory in nature, and these vibrations can take us to levels of consciousness that transcend language. One reason Sanskrit and mantras are taught in early childhood by rote (i.e., even before a child understands their meaning) is because once installed in one's deep levels of consciousness, their full effect and benefits will manifest as experience over the course of time. The mantra is sown in the person and produces effects much like a seed that evolves into a tree. When repeated over and over, it vibrates in every part of the practitioner's being and recreates within him the original reality from whence it came.

Sri Aurobindo explains:

> ....Mantra is the word that carries the godhead in it or the power of the godhead, can bring it into the consciousness and fix it there and its workings, awaken there the thrill of the infinite, the force of something absolute, perpetuate the miracle of the Supreme utterance. (Sri Aurobindo 1997:313)[29]

Reading and writing poetry impart aesthetic pleasure - a brief soaring of the imagination. A similar yet deeper experience is possible by chanting, which makes the ear a channel of cosmic reality. Mantra-s may thus be considered as energy-thought sounds. Uttering a sound-word produces an actual physical vibration, and discovery of the effect of that vibration leads to the meaning associated with it. In addition, the speaker's intention, when coupled with the physical vibration, influences the end result. The sound is the carrier, and the intention gives it additional power to produce an effect.[30]

Mantra-s are used to evoke a spiritual frequency and bring about a particular state of consciousness. They are sound frequencies that are precisely sequenced so as to evoke the inherent Shakti of vibration. Over time, the practice of chanting the mantra begins to override lesser vibrations, which become absorbed by it. After a period (which varies with each individual), the chanter reaches a level where all other vibrations are stilled so that, ultimately, he is completely in tune with the energy and spiritual quality contained in the mantra. He who is reciting the mantra becomes transformed in subtle ways. Also, the beneficial effects of a mantra accrue not only to the chanter but to all humanity and the cosmos at large.

Mantra energizes *prana*. Some healers transfer prana to patients. Self-healing can be accomplished by concentrating prana on certain organs, which can have the effect of clearing away an illness. Mantra can be a part of this process. If one repeats a mantra while visualizing an ailing internal organ bathed in light, the power of the mantra can become concentrated there with beneficial effect. This is why a child is often carefully given an appropriate name so that it will internalize its name as vibration, and over time the effect of repeating the name will bring inner transformation in subtle ways.

Discovery of Sanskrit

Yogic experiences are difficult to represent accurately in any language other than Sanskrit for, as Sri Aurobindo has noted, it is only in Sanskrit that they have been systematized.[31] Sanskrit, thus, is the 'language of Yoga'. Sanskrit philosophy states that monosyllabic sounds comprising the Sanskrit alphabet are at the origin of creation. In fact, the Sanskrit phonemes themselves reveal the nature of reality. The root sound of the phoneme references its corresponding manifestation.

Among other languages, Hebrew has similar claims and the language itself is recognized as a sacred script. There are several mystical traditions associated with the shape and sound of its letters, including a strong sense that the letters of the name of God, rendered popularly as Jehovah or Yahweh, are so sacred and so charged with spiritual energy that they should not be spoken or written in a secular context. In the Jewish tradition, however, the source of sounds is interpreted differently, and more attention is paid to the shape and form of the written language, whereas the written form of Sanskrit came much later, making Sanskrit explicitly an oral tradition. Also, it is chiefly within Kabbalah - the mystical (and non-mainstream) practice of Judaism - that the subtleties of language and sound are understood and known.

Islam, too, speaks of the special vibrations created by the Arabic of the *Qur'an*, which is one reason its memorization and recitation are considered spiritual practices in and of themselves.

Both in Jewish and Islamic traditions, Hebrew and Arabic, respectively, are usually seen as created by an external God, whereas in Sanskrit these vibrations are the Ultimate Reality itself, called *Nada Brahman*, from which 'creation' emanates.

It is important to distinguish the primordial sound/bija-mantra/phoneme that is being discussed from what, in other languages, is called a 'word'. Shabda is commonly mistranslated as 'word' but it refers to phoneme, morpheme, word, sentence, sub-sentence, discourse (Mahavakyam), para, pasyanti, madhyama (sphota), vaikhary, sabdapramnam and dhvani among many meanings. Many such phonemes combine into a sequence to create a word. Sanskrit has a dictionary of meanings of individual letters or phonemes, called *ekaksharakosha*.

A word is a composite of many alphabetic sounds. In the case of English, the dictionary offers meanings for words, yet there are no meanings for primary phonemes or the letters of the alphabet. They have evolved from human convention. In Sanskrit, however, each phoneme has rich meanings as a root sound, as well as specific effects on the consciousness. Thus, the potency of Shabda is liberating, for it is a way to gain insight into the nature of the Absolute Consciousness.

The Biblical expression 'In the beginning was the Word' would not be an accurate description of creation according to Sanskrit-based philosophies. What is more accurate is: In the beginning was the primordial sound that differentiates into multiple root sounds, which manifest further before compounding sound sequences are made possible as words. This is to say that much has happened in the creation process before words appear, and this mechanism of vibrations prior to the appearance of words allows the person meditating/chanting to go back to the source.

Only in Sanskrit does one find that each and every word can be parsed into its root sounds that contain its origin and meaning and from which it is derived. Of Sanskrit, Sri Aurobindo writes:

> Every one of its vowels and consonants has a particular inalienable force which exists by the nature of things and not by development or human choice; these are the fundamental sounds which lie at the base of the Tantric bija-mantras and constitute the efficacy of the mantra itself. Every vowel and every consonant in the original language had certain primary meanings which arose out of [some] essential Shakti or force, and [these] were the basis of other derivative meanings. (Sri Aurobindo 1996:449)

Sanskrit and Pluralism

Since every root sound has a distinct meaning, its signature is found in all the words that are derived from it. It is theoretically possible to explain the meaning of the words according to the algebraic combination of letters, syllables and roots. This transparency of root sounds and semantics follows a natural process and gives Sanskrit the ability to discover its own history. Consequently, Sanskrit is an ever-creative language in which each word is the parent and source of ideas. A letter is called *akshara,* which means 'imperishable'. Akshara is the eternal sound, and it does not perish but reveals the entire secret of speech. Another term for letter is *varna* (hue or color). Thus, every letter is heard as a sound with a corresponding visual hue as it manifests. Rishi-s are said to have *seen,* and not just *heard,* the Veda-s. The term for alphabet, *varnamala,* means 'garland of colors' or qualities or hues which an artist uses to paint reality.

Multiple Experiences of the Same Root Sound

The root sounds, depending on how they are strung and combined with others, can give rise to several words, each of which may have distinct connotations, shades of meaning, and special nuances. Since each word is discovered as the outcome of a yogic experience, a root sound or word often has multiple meanings, including even opposite meanings.[32]

Let us illustrate this with an example.[33] The root sound *dih* means 'to gather', 'collect', 'pile up'. This can be referred to as meaning #1. The experience of gathering or compiling leads to the experience of growth, increase, prosperity, and so forth. Thus, the root dih also means 'to increase', 'grow or prosper' (meaning #2). When things grow, they often cover something else, so, 'to cover' is another important meaning of dih (meaning #3). Going further, this covering may be interpreted as hiding, concealing, plastering or smearing (meaning #4). Furthermore, we can get a variety of meanings by applying prefixes and suffixes to the root word. For example, the body is called *deha* in Sanskrit and is derived from the root dih. This is because it is a cover that conceals the self within (meaning #5). We can further add the prefix *sam* to deha. Sam refers to the experience of completeness, totality and perfection, which is cognate with the English word 'sum'. Thus, the word *sandeha* (sam + deha) means 'perfect concealment' or 'doubt' (meaning #6). In a state of doubt, the consciousness is perfectly clouded, reality is covered, truth is hidden, there is no clarity of vision, and one is confused and groping in darkness. All of these are meanings of the root dih.

Figure 5 demonstrates the following: (i) a root sound has multiple levels of meanings which correspond to different but related experiences. When we analyze this closely, we find that all these meanings are interdependent and not disconnected. They form an integrated whole of many levels of experiences, all in a single root sound; (ii) These multiple meanings can each be used to derive words by adding other syllables using the rules of grammar.

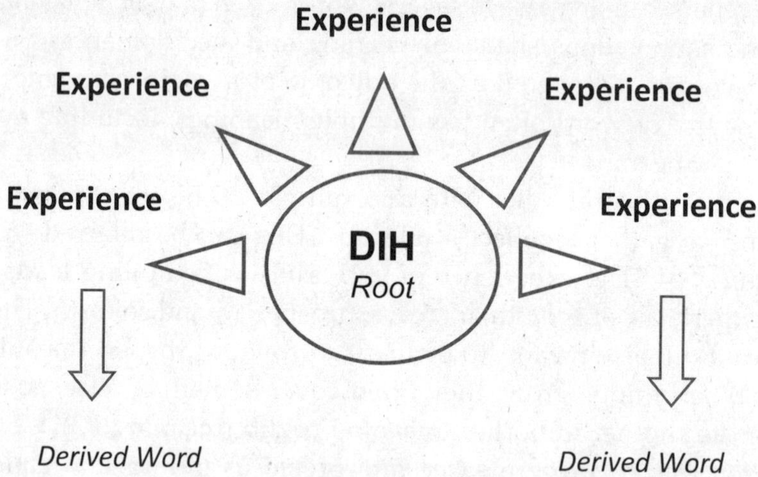

Figure 5: Multiple Experiences of the Same Root Sound

While all languages are able to create new words by combining pre-existing prefixes and suffixes, this is taken to greater heights in Sanskrit, in which the process is based on rules that are systematic, predictable and creative. When a root sound is used to create a word, the sound undergoes transformation according to established principles. By concentrating on a new word created by an expert, the listener can parse its intended meaning. This means that Sanskrit's large vocabulary is open-ended and infinitely expandable. One may think of Sanskrit as 'open architecture'. When an idea needs to be expressed, new words are created by using the root words and applying the rules of word formation.

In other languages, the initial posited association between the sound and the object it represents is more often than not, arbitrary. In Sanskrit, however, words evolve according to complex processes of association with other meanings and sounds. Unique to Sanskrit is the claim of the initial, primordial phoneme-morpheme association, also called *nama-rupa* (name-form), which stems from dharmic metaphysics of the Ultimate Reality as vibration manifesting at successive levels of concreteness. The critical implication here is that just as all primordial sounds are connected to the source in an integral unity, so are all meanings connected and interdependent; hence all objects in the universe are inseparably unified in their ultimate sense. Everything is intertwined, and nothing is isolated.

Synonyms Are Not Redundant

Owing to the prolific outpourings by Sanskrit composers, many words have a large number of synonyms, sometimes as many as twenty or more. A given synonym cannot be randomly replaced by another – not only because of the typical shift in nuance within synonyms, but also because of the distinct root-word-sound conflation in Sanskrit. From the many possible synonyms, those which best convey the exact property being described should be chosen. A deeper analysis of each word from the provided synonyms reveals that different synonyms refer to different ways of experiencing the same object, so each synonym has a specific and definite connotation. Figure 6 and the example that follows illustrate this idea.

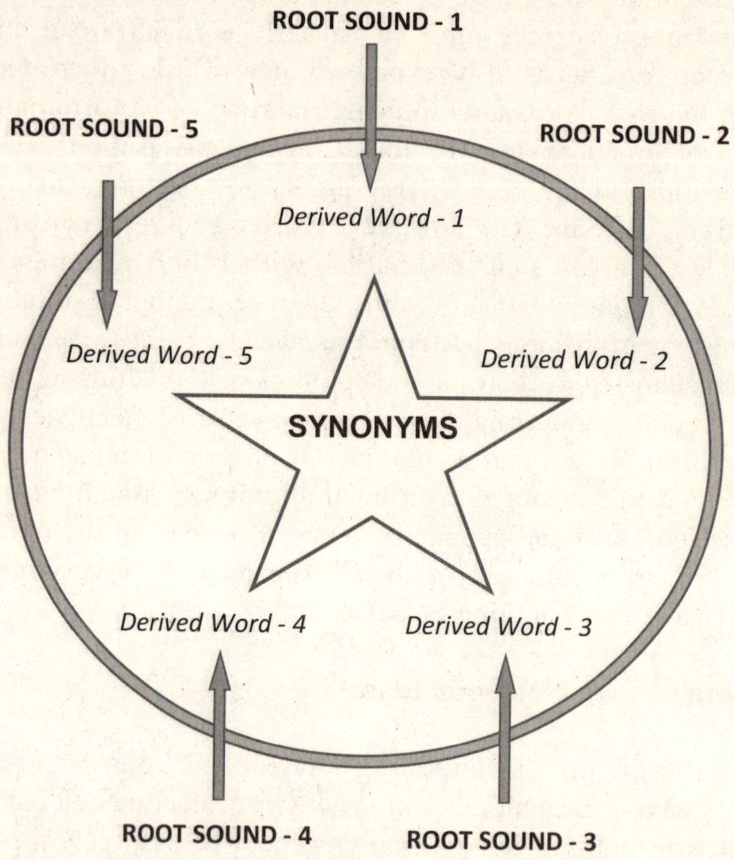

Figure 6: Synonyms Are Not Redundant

For example, thirty-four words for 'fire' are listed in the *Amarakosha*, a Sanskrit thesaurus. And yet none of them are redundant, because each captures a unique attribute. A competent writer/speaker must decide which of the provided synonyms for 'fire' is the most appropriate in a given context.

Proper nouns in Sanskrit are often definite descriptions. The one thousand names of Vishnu (*sahasra-nama*) capture all the various events relating to him mentioned in the Purana-s. There is a composition on Rama, sung at the Ramakrishna Mission centers, originally collected in the city of Varanasi, wherein the sequential definite descriptions delineate the history of His life. Thus, we find that every syllable - and every word built of a sequence of syllables - is pregnant with meanings and acts as a node in a contextual network.

Sanskrit and Contexts

Sanskrit texts, by their very nature, require interpretation in a given context. Content cannot be separated from context or given an absolute meaning. Scholar and poet, A.K. Ramanujan (1929-1993) explains:

> No Indian text comes without a context, a frame, till the 19th century. Works are framed by phalasruti verses which tell the reader, reciter or listener all the good that will result from his act of reading, reciting or listening. They relate the text, of whatever antiquity, to the present reader - that is, they contextualize it. The Ramayana and Mahabharata open with episodes that tell you why and under what circumstances they were composed. Every such story is encased in a meta-story. And within the text, one tale is the context for another within it; not only does the outer frame story motivate the inner sub-story; the inner story illuminates the outer as well. It often acts as a microcosmic replica for the whole text. (Ramanujan 1990:48)

The correct intonation of words too, plays an important role in their meaning, and these were given utmost importance in traditional oral transmissions.[34] An entire meaning could be altered by a change in accent or emphasis.[35] Accent/intonation (*svara*) has endowed Sanskrit with a rich musical quality, which is why practitioners of the oral tradition in ancient India took great care in preserving texts to the level not only of syllable but also of accentuation and intonation. This made it possible to preserve all the Veda-s, Upanishads and other shastra-s in all their original meaning and intent.

Context is also supplied by the situation, person, higher experience and intention of the speaker/writer. The same verse may have several meanings, and stories are nestled within one another. The framing story differs from one iteration to another depending on the audience, and thus different contexts are provided. For example, a couple of Jain poems describe in verse the lives of seven different monks. A literal translation of these verses into a language that is not Sanskrit-based would sound nonsensical and incoherent. When a word with a contextually determined meaning is reduced to only one of its many meanings, it is akin to assigning a specific constant value to an algebraic variable, thereby eliminating its usefulness as a variable.

Every word embodies a spectrum rather than a single value. For example, the word *lingam* is often misunderstood because it is collapsed into only one value/meaning that is taken to be its essence. Incorrectly translated as 'phallus', this has become lingam's normative usage in Western discourse.[36] However, the word lingam's range of meanings includes sign, mark, spot, token, badge, emblem and even gender. In the proposition, 'there is fire because there is smoke', smoke is the linga. Broadly, it indicates a sign or meaning referring to something other than itself. The American flag, the Statue of Liberty and national anthem are all linga for America, yet they are not redundant because they represent different aspects of America. The logo of a company is its lingam, and there may be several linga for the same entity.

Meanings change over time. Hence, insisting on fixed, constant, and isolated values is reductionist and distorting. Sanskrit grammar avoids both extremes: a fixed set of absolutes on one hand, and randomness and arbitrariness on the other, much like a computer programming language which gives rise to an infinite variety of programs while using a precise set of rules and grammar.

As a result, there is no compulsion to reconcile all the accounts of a narrative into one 'official' version (which an expansionist tradition must do in order to spread the tradition uniformly). For example, one finds numerous versions and adaptations of the *Ramayana*. There is no felt need for the lineages of various guru-s, or accounts of various avatara-s and other past events, to be organized into a linear chronology which everyone is mandated to accept. The author and collector (*vyasa*) of Sanskrit works re-contextualizes and edits the Vedic corpus anew for each *yuga*.[37]

The Indian word for a text is *grantha*, referring to the knot that holds the palm leaves together into a book. What this indicates is that the physical unity of the parts of the text does not necessarily imply that the text is a critical edition; the context of the reader's environment is the basis for interpretation. This clearly differs from the Western tradition of constructing the canonical version of every text because that is considered its 'pure' form. There are context-sensitive designs in the Indian texts, and this manner of constructing the texts is in accord with other designs in the culture. In visual representations, there is no uniquely 'true' image of a given deity. Ramanujan writes: "Not unity (in the Aristotelian sense) but coherence seems to be the end". (Ramanujan 1990:50)

The Cognizing Self is Part of the Context

The context is not separable from the person experiencing it.[38] This intertwining of subject-object is pervasive. Indian poetry is contextualized by a taxonomy of landscapes, flora and fauna, and also of subjective emotions, which Ramanujan refers to as "an ecosystem of which a man's activities and feelings are a part". (Ramanujan 1990:50)

The unity of the speaker with the environment is evident in the ease with which Sanskrit expresses action without asserting subject/object dichotomy. The ancient rishi-s were aware that the speaker is not the doer but an instrument. Sanskrit is structured in accordance with this idea and being conscious of it in language can lead to the realization of the non-doer state. In most languages, the passive voice is possible only by using transitive verbs, but in Sanskrit passive expression is natural and the preferred way, and all types of verbs, transitive or intransitive, can be passive. By contrast, in English, active speech - with the emphasis on the subject performing the action in the verb - is preferred. The difference reflects two diverse attitudes: one mindset wants to be in control of action and the other does not demand credit for the same.[39]

Mysticism and the Outer World

In higher states of consciousness, rishi-s have inquired into the nature of external objects. This inquiry led them to develop practical taxonomies of the physical world. An example is the elaborate plant taxonomy in ancient India. According to the assessment of William Jones, published in 1795, this taxonomy was more advanced than the standard Latin-based ones used by Western botanists. Jones writes, referring even to Carolus Linnaeus (1707–1778), the father of modern taxonomy:

> I am very solicitous to give Indian plants their true Indian appellations, because I am fully persuaded that Linnaeus himself would have adopted them had he known the learned and ancient language of this country… (W. Jones 1795: 237-312)

According to Hindu philosophy, each and every element in creation has consciousness, which is its nucleus (original vibration). This principle was the basis on which ancient Indian medical scientists and botanists studied plants. They combined *pariksha* (mental investigation) with discovery by intuition to produce systematic knowledge that could be subject to peer review. The thousands of names of plants available in ancient treatises are expressions of this inner process. Naming was inseparable from realizing its essence. In Ayurveda, the names allow us to understand not only the morphological characteristics of a plant but also its medicinal properties. Ancient Indian *vaidya*-s (medical scientists), could discover the exact properties of plants and their multidimensional aspects without the laboratory measurement and observational facilities on which modern empirical science relies.

Sanskrit and Dharma

Dharma and Sanskrit are deeply intertwined. Without doubt, it is an understanding of Sanskrit, its inherent harmony and generative powers that enables dharma to flower. The Sanskrit grammarian, Katyayana and the author of the *Yoga-sutra*-s, Patanjali vociferously express this view at the outset of the *Mahabhasya* (the commentary on Panini's sutra-s): that Vyakarana (grammar) can be written when the shabda, artha and their relation follow a standard. Shastra prescribes a certain form of shabda, which is already used in a particular artha, so that, when employed (with the knowledge of Vyakaranam), it would render dharma; this also implies that the opposite would give adharma.

One of the deeper goals of this book is an attempt to enable, via the theme of Sanskrit non-translatables, the larger framework of ideas and concepts of dharma into modern conversation and provoke new thinking.

Fifty-Four Sanskrit Non-Translatables

Starting with chapter 3, there are fifty-four non-translatable Sanskrit terms and their commonly used English equivalent that are compared, and their limitations discussed.

The selection of these terms and their classification has a rationale, and has not been done arbitrarily:

- The chapter on *Metaphysics* discusses words that define the fundamental nature of reality. Some very important concepts like Brahman, atma, maya, jiva and others are analyzed.
- *Cosmic Tattva* describes words that define ontological categories forming the cause of manifestation of this universe and the foundation of all that we perceive in the phenomenal world.
- *Vedic Cosmos* discusses words related to the different entities and grades of existence in the Hindu cosmological understanding of the universe.
- *Vedic Psychology* considers the constituents of the *antahkarana* including *manas, buddhi, chitta* and *ahankara.*
- *Yoga* discusses the various limbs of *ashtanga yoga* such as *asana, dhyana, samadhi* and *ahimsa,* and other key concepts.
- *Sadhana* discusses words related to the essential, practical, lived dimension of Hinduism such as *sadhana, puja,* in addition to *Karma, Jnana* and *Bhakti-yoga.*
- *Vedic Shastra* discusses critical differences between words describing *shastra* and the English equivalents which are moored in Abrahamic conceptions, key among them being shastra that cannot be translated as 'scripture'.
- *Hindu Dharma* takes on some of the most abused words, including sanskriti translated as 'Culture', *samskara* as 'Ritual', *dasa* as 'Slave', *seva* as 'Service'. This chapter also takes on the deeply hurtful translation of *Hanuman* as 'Monkey God'.
- The last chapter discusses terms specific to *kavya.*

The chapters on Cosmic Tattva, Cosmos and Metaphysics give the basis of much of the categories and operating principles for the meanings of Sanskrit words. There is much at play in these three chapters.

Darshana and philosophy are used interchangeably in the discussion of the Sanskrit non-translatables. Strictly speaking, darshana has a 'lived' and experientially verified basis, unlike philosophy. The contexts of the darshana give specific framings for the evolution of meaning of words. As discussed previously, there is nothing arbitrary about words, meanings and their relationship in Sanskrit. The three are fixed, unlike languages like English where there are no constraints on them. For instance, consider 'evolution' as a term. Nothing stops one from changing meanings of words; hence, there exists the concept of evolution of meaning 'over time'. In contrast, Sanskrit texts, though written thousands of years ago, still mean the same.

A darshana constrains and frames the meaning of a word. As an example, Figure 7 shows the evolution of prakriti in the Sankhya worldview. The cosmological basis of the Sankhya governs the meaning of many of the terms discussed.

Understanding the evolution of prakriti is central to understanding dharmic ideas of involution and evolution. We study each of the evolutes of prakriti as a Sanskrit non-translatable and the cosmic worldview of the Sankhya darshana is discussed. The diagram of prakriti describes the overall context of the Sanskrit non-translatable. Prakriti is the basis of both nature and the individual.

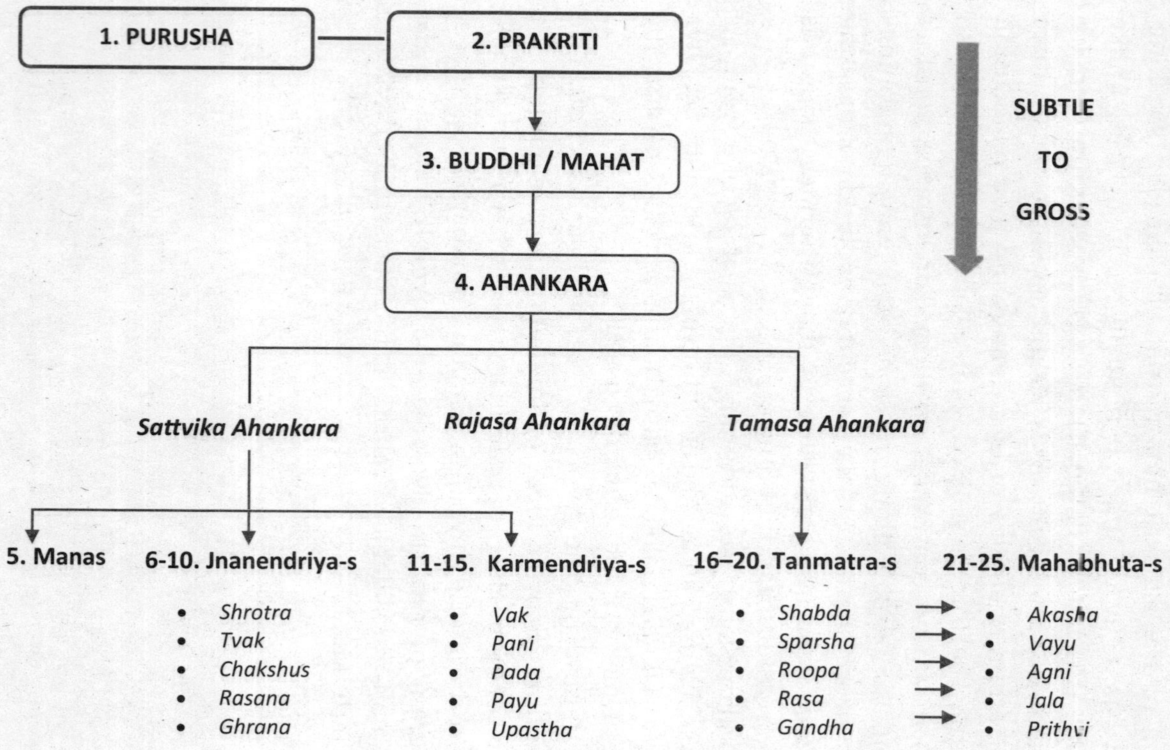

Figure 7: Twenty-five Tattva-s of Sankhya System and Evolution of Prakriti

Figure 8 depicts jiva as the conception of the finite individual in terms of its various components. Jiva, as understood in Vedic terminology has its aspects in constituents such as antahkarana and making up the *sthula sharira* and *sukshma sharira*. Along with the understanding of the evolution of prakriti, the understanding of jiva constitutes two of the most necessary fundamentals to understanding the non-translatables discussed ahead. Both, Figures 7 and 8, need to be understood together for accessing the more subtle meanings discussed in this book.

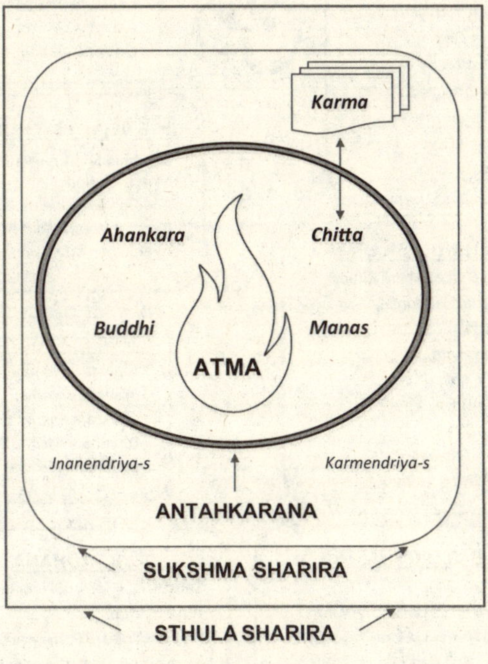

Figure 8: Jiva

The fifty-four terms in nine chapters are summarized in Figure 9. Originating from the primordial Om, discussed in the chapter on *Metaphysics*, this illustration can be used as a ready reckoner to navigate the book.

Ch 3. METAPHYSICS

Saguna/ Nirguna ≠ *Qualified / Qualityless*
Atma ≠ *Soul*
Maya ≠ *Illusion*
Jiva ≠ *Soul*
Kaivalya ≠ *Salvation*
Hinduism ≠ *Monotheism* or *Polytheism*
Om ≠ *Amen*

Ch. 4 COSMIC TATTVA

Shakti ≠ *Energy*
Prakriti ≠ *Nature*
Akasha ≠ *Space*
Agni ≠ *Fire*
Vayu ≠ *Air*
Shabda ≠ *Word*
Indriya ≠ *Sense Organ*

Ch. 5 VEDIC COSMOS

Loka ≠ *Planet*
Svarga ≠ *Heaven*
Asura ≠ *Demon*
Devata-s ≠ *Angels, gods*

Ch. 6 VEDIC PSYCHOLOGY

Sukshma Sharira ≠ *Astral Body*
Manas ≠ *Mind*
Buddhi ≠ *Intelligence*
Chitta ≠ *Unconscious Mind*
Ahankara ≠ *Ego*

Ch. 7 YOGA

Ahimsa ≠ *Non-violence*
Prana ≠ *Breath*
Chakra ≠ *Energy Centre*
Dhyana ≠ *Meditation*
Samadhi ≠ *Trance*

Ch. 8 SADHANA

Sadhana ≠ *Spiritual Practice*
Puja ≠ *Ritual*
Karma-Yoga ≠ *Path of Action*
Jnana-Yoga ≠ *Path of Knowledge*
Bhakti-Yoga ≠ *Path of Devotion*

Ch. 9 VEDIC SHASTRA

Shastra ≠ *Scripture*
Shruti ≠ *That Which is Heard*
Itihasa/Purana ≠ *History / Myth*
Tantra ≠ *Tantric Sex*
Guna ≠ *Quality / Mode*

Ch. 10 HINDU DHARMA

Hindu Samskara ≠ *Ritual*
Hanuman ≠ *Monkey God*
Sanskriti ≠ *Culture*
Agama ≠ *Ritual*
Naga ≠ *Naked*
Dasa ≠ *Slave*
Seva ≠ *Service*
Guru ≠ *Teacher*
Shraddha ≠ *Faith*

Ch. 11 KAVYA

Kavya ≠ *Poetics*
Kama ≠ *Lust*
Bhava ≠ *Mood*
Rasa ≠ *Mellow / Taste*
Prema ≠ *Love*
Leela ≠ *Pastime*
Ananda ≠ *Bliss*

Figure 9: Part 2 Overview

3

Metaphysics

Almost all Indian metaphysical systems deal with the nature of the individual self, the external insentient world, Universal Self or Brahman and the ultimate goal of man, namely, to escape from the limitations of this phenomenal life. In this chapter, seven terms commonly used in Indian metaphysics have been selected that cover these subjects, including atma and jiva, maya, and *saguna/nirguna*. The sacred syllable Om holds a very important place in all dharmic traditions, and a section is devoted to discussing its metaphysical significance. Another section highlights the distinction of Hindu dharma from Abrahamic concepts of monotheism and polytheism while the section on *kaivalya* addresses the Indian view of the final goal of human life and its distinction from the same in the Abrahamic traditions.

The Indian rishi-s had direct intuitive vision of metaphysical concepts such as atma, jiva, maya, etc., which are the fundamental truths of reality and verifiable by one willing to make an effort. In the Vedantic thought, these entities are not independent but inseparably related and dependent on the one ontologically independent principle - the Brahman. The Abrahamic idea of soul does not apply to them.

Indian metaphysics also deals with the nature of causation. Vedanta propounds the theory of causal relation called *satkaryavada* (Vedantic theory of causality) which holds that the effect does not come into existence out of nothing. Any effect is always potentially present in its cause and is only a manifestation of that potential, just as a whole tree is potentially present in a seed and manifests from it.

An important corollary that follows from the principle of satkaryavada is that the cosmos, including all the sentient jiva-s and insentient matter in it, is eternal and has not been created *ex-nihilo* at some point in time. The whole cosmos is only subject to cyclic manifestation and concealment, and not creation and destruction. Indian seers strongly believed that being cannot arise from void or non-being and vice versa. Abrahamic traditions, however, believe exactly the opposite and maintain that God created the universe and its contents.

Saguna/Nirguna is not Qualified/Quality-less

The terms nirguna and saguna are commonly employed in Hindu philosophy to describe the nature of absolute reality, Brahman. The word nirguna is usually translated as 'without qualities' or 'quality-less' and saguna as 'qualified' or 'with qualities'. Thus, we have terms such as nirguna Brahman and saguna Brahman which are often mistaken for Brahman without qualities and Brahman with qualities, respectively. This section is devoted to a clarification of these very important concepts in Indian thought and the inaccurate nature of their English translations.

Brahman is defined in the *Brahma Sutra*-s as that from which the origination, sustenance and dissolution of this entire cosmos takes place. The second sutra states that the essential characteristics of Brahman are creatorship and preservation of cosmos.[40] If Brahman is the source and cause of this cosmos, then how can it be completely devoid of guna-s?

The universe around us has many attributes and this implies that Brahman cannot be without attributes because Brahman as cause, and universe as effect, represent two different states of one and the same substance. According to satkaryavada, the effect pre-exists in its cause in a nascent form. For example, seeds yield oil because they contain it in a subtle form, whereas no amount of pressure can make sand produce oil.

The word nirguna means that Brahman is without any guna-s or material attributes. The *Chandogya Upanishad* (8.1.5) says that Brahman is free from all conditioning such as old age, death, hunger, sorrow, thirst, and so on; the Upanishadic texts deny the phenomenal attributes of Brahman but not the transcendental ones.

Nirguna does not mean that Brahman or Bhagavan is devoid of all qualities. What it means is that Bhagavan is completely free from limitations of finite existence. Bhagavan is also *nirakara* because he is devoid of material form; this simply means He is beyond prakriti and His attributes are transcendental and trans-empirical.[41]

The term nirguna lays emphasis on the negation of material qualities, whereas saguna stresses on the affirmation of transcendental spiritual qualities. Nirguna Brahman also means a manifestation of Bhagavan in which His qualities remain imperceptible and unmanifest. It is important to note here that imperceptibility of qualities does not mean their absence.

In *Bhagavatam*, it is stated that although there is only one tattva (Ultimate Reality), this indivisible tattva manifests in three different ways to the devotees according to their different capacities.[42] These three different forms of that one tattva are called *Brahman*, *Paramatma* and *Bhagavan* by the knowers of reality.

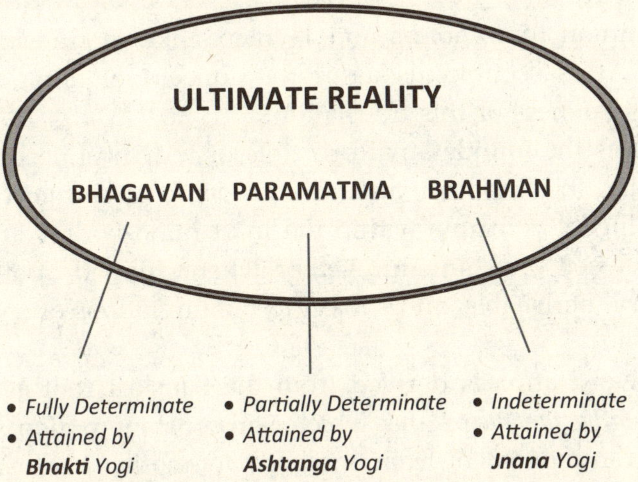

Figure 10: Ultimate Reality (Gaudiya-Vaishnava's Worldview)

Bhagavan or Brahman cannot possess material qualities because all material qualities have dualities. The Purana-s narrate that when Bhagavan Shri Krishna as a child broke the butter pot of mother Yashoda, she tried to bind Him around a mortar with ropes. However, to her surprise, any length of rope could not go around His belly, showing even as a small boy that Bhagavan can be both big and small at the same time. Thus, absolute reality is paradoxical and *achintya* or inconceivable from our worldly point of view and one should not analyze entities beyond the material realm, through material logic.[43]

Brahman is inconceivable for us because the human mind, being a product of prakriti and its guna-s, simply cannot conceive anything which is beyond prakriti. It is for this reason that shastra-s are the only valid means for gaining knowledge of Bhagavan or Brahman. It would thus be better to employ the terms nirguna and saguna as they are and not confuse them with terms like qualityless or qualified.

Atma is not Soul

It is common for scholars and laymen alike to translate atma as 'soul'; this section discusses the concept of atma and the inappropriateness of this translation.

Atma is the foundational principle of Indian philosophy and spirituality. In Hinduism, atma is considered to be the conscious and intelligent principle within the inert mind-body complex. It is the true self of a human revealed when stripped of all that is temporary, perishable, and subject to the limitations of space and time.

The word atma is derived from the Sanskrit root *ata* which means *satatya gamane* or 'that which is in constant motion'.[44] Atma is always in movement from one body to another because of the cycle of births and deaths. Hindu philosophy has at its heart the difference between atma and prakriti: while prakriti is the conditioning principle and subject to evolution, atma is immutable and remains untouched.

In the *Bhagavad Gita* (2.24), Bhagavan Shri Krishna describes atma as *sarva gatah* (all-pervading), as it is found everywhere, within different forms of life, from the largest plants and animals to the smallest micro-organisms. It also pervades the body that it occupies. According to Christian theologians, plants and animals do not have an immortal soul. Similarly, there have been debates in the Vatican on whether people in the newly discovered lands in America in the fifteenth and sixteenth centuries by Europeans and later, people of color, have a soul or not. For a long time, the West believed that women did not have a soul. As opposed to this, there has never been an iota of doubt in the Hindu dharma that all living creatures, whether plants or animals and irrespective of how enormous or tiny they may be, have atma; this is a major difference between the two concepts. In Hindu tradition, atma is clearly recognized as something distinct from the physical body.

Atma in Hinduism is beyond all gender identities and is not male, female or neuter; it is present wherever we see signs of life irrespective of the size, form, mobility of the living creature.[45] The *Bhagavad Gita* very clearly states that each conscious being is a combination of *kshetra* and *kshetrajna*.[46] Kshetrajna is another word for the atma and kshetra denotes the field of activity or, in other words, the body.

In Hindu philosophy, atma is regarded as eternal and indestructible. It is without any origination or beginning, immortal and ageless; the *Bhagavad Gita* states that an atma is never born and never dies.[47] In contrast, Christianity accepts the soul as created anew.

In Hinduism, consciousness (*chetana*) is regarded as the essential nature (*svarupa*) as well as an attribute (*dharma*) of atma. This is similar to the way heat can be considered to be the essential nature and attribute of fire, or light, that of the Sun. Consciousness being its very nature, an atma is always conscious and it is because of the atma that there is consciousness in the psycho-physical body. In contrast, there is no connection between the soul and consciousness in Western approaches. The West's ideas of consciousness linked with various manifestations of the world are comparatively underdeveloped and reliant on borrowings from the Eastern traditions.

In Vedanta philosophy, atma is characterized as sat, chit and ananda. Sat means that atma is eternal and unchangeable and there is no transformation (*vikara*) in it. Chit means that atma is conscious and can acquire knowledge of itself and external objects, while ananda means that it is free from every kind of suffering. A person suffering from some ailment or pain in the waking state becomes unaware of it in deep sleep because atma is ananda and no pain or material pleasure can touch it. Such attributes are absent in the West's characterization of the soul.

Atma is also self-luminous because it does not require anything else to know itself, just like a lamp does not require any other light source to reveal itself. It reveals itself as 'I' to each individual and so no person doubts his own existence. Atma is the controller of the body and is the knowing subject (*jnata*), agent behind all human actions (*karta*) and enjoyer (*bhokta*).

There are two kinds of atma: jivatma and Paramatma. Paramatma is the supreme person responsible for the functioning of the whole cosmos and jivatma is an integral part (*amsha*) of Paramatma, who is called the *amshi*.[48] It should be noted that amsha does not mean a spatial part of the whole because Paramatma or Brahman does not admit any spatial division. Being an amsha of Paramatma means that jivatma is totally supported by, and dependent on, Paramatma. All these qualities are alien to the Christian concept of soul.

Christianity, on the other hand, emphasizes that God decides which souls have truly accepted Christ as their savior on Judgment Day, based on which the souls are either sent to heaven or hell. The soul is thus subject not to karma but to sin, which is fundamentally and completely different from karma. Furthermore, there is neither a monotheistic God nor any Judgment Day in the Hindu tradition, and the atma is by definition, pure, untouched, beyond life and death. The relationship between atma and Bhagavan is thus fundamentally different from the Western relationship between soul and God.

There is thus clarity in Hindu philosophy regarding the nature and role of the atma. In contrast, the Christian soul is not in any sense an integral part of the Christian God but an altogether different entity. There is a disconnect and clear lack of development of the concepts of soul, consciousness and God. While there is integral unity in the former paradigm, there is a synthetically developed idea in the latter, often under the influence of other traditions. It would be grossly misleading to translate atma as soul as the two are vastly different concepts.

Maya is not Illusion

Maya is a pivotal concept in Indian thought and is often mistranslated as 'illusion', thereby creating a general misconception that Hindu philosophy is world-negating, pessimistic and unproductive. This is wholly incorrect. This section explains how maya is different from illusion.

Maya denotes limitation and due to its influence, an individual atma gets associated with physical and subtle bodies, resulting in bondage. Maya is the principle responsible for the manifestation and diversity of the material world. In many systems of Hindu philosophy (such as Sankhya and Shaiva Siddhanta), maya is identified with prakriti. The word maya is derived from the root *ma* which means 'to create or produce' and thus maya denotes the creative Shakti of Brahman or Bhagavan.

It is only the Advaita Vedanta school of philosophy where maya has been interpreted by some as the illusion through which Brahman or absolute reality falsely appears as the universe. However, even in Advaita Vedanta, maya itself does not stand for illusion but it is the cause of illusion.

An important point to understand vis-a-vis maya is that it is not an impersonal entity. Maya is the mysterious and inscrutable Shakti of Bhagavan through which He manifests this world order. Thus, maya has a feminine personality and is often referred to as Maya Devi in Hinduism. This is the reason that Hindus often name their daughters Maya, Mayavati, and so on. It would be absurd to give such names to girls, had maya meant just illusion.

Maya Shakti is two-fold in its aspects and is accordingly divided into *nimitta-maya* (or jiva-maya) and *upadana-maya* (or guna-maya). Upadana-maya acts as the material cause of this physical world. Nimitta-maya is concerned with an individual jiva and has the two-fold function of either deluding a jiva by obscuring pure consciousness or leading to mukti. Jiva-maya is called *avidya-maya* when it conceals the true nature of self. Similarly, it is called *vidya-maya* in its benign aspect when it leads to mukti.[49]

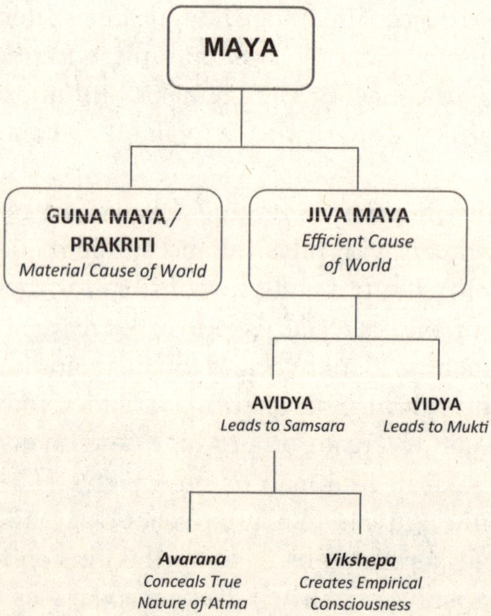

Figure 11: Maya

Bhagavan Shri Krishna says in the *Bhagavad Gita* that living beings are deluded because their ignorance covers the truth.[50] Maya makes us wrongly believe that our true identity is merely this physical body and produces cognition of the material world that keeps us trapped in samsara or cycle of birth and death. Maya functions in a manner very similar to virtual reality goggles which blocks the outside reality, even as they keep us fully engaged.

The effects of maya do not vanish on their own or according to our wish. Illusions, on the other hand, are due to defects in perception (subjective or objective) and vanish once they are rectified. Bhagavan Shri Krishna says in the *Bhagavad Gita* that maya is very difficult to overcome through one's own efforts but those individuals who surrender to Him cross very easily.[51]

Maya has the ultimate purpose of bringing a bound jiva back to Bhagavan. She impels a jiva to activity by creating diverse sense objects and also a desire for them. A jiva, upon realizing the transient nature of material pursuits, finally turns toward Bhagavan for eternal happiness and attains mukti.

Maya cannot understand itself. All the methods of Western science, being materialistic in nature, are attempts within maya to understand the world. When scientists study the physical world, they are bound to do it by using the products of maya, as the mind, intelligence, senses or any other external physical instrument are all instruments of maya. Hindu shastra-s, on the other hand, are discovered by rishi-s that transcend maya and provide a method by which a jiva can become free from maya.

Illusion is defined as a deceptive appearance, a false idea or belief and does not convey any idea of projection by Bhagavan. Maya's functioning is clear - one aspect is to conceal the truth, and the second, is to project something false in the place of truth. The concept of illusion in the West lacks such clarity without the precise metaphysical structure as seen in maya. Therefore, translating maya as illusion gives an impression that it is an unreal entity. However, Maya is a wondrous Shakti of Bhagavan and hence absolutely real.

Jiva is not Soul

It is a common perception that there is no difference between a jiva and an atma and both words are commonly translated as 'soul'. However, there is a very significant difference between the two. Atma is eternal and pure self-luminous consciousness which has no limitations or conditioning. Jiva, on the other hand, denotes an atma when it becomes conditioned under the influence of avidya or karma and falsely identifies itself with prakriti.

There are two types of atma-s: *baddha*-s and *nityamukta*-s. Nityamukta-s are those atma-s which have never been conditioned and have always remained without bondage. They are eternally free and engaged in the seva of Bhagavan in the transcendental realm. Baddha-s are atma-s which are conditioned and caught up in material bondage. Such atma-s are designated as jiva-s and are called *anadibaddha*-s, which means that their bondage has no beginning in time and is causeless. It is important to note here that bondage of souls in the Judeo-Christian tradition, in contrast, has a beginning and is caused by the Original Sin committed by Adam and Eve.

The bondage of baddha atma-s, though beginningless, has an end. These baddha atma-s can become free from their conditioning and bondage by realizing their true identity (i.e., self-realization). This liberation of a jiva is possible at any time. A soul, on the other hand, has to wait till Judgment Day to be raised to heaven.

All jiva-s are atma-s but all atma-s are not necessarily jiva-s. Jiva is a complex entity with atma at its core and many conditioning layers superimposed on it due to avidya. A conditioned jiva forgets its true nature as pure consciousness and wrongly thinks that it is the physical body, manas and buddhi. It superimposes the characteristics of body such as gender, old age, sickness, tallness, fatness upon itself and becomes a samsara-bound jiva.

This misidentification is the cause of several universal problems. People associate themselves with one particular nation or religion, leading to conflicts. However, all these characteristics actually have nothing to do with atma, which is beyond all these limitations. An atma may have taken birth as a Hindu today but it can be a Muslim in the next birth. When our physical body is made in India, we think we are Indians and if it is made in America then we identify ourselves as Americans. All these bodily identities of nationality, religion or relationship to family members are limitations which keep us trapped in this physical world. These identities belong to jiva and not atma.

It is not to suggest that one surrenders these identities and relinquish duties based on them; it is important to execute our duties and responsibilities with awareness. We can either become too deeply engrossed in them and forget our true essence as atma, or we retain an awareness of our true identity. We can perform our duties as a parent, husband, wife or as patriotic citizens of a country without forgetting our true identity as atma. This is the central teaching of *Bhagavad Gita* which Bhagavan Shri Krishna imparts to Arjuna. Bhagavan tells Arjuna that, as a warrior, it is his duty to fight but at the same time remain situated in yoga.[52] He explains yoga as a state where a person remains equanimous in every situation by abandoning attachment to success or failure. It is only attachment to results which leads to happiness and sadness; once this attachment is relinquished, these emotional states also disappear.

Kaivalya is not Salvation

This section discusses the Sanskrit term *kaivalya* which is often translated as 'salvation'. Salvation in Christian soteriology refers to deliverance of a human being from the Original Sin and its consequences brought about by faith in Christ as 'Saviour'. Salvation involves the entry of a pious Christian into heaven and the enjoyment of pleasures there.

Kaivalya is a very different concept and etymologically the word is derived from the word *kevala* which means 'only', 'alone' or 'isolated' and signifies purity. This purity is in the sense of being free from the material entanglements and conditionings of prakriti, which happens on attaining kaivalya or mukti.[53]

In Hindu moksha shastra-s, mukti is said to be of five types: *sayujya, salokya, sarupya, sarshti* and *samipya*. These five types of mukti can be broadly classified into two groups: impersonal mukti and personal mukti. Impersonal mukti occurs when a person gets freed from beginningless avidya and realizes his true identity with Brahman (Universal Consciousness) and merges into It.

When a person stops identifying with his body or ego and realizes that he is identical with Brahman, then he frees himself from the clutches of prakriti; this state is called kaivalya mukti. Such an impersonal kaivalya mukti is attained by those who follow jnana marga.

The other four types of mukti – sarupya, salokya, sarshti and samipya – are of personal nature where a jiva does not lose its individuality, as in the case of sayujya mukti or kaivalya mukti. In all these mukti-s, a person reaches the divine abode of Bhagavan with the help of bhakti. In the context of personal mukti, the word kaivalya signifies *prema* for Bhagavan.[54]

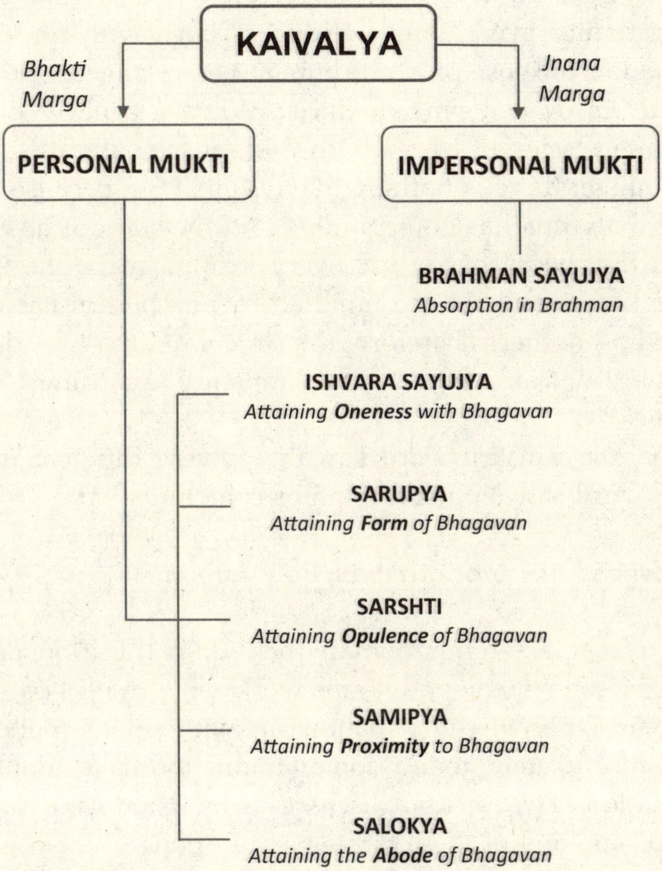

Figure 12: Kaivalya

In the *Srimad Bhagavatam* (11.9.18), Bhagavan Himself is referred to as *kaivalya* because He is eternally free and isolated from all material designations and, in a sense, is liberation personified. In the Yoga and Sankhya schools of Indian philosophy, kaivalya denotes a state of exclusiveness which lies in the separation of self (purusha) from not-self (prakriti). Thus, the word *kaivalya* may have different meanings depending on the context.

In contrast, the word 'salvation' refers to a singular concept. In Christianity every human being is born with the Original Sin. The life purpose of every human being is to get rid of that Original Sin by believing in Christ. When a believer dies, due to the intercession of Christ with God, he/she attains salvation. In Hinduism, there is nothing like Original Sin because Hindus believe that atma has no beginning and the concept does not fit in with the theory of karma. Every jivatma reaps the fruits of its own karma and a sin committed by one person has nothing to do with another. Therefore, the sin committed by Adam and Eve would not affect the rest of humanity according to Hindu principles.

Thus, the Sanskrit word kaivalya is very different from the English word salvation and requires contemplation.

Hinduism is not Monotheism/Polytheism

Western scholars tend to map the Vedic tradition onto the Judeo-Christian theological framework with categories such as monotheism, polytheism or pantheism, without any foundational basis. Unfortunately, today, some Hindus too have adopted this classification. This section discusses why Hinduism cannot be mapped onto any of these terms because none of them provides an accurate and complete description.

Hinduism, unlike Abrahamic religions, does not have just one authoritative book or one form of God. In the past, Hinduism had an apposite, and flourishing, system for understanding the shastra-s in the form of *guru-shishya* parampara. Today, with the decline of this parampara and the gurukula system, Hindus have become ignorant of their shastra-s and rely on speculations or half-baked knowledge available on the internet. Most Hindus are unable to understand the original shastra-s due to incompetence in Sanskrit and rely on English translations authored by Western scholars who are not practicing Hindus.

If the Hindu view of Ultimate Reality needs to be described in one term, it can be said that Hindus are *tattvavadi*-s. According to Hindu shastra-s, the absolute reality (tattva) is characterized as non-dual consciousness (*advaya-jnana*) by the rishi-s who achieved Its realization. Advaya-jnana is significantly not translated as 'monistic consciousness' but as non-dual consciousness because the term 'monistic' may imply that absolute reality is only one. However, the word 'non-dual' signifies that the absolute reality is indeed one, but this oneness does not negate variety or multiplicity within it. The word *jnana* means that absolute reality (tattva) is purely of the nature of consciousness.

There is no word in Christian or any theology, be it monotheism, polytheism, pantheism or any other theism, which completely describes the meaning of the term *advaya-jnana*. Monotheism is an incorrect translation because it implies only one God and no multiple manifestations and forms of that one God. There are no multiple deities or devata-s and there is no profound philosophy or framework which defines the relationship between devata-s and the absolute reality Brahman in monotheism. The doctrine of monotheism implicitly believes that God is separate from His creation and that he has created this universe out of nothing. Similarly, polytheism believes in the existence of many independent and distinct gods, completely unrelated to each other. Describing Hinduism using these terms would involve the blunder of taking a sophisticated, well-defined, and harmonious system and replacing it with a simplistic, limited, and logically inconsistent framework. It will inevitably lead to expunging many profound and fundamental concepts from Hinduism which do not fit into the meaning of these terms.

Christians eradicated polytheists in ancient Rome, Greece and other parts of the world in order to impose Christianity. These polytheists lacked any understanding of the inherent unity of every manifest thing, including their multiple gods. They had neither shastra-s nor the Veda-s. Hinduism, on the other hand, has a vast commentarial tradition to explain the profound ideas present in the Veda-s. If Hindus start calling themselves polytheists, then it would be equivalent to a tacit denial of the validity of our shastra-s.

The Ultimate Reality Brahman is described as sat-chit-ananda. Brahman is immanent but is not exhausted in the manifestation of sentient and insentient worlds, unlike in pantheism. Brahman is infinite and Its immanence does not affect Its transcendence. Brahman remains complete even after the manifestation of this universe from within Itself.[55]

Monotheism and polytheism are merely speculative concepts of a material human mind, whereas Brahman is not. Brahman can only be realized in a transcendental state when a person becomes aligned with that reality. Monotheism, polytheism, pantheism or animism may describe some part of Hindu philosophy but none of them represents Brahman completely. The concepts of Brahman, Ishvara, Bhagavan and others need to be understood on their own terms to appreciate Hindu metaphysics and one cannot replace them with merely one term from Christian or any other theology. In Abrahamic religions, there is no practical method by which monotheism can be verified or polytheism, pantheism, etc., can be falsified.

Hindu scholars should rise above their inferiority complex and not deliberately try and fit Hinduism within these Western theological frameworks for the sake of Western attention or acceptance. They should become bold enough to assert that Hinduism can only be described through the indigenous vocabulary derived from shastra-s.

Om is not Amen

Om (also called *Pranava* or *Omkara*), in Hinduism, is regarded as the most hallowed mantra that embodies the supreme reality Brahman. The meditative chanting of Om is an effective means for a person to unify with the Supreme Consciousness. Om is often compared with words like 'amen' or 'ameen' used in the Abrahamic traditions. Some Hindu guru-s claim that they are identical except for some minor linguistic variations in pronunciation. This section discusses the significance and prominent position of Om in the Hindu tradition and its non-translatability.

Western scholars and some Hindu guru-s use many kinds of seemingly logical arguments to justify the interchangeable nature of Om with 'amen'. One such argument by a very prominent Hindu guru says that the sounds 'a', 'u', and 'm' can all be produced without using the tongue and thus regarded as fundamental. The guru further argues that the combination of these three basic sounds is actually pronounced as *aam* and not as 'Om' as Hindus would like to believe. *Aam* is that universal sound which cannot be confined to any one religion. Any realized being, irrespective of his/her religion, becomes aware of this universal sound *aam*. Words such as 'Om', 'amen' and 'ameen' are linguistic and cultural distortions of this fundamental sound *aam*. The inflection of words by adding suffixes led *aam* to become 'amen' in Christianity, 'ameen' in Islam and 'Om' in Hinduism due to the influence of their respective languages and cultures.

There are several flaws in the above argument. It is against common experience to say that 'a', 'u', and 'm' are the only sounds which can be produced without using the tongue. Guttural consonants like 'k', 'g' and also vowels like 'i', 'ai' which are used in almost all languages can be pronounced perfectly without using the tongue. Thus, this logic cannot be a legitimate basis to regard only 'a', 'u' and 'm' as the fundamental sounds. Sanskrit being a rich phonetical language with a strong oral transmission culture, has emphasized and protected phonetical integrity and such distortions being the basis for something as fundamental and significant as the Omkara is highly improbable. It is very clearly stated in the Hindu shastra-s that Om comprises three constituent phonemes 'a', 'u' and 'm'. Any kind of trivialization and modification of it is not permissible in Sanskrit. Om has a very specific meaning and is irreplaceable.

Om is considered to be the very root of the Veda-s. It is the primordial sound that came out of Brahma's mouth at the beginning of creation. Om is the source and basis of all that is in existence and is the Shakti that vivifies all creatures in the universe. Om is also the basis of all speech and is the Shabda-Brahman.[56] Om is not just any word but a very powerful mantra, which makes it non-translatable and irreplaceable.

Contrary to the importance accorded to Om in the Indian tradition, words like amen do not hold much significance in the Abrahamic traditions. The word amen is uttered at the end of a prayer in Abrahamic religions to mean 'so be it'. The meaning of amen is more akin to the Sanskrit word *tathaastu*. When Hindus chant Om, they are not repeatedly saying 'so be it' or 'yes'. Hindus believe that the chanting of Om creates vibrations in a human body that resonate with the cosmic vibrations. This helps a yogi connect his consciousness with the Universal Consciousness.

Similarity in pronunciation between two words of different languages does not imply that their meaning, purpose, evolution, and functionality are also the same. The chanting and meditation of amen cannot provide the same spiritual benefits as Om. Christian theologians and saints too do not claim that simply chanting of amen would bring salvation. Similarly, no Imam or scholar in the Muslim tradition says that if one disregards all other beliefs of Islam and just chants ameen, then that alone would suffice to take one to *jannat* or heaven. On the other hand, in the Hindu tradition, chanting Om is sufficient in itself to lead a person to moksha. It is said in the *Bhagavad Gita* by Bhagavan Shri Krishna that one who departs from the body while chanting the sacred syllable Om will become liberated.[57]

It is wholly unreasonable and erroneous to equate something of paramount importance in one tradition with one of minor importance in another.

Summary of Metaphysics Non-Translatables

Metaphysics Non-Translatables			
Saguna/ Nirguna	≠	Qualified/ Qualityless	**Nirguna** Brahman refers to Brahman without any material qualities and eternal transcendence from finite existence; defining it as **qualityless** is absurd as there can be no entity without any quality at all. **Saguna** Brahman refers to Brahman possessing spiritual attributes such as satyam, jnanam, etc. The same Brahman is both saguna and nirguna.
Atma	≠	Soul	**Atma** is the conscious, intelligent principle within the psycho-physical body. It differs from the Western concept of soul which is not subject to any karma but only to sin. Atma is present in all forms of life, including plants and animals and this differs fundamentally from Christian notions of **soul**. Atma is eternal and beyond time unlike in Christianity where each soul is created anew.
Maya	≠	Illusion	**Maya** is the principle of manifestation of the material world and creates conditioning and phenomena for the atma. Maya is seen as an aspect of Shakti and has a personality. **Illusion** refers to deceptive appearance or a false idea, which is different from Maya.

Metaphysics Non-Translatables			
Jiva	≠	Soul	**Jiva** refers to the atma in a conditioned state, under the influence of avidya and karma. **Soul** is conditioned due to the Original Sin and differs from both atma and jiva.
Kaivalya	≠	Salvation	**Kaivalya** refers to the purity derived from being free of material entanglements and has many variations within it. This is completely different from **Salvation** which refers to the deliverance of a human being from the Original Sin through faith in Christ, giving entry into heaven.
Hinduism	≠	Monotheism/ Polytheism/ Pantheism	**Hinduism** believes in the inherent unity of every manifested entity. Brahman is not exhausted in the manifestation of both the sentient and insentient world. **Monotheism** has only one God but no multiple manifestations or forms of the one God – this is against dharmic ideas. **Polytheism** refers to existence of distinct, unrelated gods – this is different from the integral and unified, yet distinct entities in Hinduism. **Pantheism** espouses all things as being God but God is exhausted in immanence and there is no transcendent God which is opposite to the concepts in Hinduism.

Metaphysics Non-Translatables			
Om	≠	Amen	**Om** is the primordial sound, considered the root of the Veda-s. Om is the Supreme Reality and expresses the totality of the cosmos. In contrast, **Amen** is uttered at the end of Christian prayers to mean, 'so be it'. Hindus do not chant Om to mean 'so be it' or 'yes'; they chant it to connect with the Universal Consciousness.

4

Cosmic Tattva-s

The Sanskrit word tattva can be approximately translated as 'principle' or 'thatness'. Tattva is an aspect of reality that has basis in experienced truth; it is not a fictitious or theoretical construct but an existing reality, and a truth perceived by consciousness. With their evolved consciousness, rishi-s have been the originators of much of the Sanskrit knowledge systems. We owe them for their abilities to perceive these realities, and for their efforts in transmitting this knowledge via the unbroken guru-shishya parampara-s.

The Vedic understanding of the cosmos is in stark contrast to that of modern science as the latter does not acknowledge consciousness (purusha) as the first principle of reality. This leads to fundamental dissonances between the two worldviews in every other derivative conception. Eight compelling cosmic tattva-s are discussed in this chapter, presenting a different worldview from that of modern science. Gaining familiarity with how these tattva-s are explained and how they fit into the overall cosmic reality is critical. The following sections discuss words that depend on a reasonable understanding of these cosmic tattva-s.

The terms Shakti, Prakriti, Prana, Akasha, Agni, Vayu, Shabda and Indriya are discussed in this chapter.

Shakti is not Energy

Shakti is commonly and naïvely translated as 'energy', thus depriving the word of its profundity. Energy denotes an insentient physical force or capacity to perform activities. It can be controlled by mechanical means, as seen in the way by which we control the supply of electrical energy with a switch. In contrast, the Sanskrit word Shakti does not signify an inanimate, insentient principle as the word energy. Shakti is the divine feminine.

Western science, similar to the Charvaka-s (ancient Indian Materialists), is influenced by materialistic ideas and does not recognize consciousness as an entity distinct from matter. Science considers consciousness as an epiphenomenon or a result of matter that arises in the living body from a particular combination of material elements. Western science offers mechanistic explanations to all processes in the universe.

Kshemaraja, the celebrated eleventh century philosopher of Kashmir Shaivism, derives the word Shakti from the verbal root *shak* which means 'to be able to do something' with the affix *ti* meaning 'capability'.[58] He then adds that Shakti possesses the attributes of omniscience, omnipotence and omnipresence. Shakti is thus an intelligent sentient principle and is the ability to not only do some physical activity (*kriya*) but also to know (*jnana*) and will (*iccha*). She has a personality, unlike energy.

Kashmir Shaivism and Virashaivism frequently denote Shakti by the word *vimarsha*.[59] Vimarsha is the capability or power of Shiva (Universal Consciousness) by which He becomes self-aware and reflects on the events that occur within Him.[60] In Hinduism, Bhagavan is always accompanied by His Shakti and She is worshipped as the embodiment or personification of His grace, mercy, infinite bliss and other aspects.[61]

It is also important to understand that Shakti is not a unitary concept as there are many Shakti-s with a personality associated with each kind. For example, Krishna is often depicted as being surrounded by *gopi*-s. These gopi-s are Krishna's various Shakti-s. A description of sixteen prominent Shakti-s is found in shastra-s such as *Vishnu Purana*, and *Bhagavata Purana*. Jiva Gosvami in his *Bhagavat Sandarbha* divides these Shakti-s into three main categories: intrinsic (*antaranga*), extrinsic (*bahiranga*) and intermediary (*tatastha*). Shakti is not only a transcendental personality but also immanent and pervades the whole cosmos. We, as individuals, are an intermediary (*tatastha*) Shakti of Bhagavan.

Shakti present within the human body is called *Kundalini Shakti* in Tantra due to which an organism is enlivened. She is the source of essential life-governing currents like prana, *virya* and others and when aroused or activated, can lift a person into bliss, knowledge and ultimately, liberation. *Chakra*-s are the centers of consciousness through which the Kundalini Shakti traverses on awakening.

Removing the personhood of Shakti reduces her to the limited material concept of energy. Western scholarship prefers such inaccurate translations in order to fit Shakti into Judeo-Christian-inspired frameworks. Shakti as the Goddess or Supreme Reality is not allowed in the Abrahamic traditions. When Shakti is translated as 'goddess' with a lowercase 'g', it not only misrepresents the Hindu concept, but also finds no basis in the Abrahamic system, which does not allow female divinity. Shakti as a divine, intelligent, immanent and omniscient personality is a reminder of the West's pagan past, which Christianity brutally eliminated. Thus, the translation of Shakti into English as energy is problematic.

Prakriti is not Nature

Prakriti is a versatile and multifaceted Sanskrit word supported by deep philosophical underpinnings and many intricate technical meanings in different branches of Indian knowledge systems.[62] Unfortunately, the word prakriti is normally translated in English to the simplistic word 'nature', with the profound background and context removed in this mistranslation. The word 'nature' signifies two meanings in the English language: the physical phenomenal world and the inherent character of something.

In Sankhya philosophy, prakriti is one of two fundamental entities that ultimately exist, with the other being the inactive witnessing consciousness called Purusha. Prakriti is the primordial generative material principle which contains the whole physical universe in an undifferentiated homogenous state. It evolves through a continuous series of transformations into this world of multiplicity. When this universe gets dissolved at the end of a creation cycle (*kalpa*), then all that is insentient gets absorbed into the original material matrix or prakriti.[63]

At the beginning of a creation cycle, prakriti consists of three constitutive elements (guna-s): *sattva, rajas* and *tamas* in a state of equilibrium. Creation begins when this state, on disturbance, leads to a process of continuous transformation of prakriti into various evolutes of the physical universe, with the guna-s in varying proportions. Each subsequent evolute is more manifest than the preceding one; the transformation is from subtle to gross.

Prakriti is derived from the verbal root *kr* which means 'to do' or 'to create', 'cause' or 'produce'. Prakriti can thus be considered as the original source or cause of every material thing. The Sankhya texts also employ the term prakriti along with the term *vikriti* to commonly denote various tattva-s emerging during the process of manifestation of the physical universe.[64] Prakriti here refers to the precedent cause or the evolvent and vikriti means the subsequent effect, evolute and modification.

We reconsider Figure 7 from earlier, which explains the sequence of the evolution of prakriti. The first evolute to emerge is the *mahat tattva* and is considered as vikriti. The next evolute to emerge from mahat is *ahankara*. With the emergence of each evolute, the preceding one is considered prakriti and the emergent one as vikriti. The series of transformations show the recursive nature of prakriti and translating it as nature eliminates this technical sense.

The *Bhagavad Gita* discusses many meanings of prakriti such as the acquired material nature of an individual living being and the innate character or temperament of an individual according to which every living being performs karma.[65] The prakriti of an individual can be dominated by sattva, rajas or tamas guna depending on past karma, and influences a person's behavior.[66] It is important to note here that the concept of three guna-s is not at all suggested by the English word nature.

The word prakriti is also used in the sense of 'regaining one's consciousness', 'the notion of form', 'the idea of descent', 'the radical or crude form of any word', 'a woman', 'the male or female organ of generation', and the 'seven constituent elements of a state'. None of these are indicated by the translation of the word as nature.

Akasha is not Space

Akasha is commonly mistranslated into English as 'space', which implies a continuous three or higher dimensional physical expanse. The concept of akasha though, is elaborate, treated in every darshana and subsumes the concept of space as a part of it.

The Sanskrit word akasha is derived from the root *kash* by adding the prefix *a*; the root *kash* means 'to shine' or 'to be visible' and is used for akasha because akasha enables manifestation and thereby visibility of things in the world.[67]

Akasha is the substrate of space, time and matter and is thus not space itself but its source. It is not an inert and inactive principle like space but a potentiality which makes room for further creation. When akasha sometimes refers to space, it refers to the effect, not the cause.

Akasha is a transcendental concept and not limited to the physically observable cosmos. Different kinds of akasha which lie beyond the limits of elemental space and time also exist.[68] While Western science focuses on space as a finite concept, akasha is considered to be infinite. Yoga-Vasishtha discusses three types of akasha: *bhutakasha*, *chittakasha* and *chidakasha*.

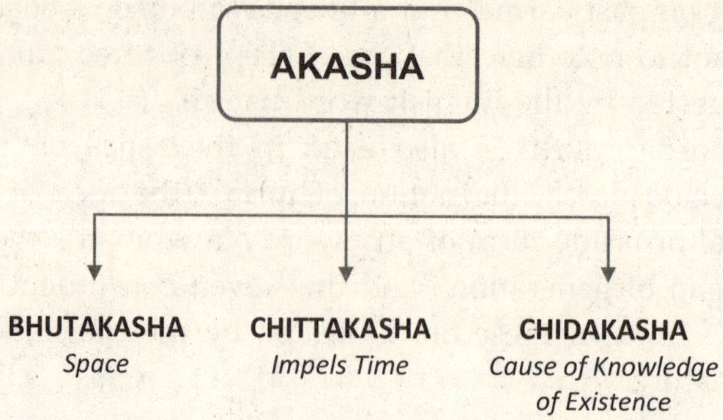

Figure 13: Akasha

Akasha is the substratum for prana, the senses and the mind as well as knowledge and ideas.[69] It is also considered as the substratum of sound. Sound, as a material wave, does not exist in inter-planetary space despite potential sources, but, as an attribute of akasha, it is present everywhere.[70] In Sankhya-Yoga darshana, akasha is considered as a penetrable, all-pervasive reality and functions as a universal medium for finite and separate entities to move freely. Translating all of these foundational concepts as 'space' is misleading and erroneous.

Agni is not Fire

Christianity paints a terrifying image of fire, as an instrument of divine punishment. Hell is Satan's barbecue. Sinners are tormented for eternity through roasting in a raging and unquenchable fire.

Agni is much more than fire. It does not merely refer to the physical phenomenon of combustion producing flame, light and heat. Agni's meanings depend on whether the level of existence under consideration is divine (*alaukika*) or mundane (*laukika*). In its primordial sense, Agni refers to Agni Devata, one of the most important Vedic deities. He is the first *deva* mentioned in the very first mantra of *Rig Veda Samhita*.[71] He has a personality and the physical fire which burns is one of his manifestations at the material level of existence.[72] Agni in the dharmic canon is considered purifying and not a hellish punishment.

According to Sri Aurobindo, Agni is the divine immortal Shakti which God has established in all mortals, which allows them to remain alive and active. He calls it, at the level of psychological sense, as the divine will and active power of Truth-Consciousness.[73] Agni devata is the source of warmth and light, which are essential for the existence of any kind of life on earth.

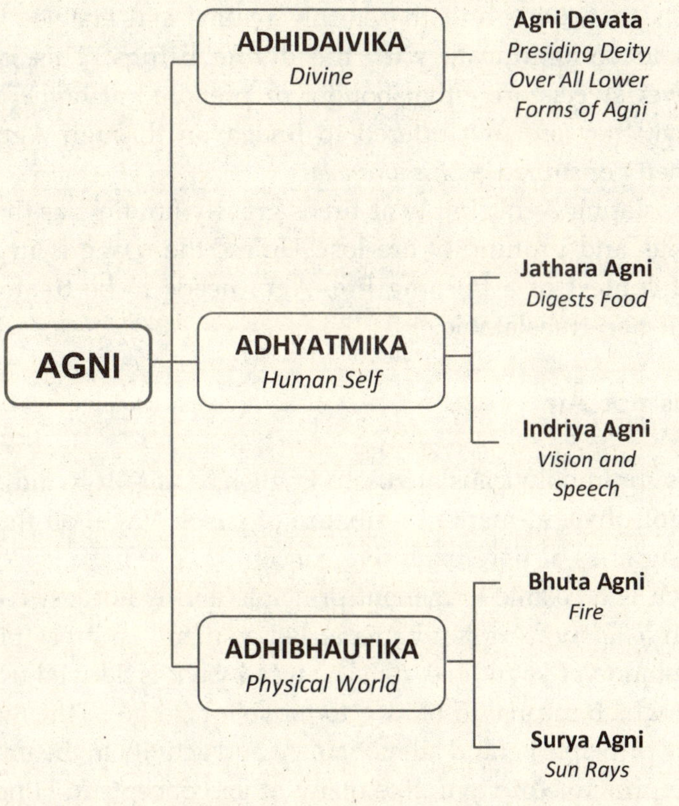

Figure 14: Levels of Meaning of Agni

The Nyaya philosophy and ancient Ayurveda texts mention different types of fires or agni-s.[74] Besides the common meaning referring to the flame generated from combustion of fuel, there is another type of agni which is responsible for the digestion of the food, called the *jatharagni* in Ayurveda or *audarya tejas* in Nyaya philosophy; it can be loosely translated as 'digestive fire'. Bhagavan Shri Krishna says in the *Gita*: "I digest the food eaten by all living beings with the *vaishvanara-agni*".[75] Nyaya accepts four types of agni: physical, digestive, lightning and agni in glittering metals such as gold.

There is yet another Agni by which we conduct a yajna who is a deity and is considered the mouth of Bhagavan Himself. He connects the divine and the earthly realms and enables human beings to communicate with the divine beings. This is why, whenever sweets are either bought or prepared at home on any occasion, they are first offered to Bhagavan through Agni, and only then consumed as his *prasada*.

Translating Agni simply as fire is grossly limiting, as the inner meanings and profundity are lost. Unless the usage is in a very limited context of a burning fire, Agni needs to be treated as a Sanskrit non-translatable.

Vayu is not Air

Vayu is commonly translated into English as 'air' or 'wind'. Air is a form of physical matter, a mixture of gases. Vayu, on the other hand, signifies a more extensive concept.

Vayu is a cosmic immanent principle and is not just confined to earth (*bhuloka*). Air can be regarded as merely a gross physical manifestation of vayu on earth. The word vayu is derived from the root *va* which means 'to blow', 'to move' or 'to go'. Thus, vayu is the very principle behind all movement and activity in the universe.

The principle of vayu, like many other concepts in Hinduism, expresses itself in three complementary aspects or dimensions of reality: elemental, phenomenal and macrocosmic (*adhibhautika*), spiritual or microcosmic (*adhyatmika*) and divine (*adhidaivika*). The word vayu, in its original and primary sense, denotes the Vedic deity, Vayu devata. He is the king of divine musicians known as the Gandharva-s, and he is regarded as the producer of sound in the Veda-s. He is considered the strongest among the devata-s and one of his chief characteristics is fast movement in all directions.[76]

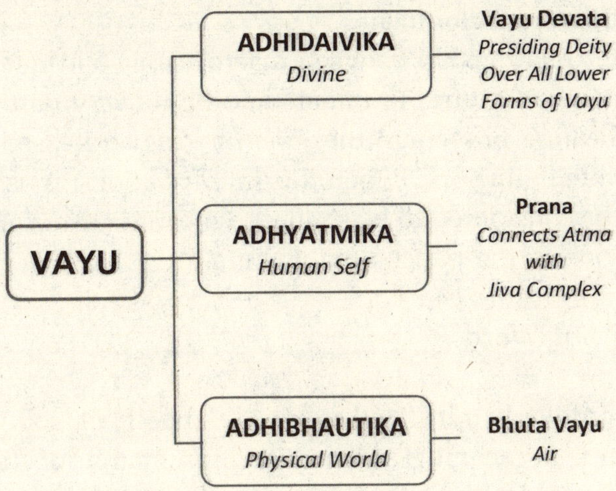

Figure 15: Levels of Meaning of Vayu

Hanuman and Bhima, who are distinguished by their physical strength, are the sons of Vayu. Vayu is also regarded as one of the *dikpala*-s (one who is the guardian of directions) and guards the northwest direction called *vayukona*. Vayu is one of the names of Bhagavan Shri Vishnu and is the creator of Agni.

Vayu and prana are related as the macro and microcosmic aspects of the same reality – what prana is for the living body, vayu is for the entire cosmos. Vayu supports the existence of all beings because of this life-giving nature.[77] According to science, anaerobic organisms can survive and grow without requiring any air or oxygen. According to the shastra-s, no organism, whether aerobic or anaerobic, can survive without the support of prana or vayu.[78]

Vayu is a technical term in Ayurveda. It is used synonymously with *vata* and refers to one of three dosha-s along with *pitta* and *kapha*. According to the *Charaka Samhita*, the pre-second century CE Sanksrit text on Ayurveda, vayu in a living person manifests in various bodily activities connected with movements. Vayu is also regarded as the cause of cellular division in the embryonic stage of human development.[79]

The inter-relationship between macrocosmic and microcosmic aspects of vayu is central to understanding its very nature. There are many healing prayers in the *Atharva Veda* addressed to Vayu which are intelligible only when this inter-relationship is realized. Vayu may be considered to be similar in meaning to air only when it denotes one of the pancha-mahabhuta-s.

Shabda is not Word

Shabda is commonly translated as 'word', 'speech' or 'sound' which is an incomplete meaning and a misrepresentation of the term.

Word, as understood in the Western tradition, is something which does not have any trans-empirical existence. It is associated with meaning arbitrarily and is man-made, transitory and destructible. Humans have been associating words with meanings over millennia and this is how language has evolved.

Shabda in the Indian tradition is eternal, divine (*apaurusheya*), indestructible and is central to man's existence including his ability to think. It is used to denote the Veda-s and other shastra-s and is recognized as one of the three pramana-s along with perception (*pratyaksha*) and inference (*anumana*). Vedic Shabda is considered innately infallible due to absence of errors from human limitations normally caused in perception and inference.[80]

According to Indian darshana-s (with a few provisions and exceptions), Shabda of the Veda-s, their meaning (artha) and the relation between the two, are eternal and not disrupted even during cosmic dissolution. The relation between Shabda and artha is innate and not based on any arbitrary convention fixed by humans. Patanjali defines Shabda as that, which when revealed, brings about meaning. It is Shabda which manifests as sound in the empirical plane through the effort of the speaker and gives rise to meaning in the mind of the listener.[81]

Shabda can have an esoteric (*guhya*) meaning along with the primary and secondary meanings. This is generally revealed by a guru when appropriate, to an initiated shishya. Shabda manifests itself at four levels in any speech process: *para, pashyanti, madhyama* and *vaikhari*.[82] The words uttered by a speaker and heard by a listener belong to the vaikhari level of Shabda. Para Shabda is the transcendent self-luminous consciousness residing in the *muladhara* chakra.

Shabda is considered a quality of akasha and means 'sound' and that which is revealed by sound.[83] The process of manifestation of Shabda begins from consciousness, which propels prana into action. Air, propelled by prana, followed by its articulation in the vocal organs, leads to the final manifestation of Shabda at the spoken level.

There are two levels of Shabda according to Bhartrhari: implicit or inner Shabda, called *sphota* and the articulate or explicit Shabda called *nada* or *dhvani*. The former is the causal basis of the latter. The manifested dhvani is temporal in nature while Shabda is eternal and divine in character. All the innumerable varieties of sounds and verbal forms such as vowels, consonants, syllables spring forth from Shabda and ultimately merge into It.

According to Bhartrhari, the idea that the world in its entirety comes from Shabda is present in the Veda-s.[84] Shabda is regarded as the Supreme Ultimate Reality and called *Shabda-Brahman*, which transcends the bounds of human experience.[85] Vak is another word for Shabda. All the objects of the entire cosmos are manifested from Shabda, making it identical with consciousness and is the substratum of all our thoughts.

Shabda is the *ashraya* or seat of various Shakti-s. Each Shabda is associated with a Shakti in the form of its meaning or artha, which makes it capable of generating the experience or knowledge of a particular object in the mind of the listener. The Shakti of denotation is inherent in Shabda just as heat is inherent in fire.

The profound meaning of Shabda is lost when translated as 'word', which refers to a unit of language uttered in a spatio-temporal context. A better Sanskrit equivalent for 'word' would be *pada* and not Shabda and the latter should remain untranslated in all contexts.

Indriya is not Sense-Organ

Indriya is often translated as 'sense-organ' or 'sense', which is yet another case of trivialization of a profound concept. The five parts of the body, which respond to external stimuli and convey impulses to the nervous system, thereby generating sensation, are referred to as the sense-organs.

The word indriya is derived from *indra* and means 'a sign' or 'an instrument' of the self (atma).[86] Indriya-s are the instrumental cause of atma's cognitions (jnana) and other experiences.

The fundamental difference between the sense-organs and indriya-s is that the former is physical in nature, whereas the latter are psychical and made of subtle matter (*sattvika ahankara*).[87] This is the reason that indriya-s have the same properties of illumination and agility that characterize sattva guna. The sense organs themselves are referred to as *golaka*-s, which are seen as the physiological locations of the indriya-s.[88] Indriya-s can perceive other objects but are imperceptible themselves and their existence is established only through inference (*anumana*).[89]

Indriya-s apprehend their objects only when they come in direct contact (*prapyakari*); otherwise, they could apprehend all objects whether distant or hidden.[90] Some indriya-s like vision (*chakshus*) apprehend distant objects because they are subtle products of ahankara and capable of expansion. Western science though, explains that vision arises when light reflected from an object falls on the eyes, making it a purely objective phenomenon. In contrast, the Indian approach to perception is subjective, although they do recognize objective aspects as well.[91] Indriya-s and the sense organs also respond differently to resistance (*pratighata*) offered by matter.

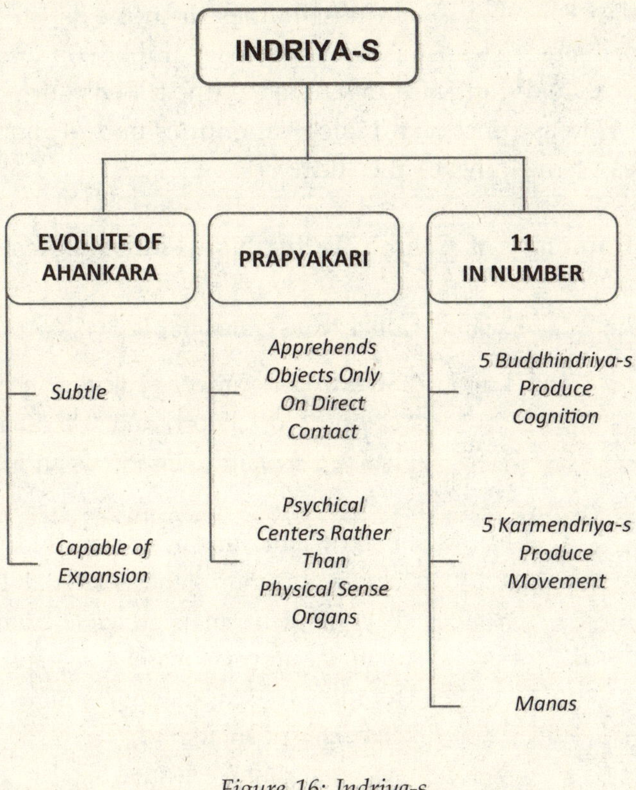

Figure 16: Indriya-s

Western physiology has five sense-organs whereas Indian darshana-s consider eleven indriya-s.[92] Among the eleven indriya-s, ten are classified into five buddhindriya-s (responsible for cognition) and five karmendriya-s (responsible for movement).[93] Manas is a class in itself and is regarded as both a buddhindriya and a karmendriya.

Sense organs, being a part of the physical body, perish at the death of a person; indriya-s do not. Indriya-s are part of the sukshma sharira of a person and not of the sthula sharira. Indriya-s are affected by the karma-s of jiva-s. This is the reason that different jiva-s have different capacities of vision, hearing, speech or mobility, even though physically their eyes or ears are similar. Upon death, indriya-s leave the physical body, along with atma and prana vayu. Such possibilities do not exist in the case of physical sense-organs, as they are inseparably connected with the physical body and are destroyed with it. Sense-organs have a limited role as functional biological entities and do not convey the planes of meaning of the indriya-s.

Summary of Cosmic Tattva Non-Translatables

Cosmic Tattva Non-Translatables			
Shakti	≠	Energy	**Shakti** is a sentient principle and has the ability to do, know, and will. Shakti also has a personality. **Energy** is an insentient principle.
Prakriti	≠	Nature	**Prakriti** is the fundamental and independent ontological principle of Sankhya philosophy. It is the generative principle from which material universe manifests. **Nature** refers to the physical phenomenal world or character of something.
Akasha	≠	Space	**Akasha** evolves from shabda tanmatra and provides a substratum for sound. Akasha is the source of space and not space itself. **Space** refers to the three-dimensional physical expanse in common usage; advanced science attributes more dimensions to it.

Cosmic Tattva Non-Translatables			
Agni	≠	Fire	**Agni** conveys different meanings at various levels of existence, including the Agni devata, digestive fire, physical fire. **Fire** only refers to the phenomenon of combustion.
Vayu	≠	Air	**Vayu** refers to the Vayu devata, prana in an individual; air is only its physical manifestation. Vayu exists even apart from bhuloka. **Air** is only a form of physical gaseous matter.
Shabda	≠	Word	**Shabda** not only refers to word, sentence, speech and language itself but also denotes the Ultimate transcendental principle. The relationship between Shabda and artha (meaning) is held as eternal by the Veda-s. Shabda is also Shabda-Brahman and is considered identical with consciousness. **Word** only refers to a unit of English language.
Indriya	≠	Sense Organ	**Indriya-s** are psychical and not identical with their seats of physiological locations in the body. Indriya-s evolve out of ahankara and are eleven in number. **Sense organs** are only five, are physical in nature and identical with their body locations.

5

Vedic Cosmos

According to Hindu tradition, the entire cosmic system of matter and spirit, with its subtle and concrete forms, is a manifestation of Universal Consciousness called Brahman or Ishvara and depends on Him for its very existence. It pervades, enlivens, and harmonizes each constituent part of the cosmos, with distinctive characteristics and plurality. The process of creation of the cosmos is the progressive descent of the Transcendent Divine Consciousness, through His Supreme Shakti, into progressively more differentiated expressions of its own Self.

Several schools of Indian philosophy regard this universe as the body of Brahman and conceive it as Cosmic Person or *Virata Purusha*. All orders of existence, whether pleasant or unpleasant, are sacred to a Hindu because they form inalienable parts of the playful self-expression of Brahman or Bhagavan.[94]

According to Hinduism, it is possible to experience the whole cosmic order within the human body itself. A person, with his/her individual phenomenal consciousness can, through appropriate methods of self-discipline and self-refinement, acquire the power to pass from one world of existence and experience to another. The term *loka* associated with this plane and grade of consciousness is discussed in this chapter, in contrast with the purely physical concept of a planet with which the term is frequently equated.

The ultimate goal of every religion is to attain freedom from the travails of material life. The terms and idioms used to denote it in one religious system cannot be casually equated with those in another. For example, the ultimate destiny for the souls of believers in the Abrahamic religions, namely, heaven or jannat, cannot be compared with *svarga*. Svarga does not refer to the place of final liberation in the dharmic traditions and is a part of the material cosmos meant for temporary enjoyment of good karma.

Further in this chapter, the terms *devata*-s and *asura*-s, commonly used to denote two important kinds of beings in this cosmos, are considered and their non-translatability is discussed.

Loka is not Planet

The idea of *loka* in Hindu shastra-s is often translated as 'physical planet'. The Purana-s sometimes describe the inhabitants of these different loka-s as traveling in various *yana*-s, or spacecrafts, from one loka to another.[95] However, this does not mean that loka-s refer to planets.

The word loka is derived from the Sanskrit verbal root *luk* which means 'to see'.[96] Hindu shastra-s describe fourteen different loka-s with gradation in the levels of consciousness of its beings.[97] A being living in a particular loka such as *svargaloka* or *tapoloka* has attained the necessary level of consciousness required for admittance to that loka. Beings residing in the *brahmaloka* have evolved to achieve a higher level of consciousness while those in the *patalaloka* are asura-s that have degenerated to the lowest level.

The gradations in consciousness is not just confined to beings in the different loka-s but also discerned among humans residing within bhuloka. These gradations also continue beyond the human level into the subtler spiritual realms with their distinct corresponding loka-s. Beings of the svarga loka have a more evolved consciousness than those of the bhuloka. A loka with a lower level of consciousness implies a more materialistic temperament of its inhabitants. A person cannot reach a higher or lower loka just by taking a flight to that loka. A loka only becomes accessible to a person when he/she has achieved the necessary qualification suited to that loka.

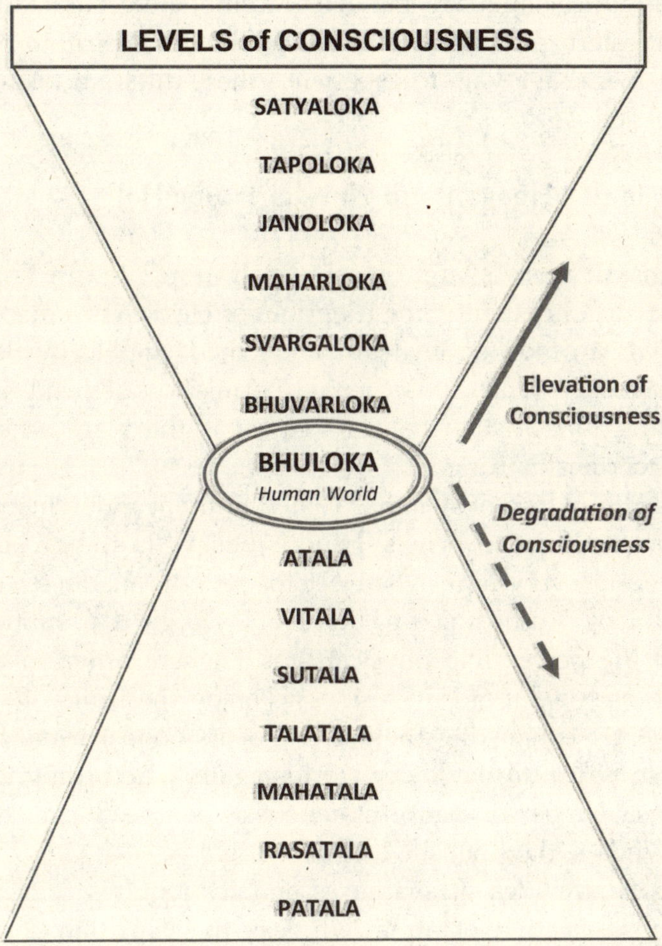

Figure 17: Loka-s

Thus, a loka is not a physical location in the observable world but a subtle realm of existence defined by a certain level of consciousness beyond the material universe. A human, while on bhuloka can experience svargaloka by elevating his/her consciousness to that level. At the same time, one must be careful not to relegate the term to metaphorical language and deny its embodied characteristics by using Western paradigms of sensory abilities. Spiritual practices like yoga enable a yogi to experience these different loka-s in the state of *samadhi*.

Svarga is not Heaven and Naraka is not Hell

The Sanskrit word svarga is commonly translated in English as 'heaven'. In Christianity, the Kingdom of Heaven is a place where a believer ascends upon death if deemed eligible by St. Peter, the gatekeeper, while those denied permission descend into hell. According to Christian beliefs, heaven is the place where God lives and rules as King.

The Hindu idea of svarga is vastly different and in many ways, contrary to Christian beliefs. Hindus believe in the cyclic nature of time and everything is subject to periodic manifestation and concealment. According to Hinduism, svarga is a subtle realm beyond the perceptible physical world where a jiva in a subtle *svargiya* body temporarily resides to enjoy the fruits of its good deeds. After exhausting the balance of its good karma, a jiva is bound to return to the lower worlds again.[98] According to Purva Mimamsa, if a person performs actions as per the dharma enjoined in the Veda-s, then he/she attains svarga.

The Hindu idea of svarga essentially requires reincarnation and transmigration of atma, whereas the Christian concept of heaven rejects reincarnation. Svarga is ruled by Indra, not God and therefore, it is not the Kingdom of God. Indra is not a specific person, but a post occupied for a limited period. According to Hindu beliefs, unlike in Christianity, it is not absolutely essential for a person to cast aside his physical body in order to gain access to svarga. Thus, the two concepts of heaven and svarga are very different and irreconcilable.[99]

Certain sects of Christianity, such as the Mormons, consider heaven a kind of retirement plan where a person can eternally enjoy amenities such as large mansions, good food, high speed internet, golf etc., according to their tastes. It would be a gross trivialization of the concept of svarga by regarding it as equivalent to such an idea of heaven.

A natural corollary to the idea of heaven is the idea of hell. In Christianity, hell is a place for eternal residence of sinful souls. In Hinduism, svarga has its antithesis in the idea of naraka, which is only a place of temporary stay meant for the purification of wrong-doers by making them exhaust their stock of bad karma.[100] An individual's good and bad karma-s done in his lifetime are finite and unique to the person. A finite cause cannot beget an infinite effect; hence the fruits of these karma-s can only be finite and never eternal. Thus, a jiva going either to svarga or naraka has to stay there only for a temporary period. The time spent by jiva-s in naraka is not only for punishment and repentance for their sins as in the Judeo-Christian framework, but to transform them through the understanding of Brahman. The entire foundational metaphysics for the two concepts is different and cannot be mapped onto each other.

Asura is not Demon

Demon is very commonly used in English to translate the Sanskrit word asura. The biblical tradition considers demons as the personification of evil and the cause of all suffering.[101] Demons are former angels that were banished from heaven after a failed attempt by them to overthrow God from his throne under the leadership of Lucifer, who was the chief angel musician of God and came to be called Satan. Hinduism does not have concepts such as devil, demon or Satan in its worldview.

The Sanskrit word asura can be understood etymologically in two ways. It can be derived from the word *sura* by adding the prefix *a* before it. Sura denotes the devata-s and asura, its opposite, means 'one who is opposed to the devata-s'. Devata-s are benign beings appointed to look after the management of this cosmos, while asura-s, driven by their malicious and destructive nature, try to disrupt it.[102] Asura can also refer to one who believes only in the enjoyment of material pleasures of life, devoid of any higher spiritual purpose.[103]

Another way of understanding the meaning of the word asura is in terms of a clan, a lineage or a dynasty. Purana-s recount that the revered sage, Maharishi Kashyapa had thirteen wives, two of whom were Aditi and Diti. The sons of Aditi are called *aditya*-s which is commonly used for the devata-s, and the sons of Diti are called *daitya*-s, which refers to the asura-s. Thus, the asura-s and the devata-s are born of the same father and are half-siblings. It is only due to their different behavioral characteristics that they are designated as devata-s and asura-s. This sense of lineage is not suggested by the English word demon or devil.

Although asura-s generally possess vices, there are instances when they have displayed extraordinary virtues. For example, Hiranyakashyapu was a cruel asura but his son Prahlada was just the opposite and amongst the great devotees of Bhagavan.[104] Prahlada's grandson Bali, also an asura, was a great devotee of Bhagavan as well.

Asura-s are sometimes shown to be recipients of valuable knowledge of the shastra-s. For example, the important ancient Indian astronomical text *Surya Siddhanta* was first revealed to an asura named Maya by Surya Bhagavan.[105] This is not the case with demons, and we do not hear of noble or righteous demons in the Judeo-Christian tradition.

The conflict between the devata-s and asura-s is also connected with the institution of yajna.[106] In Hinduism the universe is seen as a benevolent provider and a yajna is conducted to thank and give back to the cosmic process. Devata-s try to help in the yajna, and asura-s disrupt the performance of the same. This concept of yajna is not found in the Abrahamic religions and hence demons and angels cannot be distinguished on the basis of their support or opposition to yajna-s. It is thus clear that the word *asura* denotes a class of beings in the Hindu cosmology very different from the Judeo-Christian concept of demon or devil.

Devata-s are not Gods or Angels

The word devata is derived from verbal root *div*; one of the meanings of *div* is 'to praise' or 'adore'. Thus, devata-s are personalities adored and worshipped by all humans because they bring welfare to humanity. A devata is completely different from Judeo-Christian ideas of angels and gods.

Angels in Christianity and Judaism are messengers of God, that have been organized into a hierarchy based on the New Testament. The first rung of this hierarchy is seen as servants of God and their primary role is protection and care of His throne in heaven. The concept of Bhagavan is wholly different from the idea of God, as he is transcendent and omnipresent. Bhagavan is superior to devata-s and His abode is eternal and different from svarga where devata-s reside.

Angels were created *ex-nihilo* by the Judeo-Christian God. In Hinduism, however, the jivatma-s, which are eternal, manifest or emanate from Bhagavan at the time of manifestation. They acquire the body of a devata, human or any other being based on their past karma-s. A jivatma with unusually good past karma-s takes on the position of Indra devata. There is no such possibility in Christianity, as it does not even have a cyclic concept of time.

Further rungs of Christian angelology consist of angels who act as messengers of God to humans. They follow the orders of the angels in the higher rung and provide material benefits to the humans based on their authority. Angels cannot be worshipped by humans and it is considered blasphemous in Christianity to do so, whereas devata-s are meant to be worshipped and grant boons and other material, as well as spiritual, benefits.

Angels expelled from heaven due to their sins are called 'Fallen Angels', with Satan being the most well-known. These Fallen Angels incite humans to commit sins. Such a concept has no place in the Hindu worldview at all. Furthermore, angels are not allowed to wed, whereas each devata has his female counterpart representing his Shakti. These differences show that devata-s and angels are different concepts and translating devata as angel is completely incorrect.

Christianity's angelology has changed with its expansionist history. The initial *milites Christi* labeled as pagan all those who were non-Christians during the times when Christianity was advanced brutally across Europe. The pagans had diverse traditions, their own order and rituals, with some being polytheistic, pantheistic, animistic and some even monotheistic. All these divergent and different cultures were replaced by Christianity and, in the process, concepts of gods and angels were co-opted and transformed into the monotheistic Abrahamic framework.

The use of the word god (lowercase 'g') to denote Hindu devata-s has become prevalent even amongst Hindu spiritual guru-s. This is misleading as the word 'god' is used to refer to beings which have been subsumed into Christianity through its expansionist history, from the various pagan, polytheistic and animistic cultures across Europe. These gods have no unity under a single, integral framework unlike in Hinduism, where the various devata-s are connected in the Vedic cosmology and metaphysics. Using the word 'gods' to denote devata-s is misleading as devata has aspects, at many levels, such as deity of choice (*ishta devata*) and deity of a place (*grama devata*).

In recent times, authors such as Devdutt Pattanaik who write about Hindu deities, depict them as only super humans or heroes with extraordinary powers. They don't recognize their error of retaining Sanskrit terms for Hindu deities while applying Christian understanding of gods to these words. Some authors even depict Bhagavan Shiva and Bhagavan Shri Krishna as just exalted human beings of extraordinary capabilities and use specious interpretation, which is a consequence of colonial and post-colonial attempts to historicize our canon in order to provide them more legitimacy.[107]

Similar to the word 'god', sometimes the English word demi-god is also used as a substitute for the Sanskrit word devata. This translation for devata is even more inappropriate. Demi-god is defined as a being born from the sexual union of a god and a mortal being. Devata-s, on the other hand, are divine beings and hence this translation is highly misleading.

Summary of Vedic Cosmos Non-Translatables

Vedic Cosmos Non-Translatables			
Loka	≠	Planet	**Loka** is not an observable world, but an embodied plane of existence defined by set consciousness levels. **Planet** as a physical body does not convey the same meaning.
Svarga/ Naraka	≠	Heaven/ Hell	The Hindu idea of **svarga** requires transmigration and reincarnation, for it refers to a subtle realm where jiva-s stay temporarily to enjoy the fruits of their good deeds before returning to lower worlds again. **Naraka** is a temporary place for a jiva to exhaust his/her bad karma-s. **Heaven** is a place to which a Christian believer ascends and eternally lives after death. Only eligible people are granted admission while the rest are cast into **Hell** eternally.

Vedic Cosmos Non-Translatables			
Asura	≠	Demon	**Asura-s** challenge the deva-s in maintaining cosmic order, though there are asura-s who have been benevolent as well. **Demons** are the personification of evil and always incorrigibly bad.
Devata	≠	god	**Devata** is one who is an object of adoration and who manages order in the cosmos. Whereas, 'god' refers to titans/superhuman beings of the pagans that Christianity has subsumed.

6

Vedic Psychology

Vedic psychology is a system rooted in Vedic thought and underpins numerous yogic techniques present in the tradition for a person's psycho-spiritual development. It provides an understanding of human behavior and is a practical knowledge system for achieving happiness. In the Indian tradition, dharma, philosophy and psychology have remained inseparably connected. Inquiry into psychological aspects such as emotions, desires, will, perception and illusions formed an important element of Indian philosophy. The quest of the Indian rishi-s to understand and realize the self has been the cornerstone of all philosophical and psychological pursuits.

Mental health is a pre-requisite for any spiritual pursuit. The analysis of Self propelled Indian thinkers into a detailed study of human perception, desires, feelings and emotions, through which they also understood the value of concentration and awareness. Thus, training and control of will, forms an important part of Vedic psychology.

The fundamental difference between Vedic psychology and modern Western psychology lies in the subjective and intuitive methods to study man (i.e., first-person empiricism) employed by the former, as against the latter's reliance on purely experimental and inferential methods (i.e., second and third person). Indian seers derived their psychological principles on the basis of their spiritual experiences and not mere theorizing. Western psychology studies the inner states of the mind through interpretation of its outer expressions, based on pre-conceived notions and theories. In contrast, the subjective methods and theories of Vedic psychology are verifiable by a person's own direct inner experience.

The basic principles underlying the Vedic approach to human psychology include:

- The existence of Supreme Consciousness or Brahman as the essence of the entire universe.
- The atma, or individual consciousness as the essence of human personality.
- The intimate and direct relation of individual consciousness with Brahman.
- The atma as the entity which enlivens and enlightens the *antahkarana* (manas, buddhi, etc.) and the body with its consciousness.
- The principle of karma and rebirth.

The absence of these foundational concepts in Western psychology leads to many unsolved problems such as the continuity of human experience, origin and nature of mind, the relation of mind and body. Western psychologists analyze the human being through a mechanistic framework, as a brain-driven machine, the thoughts, passions and emotions of which are ultimately reducible to nerve impulses in the brain. The central and primary role of consciousness in the Vedic system is contrasted by Western psychology's view of seeing consciousness as an epiphenomenon of a bio-mechanical human brain. Vedic psychology conceives a person as a composite of physical body (*sthula sharira*), antahkarana (comprising *chitta, buddhi, manas* and *ahankara*) and consciousness or atma. Consciousness is irreducibly distinct from the physical body and the antahkarana.

The Western psychological framework is unfortunately, universally applied, replacing the insights of other cultures. This flawed approach leads to an artificial and forced mapping of the Indian psychological concepts onto the Western model, reflected in the careless translations of terms such as sukshma sharira, manas, buddhi, ahankara used in the Indian tradition, as mind, intelligence and ego. We study these terms in detail in this chapter.

Sukshma Sharira is not Astral Body

Most systems of Indian philosophy recognize the existence of sukshma sharira apart from the physical body or sthula sharira. Sukshma sharira is often translated as 'astral body', which predates Christianity and originated in ancient Greece.

According to Hindu philosophy, every jivatma is surrounded by three sharira-s, with the sthula sharira being the outermost, surrounding the sukshma sharira which, in turn, encases the karana sharira. All the thoughts of a person emerge within the sukshma sharira and it is necessary for transmigration of a jiva from one birth to another.

Sukshma sharira is subtle (*asthula*) and said to be constituted of seventeen tattva-s which include the five prana-s, five buddhindriya-s and five karmendriya-s, manas and buddhi.[108] At the time of death, atma leaves the physical body along with sukshma sharira and migrates to a higher or a lower loka according to its karma. It is the sukshma sharira which gathers the physical body around it at birth and abandons it at death. The variegatedness in human beings is because of differences in their sukshma sharira, including different physical forms. Sukshma sharira continues till the final release or mukti is attained by a jiva.

All experiences in the different lives of a jiva during its transmigratory existence leave certain residual karmic impressions or samskara-s which remain in the sukshma sharira.[109] The physical body cannot carry samskara-s during transmigration as it ceases to exist at death. Thus, sukshma sharira has a distinct individuality. According to the *Brahma Sutra,* the warmth (*ushma*) that we feel in a living body by means of touch belongs to the sukshma sharira.[110] This is the reason that bodily heat is not felt after death while qualities such as form and color continue to be perceived.

In comparison, an astral body is regarded as a vehicle to clairvoyant sight and other occult powers. It lacks any rigorous intellectual foundation like the Veda-s and its relationship with reincarnation is non-existent. The astral body is composed of finer matter and is said to be surrounded by an aura of flashing colors. It is a medium of transmission between the brain and mind and is able to move rapidly to great distances, making a person capable of cosmic travel.

The translation of sukshma sharira into 'astral body' eliminates the concept of transmigration and stored impressions from past lives. While all living beings have sukshma sharira, astral body is limited only to humans.

The digestion of the elaborate system of sukshma sharira into a simplified, though inconsistent, entity of astral body deserves a detailed study. Digestion of this kind, while distorting the Vedic framework, leaves out essential Hindu elements, making the concept itself poorly developed.

Manas is not Mind

Manas occupies a pivotal and central position in the Indian psychological tradition. It performs the role of connecting consciousness (atma) with the physical body. Perception involves 1) the contact of jnanendriya-s with the external objects; 2) jnanendriya-s with manas; and 3) manas with the atma. Thus, manas is the interface between the internal and external worlds of a human being.

The atma does not come in direct contact with anything physical and interacts with the external world through the manas. The indriya-s give all the sensorial data received by them to the manas, which acts as the central processor, reflecting on the data. The manas unifies all the data received from different indriya-s in our cognition of an object and makes them function in unison. For instance, to describe an object while we see and touch it simultaneously, the common point where the indriya-s of vision, touch and speech meet is the manas.

Manas works in a binary mode and qualifies an object of cognition with a feeling of either like (*raga*) or dislike (*dvesha*). Manas is by nature insentient or unconscious (*achetana*) and only reflects consciousness. Manas is concerned with immediate raw evaluation (*nirvikalpaka jnana*) without any rational or logical analysis, similar to a child's judgment. A quick, transient, cognitive evaluation of a given situation in a number of alternate ways is the basic function of manas.

The preferences of manas are influenced by the accumulated *samskara*-s stored in the chitta. The inclinations of manas will alter with the change of one of the three guna-s - sattva, rajas and tamas. Manas permeates the whole body, similar to consciousness and functions without space-time constraints.

Manas is a crucial factor in the experience of phenomenal awareness and body-centeredness. An uncontrolled manas overpowers the buddhi of a weak person, directing all his actions based only on raga and dvesha, which leads to the continuation of karmic cycle and bondage. A disciplined manas can thus become a source of liberation from suffering through self-realization.[111] All the methods of Yoga such as *dharana, dhyana* and *samadhi* are meant to control the manas. Similarly, in bhakti yoga, activities such as japa, puja also indirectly accomplish the same.

Western theories on the mind, range from equating it to one's true self, or one's thoughts, to being analogous to the software running the brain. Some radical thinkers even deny the existence of the mind, in contrast with the Indian psychological tradition, and view it only as a certain disposition of behavior.[112] Physicalism, functionalism, mind-body duality and dualism are all considered, but none fully studied or understood. The seat of manas in the Indian tradition is the heart whereas the Western models associate the mind with the brain. Western models of mind do not involve the entire inner cognitive apparatus (antahkarana) with manas, buddhi, chitta and ahankara, as its functional aspects. Consciousness, memory and perception are combined into a cognitive set meant by the mind. One cannot casually replace manas with a Western substitute like mind, as it would render the whole system incoherent and it would fall apart. It is unfortunate that this confused exploration often draws on the work of several Eastern traditions and concepts but seeks to incorporate it into its framework in a piecemeal manner of digestion.

Buddhi is not Intelligence

Buddhi is the chief functional aspect of the antahkarana and is responsible for producing cognition in a human being. The chief characteristic of buddhi is to discriminate and comprehend things and is commonly translated as 'intelligence'. In any cognitive act, the discrete and immediate impressions of objects by indriya-s are synthesized and assimilated by manas and then reach the buddhi, after which the ahankara unifies them. The buddhi identifies, categorizes the object, and determines the response to it.

Buddhi is unconscious by nature and only reflects the atma's consciousness. When one sees an object, the visual impressions generated by the eyes reach the manas, which synthesizes it and generates the feeling of like or dislike for the object, without any determinate knowledge about it. The impression reaches buddhi, which then compares it with the past impressions stored in the chitta. Through such comparison, buddhi ascertains and generates a determinate knowledge and resolves the action that needs to be taken regarding the object.[113]

Buddhi is the factor in the psychological apparatus which prevents a person from acting impulsively. This is highlighted in *Katha Upanishad* (1.3.3) where the atma is said to be the rider of the chariot of the human body, buddhi to be the charioteer, manas to be the reins and senses to be the horses drawing the chariot. Thus, buddhi as charioteer discharges the cognitive and emotional functions and arrives at decisions. Ahankara or the 'I' feeling comes into play whenever buddhi makes a positive or a negative judgment. Thus, cognition consists of the following steps:

1. The indeterminate knowledge that there is some object
2. The buddhi determines the object
3. The ahankara self-arrogates the knowledge
4. The buddhi decides the appropriate response

Buddhi is predominantly sattvika and manifests through tendencies such as virtue (dharma), wisdom (jnana) and non-attachment (*vairagya*) in man. The actions of the manas leave a karmic trace whereas buddhi fixes one in the calmness of self-knowledge, removes desires and impulsive responses, leading to calm discrimination and absence of karmic reactions.[114] A person who acts under such an influence of buddhi and achieves realization is called *buddha* or 'the awakened one'.

Buddhi is very different from the Western concept of intelligence which can be measured with the help of Intelligence Quotient (IQ) tests. Buddhi's role of providing determinate knowledge differs from the West's definition of intelligence which borrows from disciplines such as psychology, learning, philosophy and others. The process of cognition and the role of buddhi in it is well defined whereas it remains open-ended in the Western model of intelligence. Intelligence in the West is associated with the mind and the brain, whereas buddhi is not a part of the brain but of the sukshma sharira.

Chitta is not Unconscious Mind

Chitta in Vedic psychology is a foundational part of the conditioned jiva and denotes the repository of karmic samskara-s in the antahkarana, which is wrongly translated as the 'unconscious mind'.

Chitta is the individualized mahat tattva for one particular atma. Mahat tattva is all-pervading and the part an individual uses to store his/her own experiences and memories is called chitta. It is within the chitta that consciousness or chetana first permeates from the atma. The word chitta and chetana derive from the same root *chitti* which means 'to be conscious' or 'to be aware'. Chitta is thus the foundation on which the complete psychological complex of an individual is built.

Chitta is located in the heart region where the atma is believed to be located and is constant through the different lives of a jivatma. It stores memories of all experiences as samskara-s. Chitta is responsible for the distinct personality of each individual. One can think of the chitta as similar to a hard disk that stores past impressions unique to the person. According to the law of karma, the effect of any karma is not always instantaneous. The cause generally remains registered and dormant in the chitta for a long time before giving rise to its effect in suitable environment.[115]

The various spiritual sadhana-s are meant to ultimately free a person's chitta from all its samskara-s. Patanjali's *Yogasutra* says that yoga is the quietening of all the activities of chitta leading to the *drashta* or seer becoming situated in his own pure self-luminous consciousness.[116] Dharmic society created its social order to regulate the chitta for good samskara-s for all its members.

Similar to how one can transfer contents between two hard disks, the conditioning and content of one chitta can be transferred to that of another. This takes place all the time during interaction between people. Yogi-s and accomplished guru-s can manipulate chitta-s and even delete karma-s stored in the chitta to eliminate their consequences.

According to Freud (1856-1939), the founder of psychoanalysis, the unconscious mind is a reservoir of thoughts, wishes, feelings and painful memories from one's present life. Western psychologists do not believe in the law of transmigration and reincarnation of the atma. The unconscious mind thus, has nothing to do with one's past lives and has no karmic record. In contrast, the chitta is the storehouse of samskara-s from the past and present lives. Chitta cannot thus be surgically clipped out from the Vedic psychological complex and transplanted into the Western theories of mind.

Ahankara is not Ego

Ahankara is that constituent of the antahkarana which initiates the process of individuation and gives identity to the psycho-physical framework of a person. The word ahankara means 'that which gives a sense of *aham*' or 'I-ness' and is erroneously translated as ego. Consciousness without any sense of I-ness would not be self-aware and hence meaningless. Ahankara's function is to personalize various experiences by linking them together as 'my own'.

Ahankara is the self-arrogating principle that brings subjectivity into the activities of all body parts and associates them with the person. Ahankara generates a unique identity in a person in the form of empirical self. When one says, 'I am', it implies that one is neither an object nor any other person but a distinct individual. Every action needs an agency and that is the ahankara. It is not possible to give up ahankara completely as long as one is connected to the material body and one can only minimize some of its activities.

A person becomes caught in a self-perpetuating karmic cycle because of ahankara. As long as one acts with a sense of doership due to ahankara, he creates more karmic impressions in the chitta. These, in turn, shape one's unique identity and further strengthen their notion of empirical self.

The surrender of ahankara, only to Bhagavan is one of the means of its purification. Deluding oneself, especially in the absence of proper sadhana or guru, and indulging in actions without purifying one's psyche, leads to disastrous consequences for oneself and others, and the accumulation of colossal bad karma.

Besides the meaning of ahankara as the self-referencing system at the individual level, the term has another similar meaning at the cosmic level. In Sankhya metaphysics, ahankara is the third evolute in the chain of evolution of prakriti and develops out of mahat tattva. It is the cosmic individuating principle responsible for limitations, separation and variety in the universe. Ahankara in an individual body is a material thing and a part of the cosmic ahankara.

Ahankara needs the consciousness from atma in order to function. The atma's sense of 'I'ness is spiritual and when connected to a particular body, gets superimposed onto the material ahankara and they function as one single unit.[117] This sense of unity leads to conditioning and identification with the mind-body complex and the actions performed by them. If one rises above ahankara, then everything becomes Universal Consciousness, because without ahankara, there is no conditioning and no limited existence.

Ahankara gives rise to both positive and negative traits in a person's behavior. According to Sankhya philosophy, there are three types of ahankara: sattvika ahankara, rajasika ahankara and tamasika ahankara. Sattvika ahankara leads a person towards good deeds, tamasika ahankara towards inertia and dullness and rajasika ahankara towards aggressive domination. Yoga helps transform tamasika and rajasika ahankara into sattvika ahankara before transcending ahankara itself.

It is not possible to give up ahankara completely, as any sadhana to transcend it still creates karmic impressions which perpetuates the samsara. Bhagavan Shri Krishna says that even sattvika ahankara binds one to the material world in subtle ways.[118] Therefore, sadhana, such as bhakti-yoga aims to transform it by considering only Bhagavan as the real doer of all one's actions.[119]

In Western psychology, Freud's concepts of id, ego and superego dominate discussion on the subject. The id, which Freud considers as the first division of the mind to develop, contains two biological drives - sex and aggression - that are the source of all psychic or mental energy. The id's goal is to pursue pleasure and satisfy biological urges. The ego, as the second division, develops from the id during infancy. The ego's goal is to find safe and socially acceptable ways of satisfying the id's desires. The superego, the third of Freud's division of the mind, develops from the ego during early childhood. The goal of the superego is to apply the moral values and standards of one's parents and society in satisfying one's wishes. Freud considered a large part of the ego's material to be conscious, such as information we gather in adapting to our environments. A smaller part of the ego's material is unconscious, which stores repressed desires.

Ahankara, unlike ego, does not come into existence during infancy or childhood but is something every sentient being is born with. Ahankara is not concerned solely with the satisfaction of desires in a morally acceptable way as is the ego. Apart from the Freudian psychoanalytic model, other Western psychological models too fail to compare with the entire complex of antahkarana, interlinked with the dharmic cosmological framework in the Indian tradition. The mistranslation of ahankara as ego especially distorts the profound meanings of core Indian metaphysical concepts, necessitating it to be used as a non-translatable.

Summary of Vedic Psychology Non-Translatables

Vedic Psychology Non-Translatables			
Sukshma Sharira	≠	Astral Body	**Sukshma Sharira** is subtle, made of seventeen tattva-s. At the time of death, the atma leaves the concrete physical body along with its sukshma sharira and migrates according to its karma. Sukshma sharira has a distinct individuality. **Astral body** is a vehicle of clairvoyant sight, occult powers and is finer than physical matter. Translating sukshma shakira as astral body destroys the concept of transmigration and storing of karmic impressions.

Vedic Psychology Non-Translatables			
Manas	≠	Mind	**Manas** connects the atma and the concrete body in a linear relationship. It qualifies an object of cognition with a like/dislike feeling. Western theories on the **mind** are varied and even conflicting. Consciousness, apart from the mind is not considered; Western theories also do not have an equivalent cognitive apparatus to the indriya-s and the antahkarana.
Buddhi	≠	Intelligence	**Buddhi** is the chief form and functional aspect of the antahkarana that produces cognition. Discrimination is the main function of the Buddhi. **Intelligence** is not precisely defined and refers to something that can be measured and the dharmic concept of Buddhi has little to do with this.
Chitta	≠	Unconscious Mind	**Chitta** is the individualized aspect of mahat and is the foundation of the complete psychological complex of an individual. It retains memory in the form of samskara-s and is responsible for the distinct conditioning of each individual. Chitta is very different from the **unconscious mind** which does not consider the laws of transmigration, rebirth and karma.

Vedic Psychology Non-Translatables			
Ahankara	≠	Ego	**Ahankara** is a component of the antahkarana responsible for the individuality and agency of a person. It is also the individuating principle responsible for limitations, separation and variety in the Universe. **Ego**, unlike ahankara which is ever-present, comes into existence during infancy or childhood. Ego's goal is to find safe and socially acceptable ways of satisfying desires.

7

Yoga

Yoga is one of the six systems of Hindu darshana-s. It is derived from the verbal root *yuj,* which means 'to unite'; Patanjali defines yoga as cessation of all thought process and becoming situated in one's own self. Yoga was discovered and developed by the austere and wise Indian seers of the past; the *tapasya* performed by them through truthfulness, ahimsa, abstinence and devotion to Bhagavan were transformed into the systematic methods such as *dharana, dhyana,* and *samadhi.*

Yoga is characterized by a permanent, sublime state of consciousness (samadhi), where a person attains complete control over the senses, mind and body. It is a grave error to translate this highest yogic state (samadhi) as 'trance'. Trance is an abnormal (tamasika) state of mind under the influence of drugs or alcohol, where a person has no control.

Patanjali describes eight stages in his ashtanga-yoga: *yama, niyama, asana, pranayama, pratyahara, dharana, dhyana* and *samadhi.* The attainment of each of these involves rigorous and strict sadhana. These eight terms carry deep and specialized meanings for which no English equivalents exist. However, many modern yoga instructors commonly and senselessly translate the last five as meditation. The word 'meditation' does not even begin to accurately represent the meaning of any of these terms individually and using it indiscriminately for all five is a crude distortion.

Ahimsa forms an important part of the first stage or limb of Patanjali's ashtanga yoga called yama; this chapter considers its mistranslation as 'non-violence'. In the yogic system, any disease or pain in the body happens due to the imbalance of prana and control of it (pranayama) is an important element in yoga sadhana; this chapter discusses its mistranslation as breath. *Chakra* is another important concept in the yoga tradition, commonly mistranslated as energy-center or energy-wheel.

Yoga is widely popular across the world, mainly focused on the physical and auxiliary aspect of asana-s. With this increase in popularity, the risk of misinterpretation and mistranslation of the yogic terms through self-styled yoga instructors and their eventual digestion into popular culture has also escalated, necessitating their recognition as non-translatables.

Ahimsa is not Non-violence

Non-violence is commonly defined as the use of peaceful means to bring about political or social change. The principle of non-violence denotes the practice of being completely harmless and kind to other living beings. The traditional Hindu concept of ahimsa also emphasizes the qualities of kindness and harmlessness, but not absolutely or unreservedly. In the pragmatic world, some use of force becomes inevitable to ensure that truth and justice prevail.

Etymologically, the word ahimsa derives from himsa by adding the prefix *a*. It is a common misconception that the prefix *a* or *an* is used to give the opposite meaning to a word. For example, jnana means 'knowledge' and ajnana means 'ignorance'. However, the prefix *a* has six meanings and one of them means 'less' or 'small'. In case of the word ahimsa, it means minimizing himsa or violence and not complete absence of violence.

According to the Hindu view, there is always some himsa involved in the continuation and preservation of life and this is not regarded as violence.[120] However, himsa, though unavoidable, can be minimized through governing principles called *ahimsa dharma*. Non-violence cannot be regarded as an absolute rule independent of context. The ideas of ahimsa are derived from the shastra-s which recognize that total elimination of violence is impossible and unnatural, and that the only pragmatic solution is minimization of violence. Bhagavan Shri Krishna inspired Arjuna to fight the righteous battle at Kurukshetra, because taking appropriate, punitive action against adharma is an act of ahimsa, and an intrinsic part of the Kshatriya dharma whereas inactivity is an act of himsa.

Gandhi mistranslated and digested the word ahimsa into 'non-violence'. His teachings and methods are based on non-violence and not ahimsa.

The word *himsa* either cannot be translated as 'violence'. Himsa is not limited to physical harm but includes other manifestations as well. The legal text, *Manusmriti* states that there are three forms of violence or himsa: physical, verbal and mental. Though the term violence has acquired expanded meanings in the West, physical violence still constitutes its dominant meaning. In the Indian context, himsa and ahimsa applies to each of the three sharira-s and one can determine the exact nature of harm and path of healing, within the psycho-physiological complex of the Indian system. Violence and non-violence, on the other hand, are related to a completely different Western framework of mind-body complex. Thus, ahimsa and himsa should not be decoupled from the Indian tradition with inadequate and misleading translations.

Prana is not Breath

Prana is derived from the root *an,* which means 'to breathe,' and has the prefix *pra* used for the word to mean 'that which comes before breath' or, 'that which gives rise to life'. Prana is often translated into English as 'breath' or 'vital air'.[121] The word 'breath' signifies the physical movement of air during respiration and is a sign of life. Prana is not just breath but is the basic force of life responsible for activating the psycho-physical body, including breath.[122]

Prana is the bridge linking atma and antahkarana along with the physical body. Atma sustains life only through the prana, as the former transcends space-time and cannot directly influence anything material such as the manas or the indriya-s. Prana first imbues chitta with consciousness, which then transfers it further down to ahankara, manas, buddhi, indriya and eventually the entire body is permeated. Prana, unlike breath, is not just confined to the respiratory system of the body but is a force that vitalizes different sections and makes them function in a coordinated manner. Prana's role of channeling consciousness into the psycho-physical body of a living being cannot be captured by the word 'breath'.

Prana assumes five differentiated forms and pervades the whole body as prana, apana, vyana, udana, and samana. Prana in the form of vyana maintains cardiac activity and is responsible for blood circulation; samana activates the intestine and is responsible for the digestion of food. Prana is responsible for any voluntary or involuntary movement and activity in the body.[123] When a part of our body is given anesthesia, we lose consciousness in that part because the flow of prana gets obstructed.

Prana is the cause of all energy that we see; it is present in air as well as in food. When we eat food or breathe in air, we are taking in prana from them into our bodies. Natural environments of an ocean, lake, river and mountains rejuvenate one because more prana is available at such places. Fresh food has more prana than artificially preserved frozen food; one can lose prana by overeating and gain it by fasting, which helps balance prana. The source of all the prana in vegetation and other life forms on earth is the sun; some Indian yogi-s have been known to practice *Surya-yoga,* the yogic method of surviving only on the prana from the sun.

Mantra-s function as storehouses of prana which can be tapped into by adept sadhaka-s for gaining energy and vitality. Disease is considered as a deficiency of prana in the affected part of the body and mantrika power brings healing through its replenishment. Pranayama is another yogic method of controlling prana and has the ability to cure diseases. Pranayama also influences the chitta and can become instrumental in removing karma. Prana is also obtained from loving relationships. None of these ideas are conveyed through the mistranslation 'breath'.

Chakra is not Energy Center

The term chakra used in tantric yoga, though popular in Western lexicon, is poorly understood by the English-speaking world. Chakra-s have been, unfortunately, studied by some only through independent reading, without any guidance from a proper guru, resulting in theoretical and inaccurate understandings, as exemplified by psychologists such as Carl Jung (1875-1961).

The primary focus of Vedic philosophy has been the phenomenon of consciousness. As discussed earlier, the presence of atma imparts consciousness to the insentient human body. The tantric yoga tradition considers the chakra-s to be the seats or *loci* through which consciousness radiates into the human physical system. These chakra-s are not anatomical locations in the physical body and are only experienced by yogi-s during dhyana. Chakra-s are a part of sukshma sharira, are not identical with nerve plexuses and disappear at death.

Generally, seven chakra-s are commonly recognized across tantric yoga schools: *muladhara, svadhishthana, manipura, anahata, vishuddha, ajna* and *sahasrara.*[124] They are located along the central nervous system, between the muladhara at the base of the spinal column to the sahasrara at the crown. In tantric texts, each chakra is symbolically represented as a lotus flower with a particular number of petals because Shakti (consciousness) radiates outwards from a chakra in petal-like emanations. Thus, a literal translation of chakra as 'wheel' or 'center' is a complete distortion of its meaning.

The status of chakra-s as active, inactive or partly active represents the levels of spiritual consciousness attained by the sadhaka and reflects his natural abilities and interests. As the consciousness of a person rises higher, the veils obstructing the chakra-s get progressively lifted and the sadhaka becomes freer from lower material nature. The chakra-s are associated with their corresponding loka-s and the rise of the Kundalini Shakti also brings about the level of consciousness of the associated loka.

The highest chakra sahasrara symbolizes the plane of transcendence and a person attains the state of samadhi when consciousness reaches this chakra. This ascent of consciousness from the muladhara to the sahasrara, aided by yogic techniques, is the rise of the *Kundalini Shakti*. This progressive ascent through the chakra-s allows the Shakti to absorb all twenty-four material tattva-s until She enters the sahasrara and becomes one with the Universal Consciousness.

Each chakra representation has petals that represent sound vibrations in the form of Sanskrit syllables. Every represented syllable has a certain Shakti in it and the sum total of all the syllabic sounds in the petals of a chakra is the mantra of that chakra. The center of each chakra has a letter that represents the root (*bija*) of the mantra, the chanting of which assists in uplifting consciousness. There is a divinity related with each chakra, representing the forces manifest and latent in it.

A common mistranslation of chakra is 'energy center'; chakra-s represent particular forms of consciousness and are not merely physical energy centers. Energy is a material and insentient concept, with no well-defined connection with consciousness. Calling chakra-s merely 'energy centers' is a gross trivialization of their profound meaning. The concept of chakra is interconnected with many other concepts such as loka-s and mantra-s in the Indian knowledge system, which contribute to its proper comprehension. This interconnected and internally consistent philosophy is distorted when isolated parts from it are mapped on to a different system.

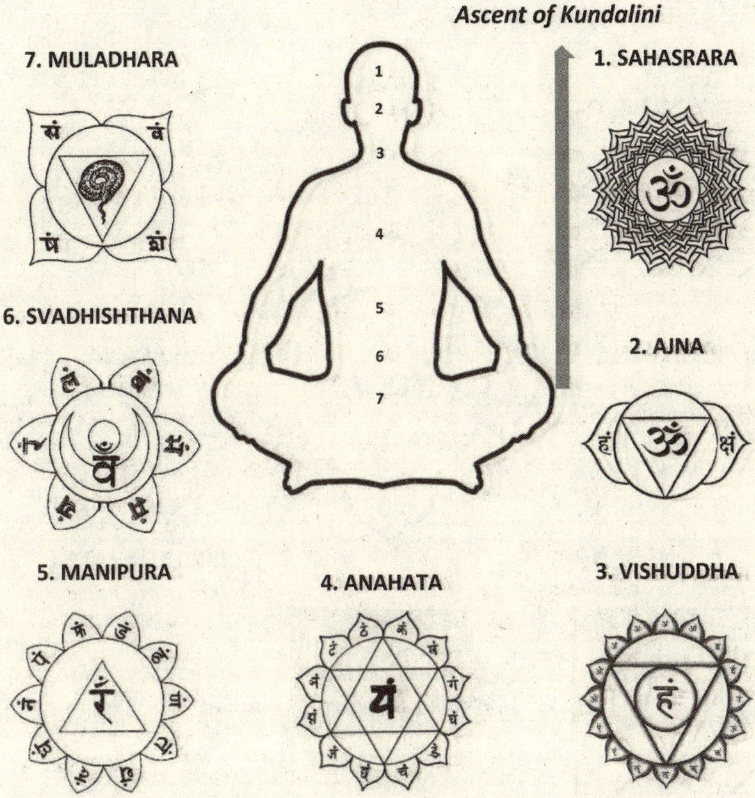

Figure 18: The Seven Chakra-s

Dhyana is not Meditation

The word dhyana is derived from the Sanskrit root *dhyai* to mean 'think' or 'contemplate'. According to Patanjali, dhyana refers to fixing one's mind on a specific object without any deviation.[125] Meditation includes techniques to promote relaxation, build internal energy, life force and develop compassion; it is also used to refer to deep thinking on a particular subject.

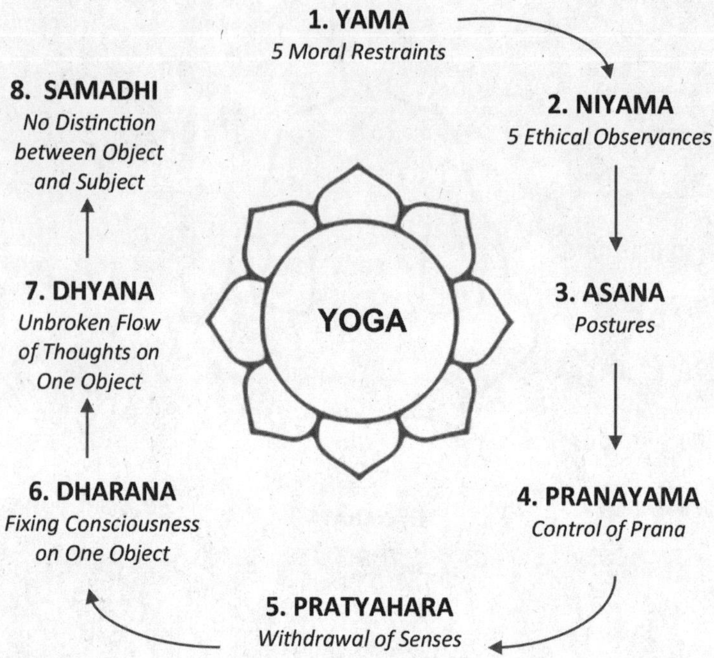

Figure 19: Yoga

In dhyana, the purpose is not to specifically develop qualities such as love and compassion; they emerge spontaneously from dhyana and preceding stages in yoga sadhana. A yogi's chitta becomes withdrawn from all sense desires in pratyahara. Compassion develops due to practice of ahimsa, cleanliness (*shaucha*) and truthfulness as required in the first two steps of yoga sadhana, namely, yama and niyama. Each of the stages in the figure above has a unique purpose in yoga and labelling all these terms as meditation is a serious case of reductionism and over-simplification.

It is akin to mixing assorted remedies for different diseases and referring to them all as one 'medicine'.

Samadhi is not Trance

The word samadhi in Indian philosophy denotes a transcendental state of super-consciousness in which a person goes beyond the barriers of his/her normal cognition based on the psycho-physical mechanism. Samadhi is often translated using words such as 'trance', 'hypnotic state' or 'altered state of consciousness'. This section highlights the distinction between samadhi and other banal translations.

Trance is defined as a half-conscious state, characterized by a dazed condition or absence of response to external stimuli, typically induced by hypnosis or drugs. Samadhi is the very antithesis of trance; it is an elevated state of consciousness in which a person's awareness is beyond the ken of the wakeful state. Samadhi transcends the limitations of space-time and makes accessible the sensorial and the super-sensorial realities of the present, the past as well as the future. In samadhi state, a yogi gains knowledge of the principles underlying and controlling the harmony of the cosmos called *ritambhara prajna.*

The word samadhi is derived from the Sanskrit root *dha* by adding the prefixes *sam* and *aa*. The root *dha* means 'to fix' or 'concentrate' and *sam* denotes 'complete' or 'perfect'. Samadhi brings together all the dissipated and scattered forces of manas. It is attained by intense contemplation on an object and is a state where the sadhaka, the object of his contemplation and the act of contemplation lose their distinctions. Thus, in the state of samadhi, all the fluctuating mental states (*chitta vritti*-s) become still.

The Yoga-sutra-s mention several samadhi states which are broadly classified into *sabija samadhi* and *nirbija samadhi*.[126] Sabija samadhi is attained by concentrating the chitta on some object or idea such as a mantra, a sound or light. In nirbija samadhi, there is no object before consciousness, and the ego gets completely dissolved.[127]

Maharishi Patanjali speaks of a very important method in yoga sadhana called *samyama,* which is the simultaneous application of the last three yogic states of dharana, dhyana and samadhi on an object.[128] During samyama, a sadhaka enters into the state of samadhi while retaining full awareness of the external world. When the object of samyama is Ishvara, it leads to emancipation and unlimited ananda for a sadhaka. Similarly, the performance of samyama on the Sun gives knowledge of the different realms of the entire universe or cosmos.[129] Thus, samadhi is an extremely consummated and accomplished state and cannot simply be called trance. Nobody in a bewildered and confused state of trance can attain knowledge of the entire cosmos.

Samadhi gives a yogi mastery and control over the forces of nature, which cannot be induced by drugs or hypnotism as in the state of trance. Trance is merely a tamasika state with a distorted vision of reality, often accompanied by a false sense of joy or exhilaration. A person in a trance suffers from an undisciplined and deluded mind with which it is impossible to attain any higher state of realization. A person goes into a drug-induced trance to escape the worldly reality, whereas a yogi goes into samadhi to rejuvenate and re-engage with worldly reality. A person becomes capable of achieving samadhi only after a highly disciplined life of sadhana. There are no shortcuts such as drugs or hypnotism for attaining samadhi.

Summary of Yoga Non-Translatables

Yoga Non-Translatables			
Ahimsa	≠	Non-violence	**Ahimsa** emphasizes kindness and harmlessness, but recognizes that himsa is not completely avoidable. **Non-violence** requires the unconditional use of peaceful and harmless means 'to bring change'.
Prana	≠	Breath	**Prana** connects the consciousness of atma with the inert psycho-physical body of an individual. It is not just confined to the respiratory system but pervades the whole body. **Breath** signifies the air inhaled or exhaled during respiration.
Chakra	≠	Energy Centre/ Wheel	**Chakra-s** are considered to be seats through which consciousness radiates into the human physical system. Chakra-s are not anatomical locations in the physical body perceptible to the human eyes. The word **energy** need not have any connection with consciousness, as insentient machines also have energy and capacity to do work.

Yoga Non-Translatables			
Dhyana	≠	Meditation	**Dhyana** is a specific limb of ashtanga yoga revealed by Maharishi Patanjali. **Meditation** is a term used indiscriminately to denote the latter five limbs of yoga, collapsing many technical aspects of the sadhana into one ill-defined word.
Samadhi	≠	Trance	**Samadhi** refers to a transcendental state of super-consciousness where a person goes beyond the barriers of egocentric psycho-physical setup. **Trance** refers to a half-conscious state characterized by absence of response to stimuli, typically induced by drugs or hypnosis.

8

Sadhana

The essence of Hinduism lies in the immediate intuitive experience of the divine, which requires a sadhaka to follow certain essential forms of discipline known as sadhana. Bhakti, yoga, jnana, *nama-japa*, *sangita* are some forms of sadhana depending on the temperament of a sadhaka. Sadhana is commonly translated as 'spiritual practice' or simply, 'practice'. This chapter evaluates this translation, along with those of other major forms of sadhana-s.

Sadhana is not Spiritual Practice

Sadhana comes from the Sanskrit verbal root *saadh* which means 'to reach a goal'. Sadhana is the experiential side of Hinduism and a process by which a sadhaka reaches the goal of spiritual perfection (moksha) in his/her spiritual journey. On the other hand, the word 'practice' denotes a customary, habitual, or expected way of doing something and can be related to anything such as practicing a sport. However, these self-gratifying actions cannot be called sadhana because the word is used only in the context of attaining moksha. Indifference or absence of desire (vairagya) towards worldly possessions or fame is an important element in any sadhana.

Sadhana may refer to different paths such as the *karma marga* if a person is a karma yogi or *bhakti marga* if one is engaged in bhakti activities such as japa, *kirtana*, puja, or contemplation on divine *leela*-s of Bhagavan. Sadhana is a conscious effort at manifesting the divine qualities within an individual and is limited to humans. The word 'practice', on the other hand, can be used even in the case of training animals.

The word practice can denote an activity which is the very antithesis of sadhana; for example, one may practice how to smoke, but there is no such thing as sadhana of smoking. Sadhana leads to an expansion of one's consciousness; any activity which makes one more selfish and contracts his/her consciousness by increasing the feelings of 'I' (*ahanta*) and 'mine'(*mamata*) cannot be called sadhana.

Sadhana is a way of life in accordance with dharma and Hindu shastra-s and one cannot devise one's own sadhana based on wishful thinking. Only one who has realized the ultimate truth and crossed different stages towards moksha through the shastra-s can guide an aspirant in sadhana. Some proponents of spirituality declare their disbelief in any *shastra pramana* and teach sadhana to followers without reference to any shastra. They claim their sadhana to be a new creation based on their independent experience. Bhagavan Shri Krishna in the *Bhagavad Gita* says that those who act as per their own desires, discarding the injunctions of the shastra-s, attain neither perfection, happiness, nor moksha. Thus, claims of sadhana-s independent of shastra-s are in direct violation of the teachings of the *Bhagavad Gita*. People sharing their own independent methods of attaining perfection are free to sell their independent spiritual program but should call it practice and not sadhana.[130]

Puja is not Ritual

Puja is a form of sadhana in Hinduism through which a devotee expresses prema and bhakti towards a personal deity. The word puja derives from the root *puj* which means 'to honor or to respect with devotion' and this section discusses its mistranslation as 'ritual'.

Ritual refers to a sequence of activities, religious or non-religious, involving gestures, words and objects performed in a prescribed order according to a particular tradition. The purpose of puja is not perfunctory continuation of a certain tradition, but an expression of prema to establish a relationship with the deity.

The articles used in a puja such as incense (*dhupa*), lamps (*deepa*), flowers (*pushpa*) and activities such as singing, and chanting are for the pleasure of the deity and to create an atmosphere of ananda. The offerings in a puja express the devotee's prema and gratitude towards Bhagavan and lead to transformation and purification of his self. The *vigraha* of a deity to whom puja is offered is identical with the personhood of the deity and personifies Ultimate Reality for the bhakta.

Karma-yoga is not Path of Action

Karma-yoga is regarded as one of the means for the attainment of moksha in Hinduism and is popularly translated as 'path of action'.

The word karma has two meanings: a) any action or activity of a person in present and past lives; and b) activities prescribed by the shastra-s, performed with a certain mental attitude, such as yajna-s, recitation of mantra-s, worship of a deity and other dharmic activities as used in the compound word karma-yoga. The word 'action', on the other hand, is used to denote anything performed by an individual in his life as the concept of past life or karma is absent among the adherents of Abrahamic religions; the word 'action' is narrowly confined in its scope to just one life.

The mistranslation 'path of action', at best refers to mundane activities of a person performed to perfection, but are of no consequence from the lens of karma-yoga, as they do not lead to spiritual upliftment. As per the law of karma, all actions cause reactions and perpetuate the cycle of samsara. 'Path of action' gives the freedom of action but not the freedom from action, i.e., it can never grant a person liberation or moksha.

Bhagavan Shri Krishna in the *Bhagavad Gita* defines karma-yoga as the art of working in proper consciousness.[131] Karma, which normally keeps one bound to samsara, can also act as a means to escape it. In karma-yoga, a person engages in worldly activities at the physical level, but at the psychological level he/

she surrenders all desires for the enjoyment of fruits of actions and offers them to Bhagavan.[132] Desire and ego are the common motivational forces for all human karma-s (*sakama karma*). Karma-yoga acknowledges this relationship between desire and karma and works towards transcending it by eliminating the attachment to the fruits of actions (*nishkama karma*).[133] Nishkama or desireless karma done in accordance with the shastra-s is dharma; even the sense of doership of action called *kartrtva bhava* is a sign of ignorance.

Hinduism classifies all karma-s as sattvika, rajasika and tamasika; it is only sattvika karma-s performed as an offering to Bhagavan which help a person to transcend the three guna-s of prakriti and not merely performing good deeds. In Christianity, emphasis is laid on the performance of good deeds which when performed in accordance with the Christian ethical principles, secures a believer a place in heaven. However, in karma-yoga the focus is not only on the nature of action but also the agency and inner attitude of the person. The *Bhagavad Gita* says that only an atma bewildered by a false identification with the body thinks itself to be a doer when, in reality, all actions happen by the impulse of the three guna-s.[134] Karma-yoga culminates in the complete harmonization of personal will with the Supreme Divine will and realization of oneself as an instrument of It.

Karma-yoga is thus, a process very different from the 'path of action' in which one remains bound to this material world and begins when one surrenders the 'path of action' to seek liberation from material bondage.

Jnana-yoga is not Path of Knowledge

Jnana-yoga is prescribed in the Hindu shastra-s as a means for moksha. It is commonly translated as 'the path of knowledge' and this inaccuracy is considered here.

Knowledge is defined as facts, information and skills acquired through experience or education. In general, it denotes awareness of any material object, a quality, an act or an emotion by bringing them into relation with the knower; knowledge thus reveals empirical reality. On the other hand, jnana in the compound term jnana-yoga does not refer to the conditioned and limited knowledge of empirical life. Jnana normally refers to any kind of cognition but in the context of jnana-yoga, it refers only to the realization of the essential nature of self as identical with the Brahman called *Brahma-jnana* or *atma-jnana*. The subject-object dichotomy which persists in all cases of knowledge is transcended in jnana-yoga.

In the Indian tradition, jnana refers to both empirical knowledge (*apara-jnana*) and transcendental knowledge (*para-jnana*).[135] Jnana-yoga is not only the process of knowing but is a sadhana and involves sadhana-*sadhya* relationship. Jnana is the sadhana, and realization of identity with Brahman is the sadhya. 'Path of knowledge' does not convey the sadhya and the relationship. The sadhana of jnana-yoga does not merely involve intellectual study. According to Advaita Vedanta, a sadhaka of jnana-yoga must possess qualifications including the ability to discriminate between eternal and transient entities (*viveka*) and non-attachment to worldly objects (vairagya) along with other requirements.[136] No amount of knowledge on worldly matters aids the path of jnana-yoga, and the sadhaka needs to follow the sadhana-chatushtaya of Advaita Vedanta or similar prescription from classical yoga and observe strict adherence to moral and ethical codes from these paths.[137]

A man of knowledge may be harmful to society, but a jnana-yogi embodies wisdom and enlightenment for society. Jnana-yogi-s are those who have risen above worldly pleasures and pain. Thus, jnana-yoga, which deals with transcendental matters should not be reduced to mundane levels as 'path of knowledge'.

Bhakti-yoga is not Path of Devotion

In Hinduism, Bhakti-yoga is one of the simplest means for attaining moksha. Given its all-inclusive and uncomplicated nature,

Bhakti-yoga has attained popularity worldwide as a means to God-realization. Bhakti-yoga is commonly translated as 'the path of devotion' which is an over-simplification of the Sanskrit term. The word 'devotion' can be used in a purely secular sense, as in the case of devotion towards one's family members, business or job. However, the word bhakti is used specifically for Bhagavan.

Bhakti, commonly translated as devotion, derives from the verbal root *bhaj* which means 'to offer seva'.[138] The sadhana of bhakti-yoga requires two entities - a *bhakta* who practices bhakti and Bhagavan who is the recipient and object of bhakti. In bhakti-yoga, the supreme goal of human life is to attain unbounded prema for Bhagavan, devoid of any self-interest, which leads to, and culminates in, divine communion.[139]

Bhakti-yoga is founded on an individual's emotional relationship on a personal basis with the Supreme Being and is not possible with some impersonal force, energy or principle. Bhakti-yoga essentially requires a divine personality, with attributes and form (*nama-rupa*), to adore with shraddha. This finds expression through various stunning and diverse forms and traditions in Hinduism, for instance, seen in temple architecture and murti-worship; the latter is especially prohibited in Abrahamic religions and regarded as idolatry and sacrilegious.

In different sampradaya-s of Hinduism, bhakti-yoga is used as a technical term to denote certain practices to be followed by a bhakta. For instance, in the Sri Vaishnava sampradaya, the practice of bhakti-yoga involves a seven-fold discipline called *sadhana-saptaka*, to steadily direct the mind towards Bhagavan.[140] Similarly, the Gaudiya Vaishnava sampradaya, following Bhagavatam, explains bhakti-yoga as constituting the following nine-activities: listening to the leela-s of Bhagavan (*shravana*), chanting Bhagavan's names (*kirtana*), constantly remembering Bhagavan (*smarana*), offering seva at Bhagavan's feet (*pada-sevana*), worshipping Bhagavan (*archana*), offering obeisance to Bhagavan (*vandana*), considering oneself as a dasa of Bhagavan (*dasya*), considering Bhagavan as friend (*sakhya*), and complete surrender to Bhagavan (*atma-nivedana*). Thus, bhakti-yoga is complex and cannot be translated as 'the path of devotion'.

Summary of Sadhana Non-Translatables

Sadhana Non-Translatables			
Sadhana	≠	Spiritual Practice	**Sadhana** is the process of attaining the spiritual goal of moksha. Self-gratifying actions cannot be referred to as sadhana. The word **practice** applies to a range of things, from sports to music and art, and refers to the habitual and expected way of doing something.
Puja	≠	Ritual	**Puja** is a form of spiritual sadhana where a devotee expresses his bhakti towards a personal deity. **Ritual** involves procedure which may or may not be religious, with a sequence of activities, in accordance with some custom or tradition.
Karma-Yoga	≠	Path of Action	The compound word **karma-yoga** refers to works performed as prescribed by the shastra-s, with a selfless mental attitude. **Path of action** refers to ordinary activities which cause reaction from the perspective of karma, leading to further entanglements in the material world.

Sadhana Non-Translatables			
Jnana-Yoga	≠	Path of Knowledge	**Jnana-yoga** refers particularly to the path of yoga which leads to the awareness or realization of the essential nature of self as identical with the ultimate Brahman. The subject-object dichotomy which persists in cases of knowledge is transcended in jnana yoga. **Knowledge** refers to information, facts, skill acquired through experience, revelation of empirical reality.
Bhakti-Yoga	≠	Path of Devotion	In **bhakti-yoga** the supreme goal of human life is to attain unbounded prema for Bhagavan devoid of any self-interest, leading to divine communion. Bhakti-yoga essentially requires a divine personality, with attributes and form, to adore. The word '**devotion**' can be used in a purely secular sense, to convey devotion towards one's family members, business or job; however, the word bhakti is used specifically for Bhagavan.

9

Vedic Shastra

Shastra refers to the corpus of authoritative texts in the Hindu tradition which have served as the guiding force for millennia. Vedic shastra broadly refers to the Veda-s, the Upanishad-s and all the allied sacred texts including the Vedanga-s, Itihasa-s, Purana-s and Smriti-s. These shastra-s have been traditionally studied and transmitted orally by one generation to the next, by learning from qualified guru-s ensuring protection from distortion. This chapter considers the mistranslations of terms such as Shastra, Shruti, Itihasa, Purana, Tantra and guna.

Shastra is not Scripture

In Abrahamic traditions, the word 'scripture' refers to a book which God reveals for the guidance of all humans through a chosen person - a prophet - at a particular time in history. Any revision to the scripture is allowed only through a new prophet sent by God. The instructions received through such past revelations constitute the scriptures. A scripture is sacrosanct and frozen in a particular historical time and there is no scope for any alteration of its content.

Shastra, however, is not something Bhagavan revealed to any chosen person at a particular time in history. Shastra-s are classified as *Shruti* and *Smriti*. Shruti-s (Veda-s) denote texts which are eternal (*nitya*) and not created by anyone at any point in time (*apaurusheya*). Shruti-s are only perceived by the enlightened rishi-s through supranormal means. Smriti-s refer to sacred texts written by ancient rishi-s to explain the Shruti-s and derive their authority from them.

The most fundamental shastra is the Veda, and manifest in the same form at the beginning of every *kalpa* (creation cycle), similar to the descent of Bhagavan (*avatara*).[141] *Brihadaranyaka Upanishad* (2.4.10) says that the shastra-s such as Veda-s, Itihasa-s and Purana-s, are the very breath of Brahman and are similarly eternal. In contrast, the coming of Jesus created Christian scriptures which did not exist before; thus, its teachings are part of history. The Veda-s are ahistorical and there was never a time when humanity was bereft of them. This feature of eternal truth vis-à-vis historical truth highlights a very fundamental distinction of shastra-s from scriptures and emphasizes the inappropriateness of using the word 'scripture' for Hindu shastra-s.

Conversely, it is misleading to use the word shastra for the scriptures of Abrahamic tradition because in Hindu tradition, a text is regarded as authoritative and a part of the shastra-s only when it is in conformity with the Veda-s. The Bible and the Quran, which do not share ideas that are basic to the Veda-s such as the eternality of the atma, law of karma and reincarnation cannot be considered shastra-s. Only those parts which are in conformity with Veda-s can be accepted as shastra.

While scriptures were dictated to chosen prophets, without any regard to merit, the Veda-s as impersonal knowledge at the adhyatmika level, become an object of cognition when one has purified oneself through rigorous sadhana and tapasya. Such a spiritually qualified and enlightened person is called a rishi in Hindu tradition. Rishi-s are highly revered and worshipped, whereas in Abrahamic traditions, the worship of a prophet may be regarded as blasphemy. While scriptures are not personified, the Veda-s have a personality.[142]

Another important distinction between the shastra-s and the scriptures lies in the way they are learnt. Indian tradition of learning has been primarily oral through conscious choice, and the Veda-s were accurately transmitted and preserved through the unbroken lineage of guru-shishya parampara.[143] Abrahamic scripture derives from, and rests upon, the idea of a written text documenting the decrees of God for man while the Veda-s embody the oral tradition.[144]

The Smriti-s are dynamic and adaptable to reinterpretation for different epochs, preventing their irrelevance with time.[145] Scriptures, in contrast, lack these evolving aspects, making them frozen at a particular historical time and reducing their relevance in the modern world. The dynamic aspect of Hindu shastra-s is completely lost when they are translated as scriptures, adding to the reasons why the shastra is a Sanskrit non-translatable.[146]

Shruti is not 'That which is Heard'

Shruti is a profound term in Sanskrit, commonly mistranslated as 'that which is heard'. Shruti is used to signify the intuitive hearing experienced during samadhi and not merely something that is auditory. Ancient Indian rishi-s experienced a resonance with the subtle and supra-physical cosmic forces, leading to the manifestation of the Vedic mantra-s which are referred to as Shruti-s.[147] Since Shruti-s and Veda-s are synonymous, the Shruti-s are nitya and apaurusheya; Hinduism is called *sanatana* (eternal) dharma because it based on the Shruti-s.

According to tantric texts there are two types of sounds - *ahata* and *anahata*.[148] The ahata is produced when two things strike, such as the sound uttered by a person while speaking. However, the sound of the Veda-s is *anahata,* which means that it is not produced by any conjunction of objects. Anahata sound is beyond the realm of senses and is eternal. Anahata Shabda is silent to the physical ears of an ordinary person but can be perceived by yogi-s in samadhi.

The process for the correct pronunciation of the mantra-s in the Shruti-s involves a deep knowledge of phonetics (*shiksha*), which activates the nerve centers of the listener and affects the universe. A change in intonation can completely alter the effect produced by a Shruti mantra on the listener and hence, guidance of a learned guru is essential.

According to Indian philosophy, Vak has four levels and Figure 20 shows its forms from most concrete (*vaikhari*) to subtlest (*para*) manifestations.

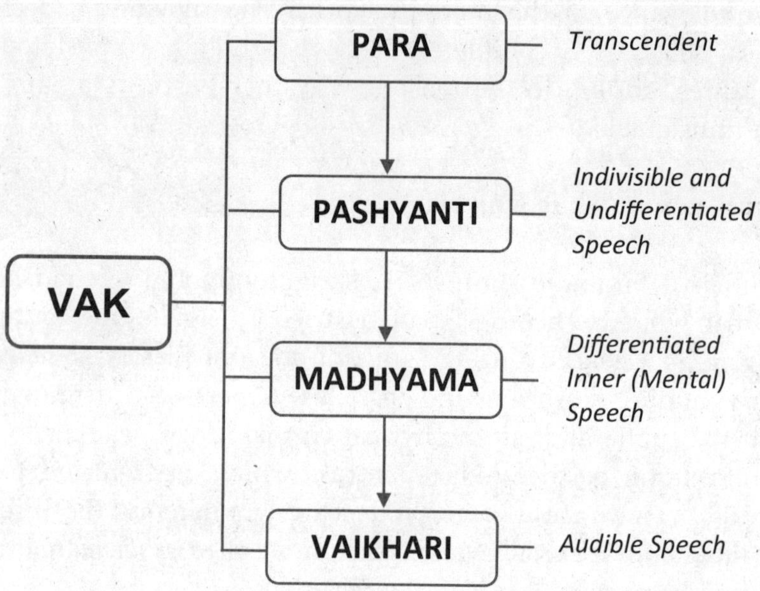

Figure 20: Vak

Para Vak is nothing but the Shruti-s. Indian thought has four levels of speech or language and corresponding levels of hearing. Shruti is not something heard at the vaikhari level but at the level of Para Vak, by rishi-s. Considering the profound implications of mistranslating such a term, Shruti is a prime example of a Sanskrit non-translatable.

Itihasa/Purana is not History/Myth

In Indian tradition, Itihasa and Purana denote a corpus of texts which are foundational to the Indian ethos in all aspects. There are two Itihasa-s - *Ramayana* and *Mahabharata* - whereas the Purana-s are many in number, with eighteen of them regarded as more exhaustive and important. *Itihasa* and *Purana*, have been misinterpreted due to their mistranslation as 'history' and 'myth' respectively.

History is regarded as knowledge relating to past events connected to a particular people, country, period or persons, usually written as a chronological account. Itihasa-s and Purana-s also contain historical facts, but are neither merely books of history, nor tales of fantasy (myth). Itihasa-s and Purana-s are a part of the Vedic literature and regarded as the fifth Veda.[149]

Purana-s are regarded in Hinduism among the fourteen or eighteen branches of traditional knowledge.[150] Purana-s are vaster in time, spanning numerous kalpa-s and their narrative is not linear in time as in the case of history.[151] They narrate incidents from different yuga-s to spiritually enlighten a person and have information related to geography, astronomy, political theory, culture, economics, philosophy and several other streams of knowledge and not merely reporting historical facts. A Purana by definition contains five subjects: creation of the universe, secondary creation and dissolution of the universe, genealogy of gods and our ancestors, reigns of various Manu-s and events during those reigns.[152] The word Itihasa, etymologically means 'so it has been'; *Amarakosha* (1.6.4) defines Itihasa as a text which narrates events that occurred in the past.

The word *Itihasa* can be broken down into three units: *iti*, *ha* and *asa*. *Iti* means 'thus', *ha* means 'was' and *asa* means 'expansion'; thus, Itihasa means 'expansion or elaboration of an incident which happened in the past'.[153] Maharishi Valmiki in the *Ramayana* and Maharishi Veda Vyasa in the *Mahabharata* have used historical facts for pedagogical purposes. The Indian conception of Purana-s and Itihasa-s can be regarded as an interpretative account of past events in a cultural or a spiritual context.

This unique and insightful method of narration has made the Purana-s and the Itihasa-s timeless literary works. The renowned etymologist Yaska, in his work *Nirukta* (111.19), has defined 'Purana' as *pura navam bhavati* which means that anything old which becomes new is known as 'Purana'. Thus, although the Purana-s and the Itihasa-s narrate very old incidents, they are also new in the sense that the principles illustrated by them are eternal and ever-applicable in a person's life. The *Bhagavad Gita,* which is a part of the *Mahabharata,* describes among other things, the way a human mind functions and is as relevant today for anyone as it was in the past.

Purana-s and Itihasa-s convey the knowledge of the Veda-s in a lucid and engaging manner to everyone.[154] The Western genre of history has no underlying foundation in anything equivalent to Shastra, unlike the Purana-s and Itihasa-s have in the Veda-s. Maharishi Veda Vyasa selected numerous interesting and actual incidents from the past and narrated them in the *Mahabharata* in a way that anyone hearing them would gain some wisdom. These stories teach the principles of the Veda-s without the accompanying rigor and intensity, while they can be remembered more easily than the abstract mantra-s or sutra-s in the Veda-s.

The different Purana-s relate an incident from a kalpa with a different prakriti to cater to the needs of tamasika, rajasika and sattvika people.[155] This is because people have an inherent attraction towards an incident if it is molded and presented according to their own prakriti.[156]

Tantra is not Tantric Sex

Tantra-s are Hindu shastra-s, with unique metaphysical doctrines, based on the experiences of seers and yogi-s. Tantra-s deal with sadhana-s for elevating a person's consciousness but are unfortunately misconstrued as being about sex, black magic and rituals.

Hindu shastra-s consist of two broad complementary divisions: Veda-s (*nigama*) and Tantra-s (*agama*).[157] Tantra is derived from the root *tan* which means 'to spread out' or 'expand'; thus, Tantra is a shastra which leads to the expansion of one's knowledge or consciousness.[158] The Tantra-s are not subject to *vaidikachara* and do not require a person to be born in a *varnashrama* system or to go through the *upanayana samskara* for commencing their study unlike the Veda-s. There is no restriction of birth, gender, place or age to begin the study of Tantra-s.[159]

The revealed knowledge of the Veda-s is confirmed by the experiential knowledge of the Tantra-s.[160] Tantra-s are not only manuals of sadhana-s but also present a well-developed theory of epistemology and ontology, which is in consonance with the Upanishad-s. Tantra-s deal with a variety of subjects such as the description of the Supreme Being Brahman, the principles of creation, maintenance and destruction of the universe, the worship of devata-s, construction of temples, the various chakra-s in the human body, dharma, mantra, yantra, medicine and astrology.

The approach of Tantra-s for transcending this material world is unique. They do not favor the mortification of mind and renunciation of this material world, instead accept the bodily instincts positively. Tantra-s attempt to integrate the limited sensory perceptions of the individual with the cosmic forces of the universe. They do not hold desire and moksha in opposition but use the desire itself as a means to self-realization.[161] Tantra-s do not directly prescribe a life of self-abnegation but allow a person to engage in worldly life with awareness.

There are three broad divisions of Tantra-s: *Shakta*, *Vaishnava* and *Shaiva* to help transcend the three guna-s of prakriti: sattva, rajas and tamas.[162] A very fundamental tenet of Tantra-s is *yat yat ande tat tat pinde* which means that whatever exists in the vast world outside also exists within an individual body.[163] The ancient Indian *Tantrika*-s were scientists investigating the deepest mysteries of the cosmos in the laboratory of their own bodies.

Tantra has been equated by the West to sex, erotica and black magic and this completely wrong and misleading interpretation is now imported to India and accepted by Indians. The misconceptions in creating such a view of Tantra is partly due to the incompetent and literal translation of the tantrika terms by Western scholars. For example, bhuta shuddhi has been translated by the well-known nineteenth-century English scholar Monier Williams as 'removal of demons'.[164] The symbolic language of the Tantra-s is lost on many Western scholars, who take an uncritical view of the texts in the absence of initiation and guidance from a guru. The symbolic language of the Tantrika texts is to prevent their misuse by unqualified people, who only seek sensorial gratification and not moksha.[165]

Many great Indian saints from various sampradaya-s such as Adi Shankaracharya, Yamunacharya, Shrila Jiva Gosvami and Ramakrishna Paramahamsa, followed the Tantra-s and achieved God-realization. The legitimate spiritual path of the Tantra-s, aided by the easier accessibility to knowledge and pecuniary motives, has unfortunately been reduced to hedonism and marketable products. Tantra is an invaluable dharmic asset and part of its heritage; its protection from such distortion is deeply important and a primary responsibility.

Guna is not Quality or Mode

The word guna is often translated as 'mode' or 'quality' irrespective of the context and the many technical meanings associated with it. Prakriti, is composed of three constituent elements: sattva, rajas and tamas (its guna-s); the sense here, denoted by guna is that of a constituent or a component part. It is important to note that these three guna-s themselves have certain qualities inherent in them.

According to Nyaya-Vaisheshika, it is *dravya* or a substance which has some quality inherent in it. However, quality itself is qualityless. For example, when sugar is considered sweet, the sweetness is a quality found in the substance sugar, but sweetness itself does not have any quality. Thus, guna is not the quality itself but the substratum of qualities. Each of the three guna-s of prakriti manifest certain characteristic qualities: from sattva guna arises equanimity, from rajas arises greed and from tamas guna arises delusion and ignorance.[166] The diversity in this world is due to the difference in the proportion of three guna-s in the constitution of various things.[167] Unfortunately, English translations of the sankhya texts replace guna with 'quality' or 'mode', which is evidently a case of mistranslation.

Indian thought also considers sattva, rajas and tamas guna-s as the three Shakti-s of prakriti. Other meanings of the word guna include: multiplication as seen in Jyotisha Shastra and *ganita,* a class of vowels (a, e [ए] and o [ओ]) as seen in Panini's *Ashtadhyayi.*[168] In the *Arthashastra* (7.1), guna is used as a technical term to denote the six forms of state policy dependent on a king.[169] None of these different technical meanings of the word *guna* have any connection with the word 'quality'. It is the complete elimination of several different meanings from different branches of Indic knowledge systems that is achieved by mistranslating guna as 'quality' or 'mode'.

Summary of Vedic Shastra Non-Translatables

Vedic Shastra Non-Translatables			
Shastra	≠	Scripture	**Shastra-s** refer to the corpus that is treated as eternal knowledge, complete, true, and timeless. Historicity and prophethood, key agents in creation of scriptures, have no meaning in Hindu shastra-s. **Scripture** refers to the book which God reveals for the guidance of human beings through a prophet in history. Only prophets revise the scripture, otherwise it is frozen in time and sacrosanct.
Shruti	≠	That which is heard'	**Shruti** signifies the intuitive hearing during samadhi and not merely physical hearing though ears, which is what '**that which is heard**' misrepresents.
Itihasa/ Purana	≠	History/ Myth	**Itihasa-s** and **Purana-s** contain historical and chronological facts but are not merely books of **history** with no relevance to the present and are definitely not tales of fantasy as is meant by **myth**. Both are seen as sources of traditional knowledge and are a part of Vedic literature.

Vedic Shastra Non-Translatables			
Tantra	≠	Tantric sex	**Tantra** refers to shastra-s which have been based on experiences of seers and yogi-s. Tantra-s are complementary to Veda-s; the former is based on induction while the latter is based on deduction. Initiation and a guru are required to learn Tantra and hence it is written in a language that needs deciphering. Mistranslation of Tantra as **Tantric sex** reduces a spiritual path to perverted hedonism.
Guna	≠	Quality/ Mode	**Guna** has several technical meanings in Hinduism, including constituents of prakriti, a class of vowels and forms of state policy (in *Arthashastra*). **Quality/Mode** refers to a generic attribute which takes away from the particular meanings of Guna.

10

Hindu Dharma

Dharma is a term intrinsically unique and central to the Indian civilization. It is derived from the Sanskrit root *dhr* which means 'to support' or 'sustain'; dharma thus means 'that which supports or upholds the world and its beings'. Hinduism is called *sanatana dharma* (i.e., the eternal dharma) which supports the physical, social and moral order of the entire manifested world. Sanatana (eternal) here is not a qualification of dharma; it means that whatever is eternal is dharma and also that what we call dharma, has to be eternal. Dharma defies an exact rendering into English or any other language; it does not refer to a system of abstract ideas or beliefs having no essential connection with life nor is it a set of rules to be blindly followed in daily life without any understanding of the basic principles. Hindu dharma is actually the Hindu way of life.

Hindu dharma is very wide and universal in its scope. It is not based on the message of any single prophet or Avatara or on the teachings of any one sage, saint or religious reformer. Although the Veda-s are regarded as the authority in Hindu dharma, the *Manusmriti* (2.6) regards the traditions and practices of those who know the Veda-s, the conduct of virtuous people and an individual's conscience as important sources. Hindu dharma is thus founded on the varied experiences and teachings of muni-s, rishi-s, acharya-s and bhakta-s, making it nurturing of diversity, naturally assimilative and a highly efficient system with an open architecture for adaptation.

A few terms related to Hindu dharma and their mistranslations are considered here.

Samskara is not Ritual or Ceremony

Samskara-s refer to the various purificatory actions done for sanctifying and refining the body, mind and intellect of a person. The performance of these samskara-s is essential to make an individual a practicing Hindu. Most Western scholars generally translate samskara as 'ritual'; ritual or ceremony refers to a series of actions performed that may or may not have a spiritual consequence. The flag ceremony in most countries and taking the oath of office are examples of rituals and ceremonies which have no spiritual consequence and are secular in nature.

The word samskara is derived from the verbal root *kr* by adding prefix *sam* and it means 'purification' or 'embellishment'. Hindu dharma believes that it is rare for a jiva to gain birth in a human body and hence it takes great care to protect and nurture the body and mind of an individual. Samskara-s aid this by purifying and embellishing the body, mind and intellect of a person to make it a worthy dwelling place for the atma.

Samskara-s can be likened to the process of installation of software on a computer and are meant to efficiently run a human body. A total of forty-one samskara-s is required to be performed at various milestones in a person's life to consciously mold and refine one's character. *Garbhadhana* is the first one and the final samskara is *shraaddha* or *antayeshti* which is done after the death of an individual. Shraaddha is also performed annually for a person by his descendants in perpetuity. Garbhadhana is done at conception to attract a good atma to take birth and purify the minds of the prospective parents before conception.[170]

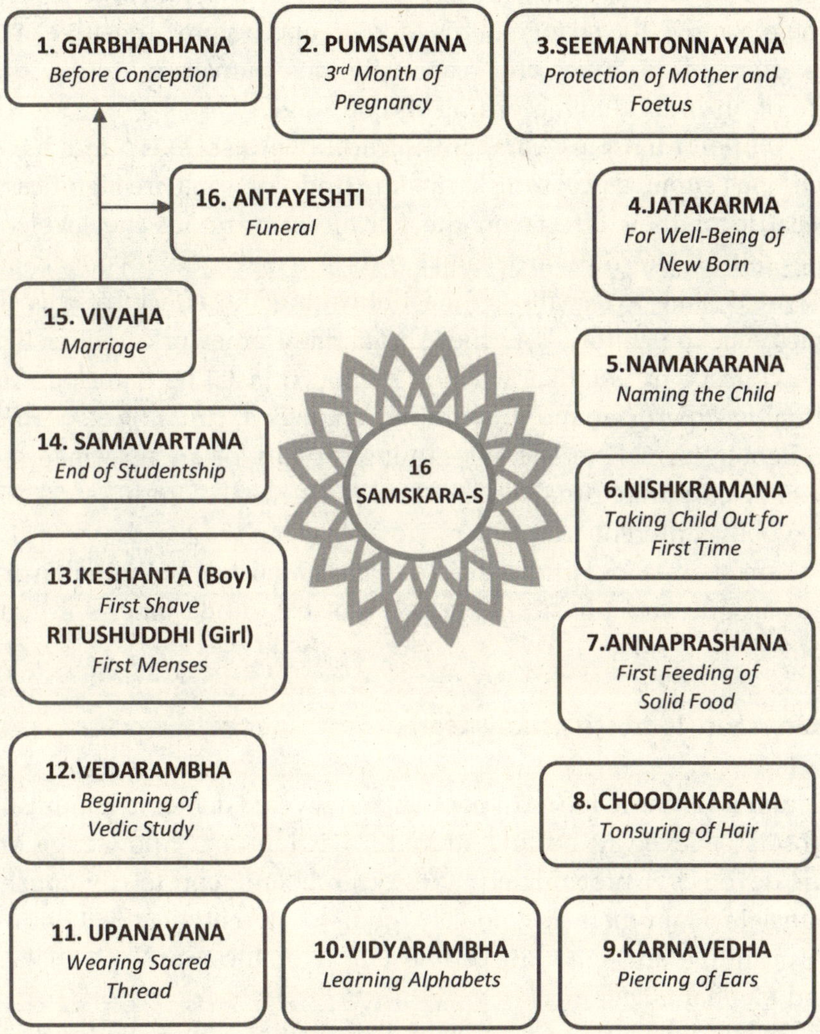

Figure 21: Sixteen Samskara-s

Samskara-s are not irrational and futile priest-craft but give a sense of identity to an individual, when performed at various milestones in a person's life. The samskara-s at different ages of an individual, such as initiation (*upanayana*), tonsuring (*mundana*), end of studentship (*samavartana*), marriage (*vivaha*) and others, help one recognize the change in his identity and become sensitive and aware of one's duties and responsibilities. Samskara-s guide the life of an individual according to one's age.

While rituals in Abrahamic traditions also exist and have religious significance, samskara-s in Hindu dharma are significant because of their effects on the karmic imprints at the level of the chitta. The outward samskara-s are believed to create an elevated state externally, while imprinting the effects of this in purifying the chitta.[171] As the Abrahamic framework neither has the concept of antahkarana nor karma, translating samskara as ritual is superficial and misleading. The word 'ritual' is also used to denote formalism such as signing a treaty or an agreement as seen in 'corporate ritual' and 'bureaucratic ritual'. Hindu samskara is wholly different from this.

Samskara-s for Hindus are the experiential side of their dharma and an outward physical expression of the subtle inner spiritual forces.

Hanuman is not Monkey God

Hanuman is one of the most popular and revered deities in Hinduism who is believed to bestow strength, wisdom and knowledge on His devotees. Unfortunately, Western scholars tend to frivolously translate Hanuman as 'monkey god' to stereotype the Hindus as primitive and ignorant people who worship monkeys, snakes and elephants.

In Hinduism, there are certain deities whose divine bodies may bear some resemblance in their external features with particular creatures in our mortal world. However, it would indeed be unintelligent to regard a deity as simply a monkey or an elephant on the basis of this partial external resemblance. Hanuman is described as a *vanara* in the *Ramayana*. Vanara-s were devata-s who incarnated to help Bhagavan Shri Rama; they took birth in bodies with partial resemblance to monkeys and humans.[172] Thus, to translate Hanuman as 'monkey god' or Ganesha as 'elephant god' only betrays the ignorance and intention of the translator.

Hanuman is a highly learned devata, erudite scholar and widely acclaimed for his knowledge of Veda-s and Vyakarana.[173] This is in obvious contrast to a monkey, which is a very rajasika creature, unlike Hanuman, who embodies pure sattva guna.

Hanuman is also called *Kapisha* and one of the meanings of the word *kapi* in Sanskrit is 'monkey'. However, the word kapi also means 'one who resembles or has a complexion like that of a monkey or an ape'. *Vanara*-s were a different type of human beings and the word vanara itself is derived from the Sanskrit word *va* and *nara* which means 'slightly like human being'. Another Sanskrit word which is used to denote vanara-s is *kimpurushah*, formed by a combination of two words *kim* and *purushah*. Purushah again means 'human being' and kim means 'what' and is used here in the sense of amazement. Vanara-s may have been a different species of human beings that is no longer extant, which had some physical features of monkeys.[174]

Hanuman is a great bhakta of Bhagavan Shri Rama and is considered as an avatara of Bhagavan Shiva who appeared on earth to assist Bhagavan Shri Rama in His fight against the evil asura-s.[175] Hanuman is considered among the seven *chiranjeevi*-s (immortals) in Hinduism who are ever present physically on earth.[176]

Sanskriti is not Culture

Sanskriti is commonly and loosely translated as 'culture'. Culture is defined as the quality in a person or society that concerns excellence in arts, letters, manners and scholarly pursuits.[177] Sanskriti, on the other hand, is not just confined to the material world and includes the pursuit of a higher purpose. Samskara and sanskriti are cognate words; sanskriti is a means to create samskara-s that will transform a person into a valuable member of society.

Sanskriti comes from the Sanskrit root *kr* which means 'to do' or 'to make', and the prefix *sam* conveys a sense of embellishment or some additional improvement. Etymologically, sanskriti refers to actions done for the holistic refinement and perfection of all the potentials within a human being. The Sanskrit word prakriti means 'the raw natural life without any refinement', such as the way animals live.

Sanskriti embraces all the aspects of an individual's life and is not merely confined to fine arts. Sanskriti provides the guiding principles for an individual to cultivate innate potentials for individual and social refinement. Sanskriti is for the harmonious perfection of all the four varna-s in the traditional Hindu society.

Purushartha-s in dharmic traditions recognize man's needs and provide a framework for their legitimate pursuit and development. This social set-up is based on the Vedic foundation and sees divine manifestation everywhere, thus creating a life-affirming view not subject to extremes of nihilism or hedonism. Dharmic society leverages its Vedic psychology to guide and direct man's daily life for optimal individual and collective well-being, while keeping the spiritual goal of moksha as the overarching aim. It is this unique set-up which incorporates profound concepts of rasa and samskara-s, to create a vibrant way of life, i.e., sanskriti. Hindu sanskriti, therefore, is an inseparable part of the integrally unified Hindu dharma. Aesthetic and sensual pursuits in sanskriti are thus under this framework, differing from 'culture,' which is ill-defined in comparison, devoid of any unified or singular metaphysical foundation, and is a case of Western synthetic unity.[178]

Sanskriti is not just concerned with one life span of an individual but considers an atma's journey through several births. However, Western culture assumes just one life, to be spent in pursuit of material pleasures. Such a culture can be arbitrary, at the individual's discretion, and include choices that might be harmful to the individual and society, reflected in the frequent usage of words such as 'pop-culture' or 'drug-culture'. In the

Hindu culture, such hedonism and destructive behavior is called *vikriti,* which is the opposite of sanskriti. In contrast, the word sanskriti can only be applied for deeds with the motive of spiritual upliftment of an individual and society. Sanskriti should be used only for positive lifestyles based on dharmic principles, and vikriti for abusive forms of lifestyles.

Agama is not Ritual Text

Agama-s are a vast body of literature and not accurately studied or even compiled in modern times. They provide procedures for temple worship, temple-architecture, town-planning, fine arts, administration, healing with the use of Shakti-s, even bringing rain, and virtually every domain of practical living connected with temples in the Hindu society. They also describe the various utsava-s or festivals to be celebrated and the processions to be conducted at temples. Veda-s and Agama-s are complementary to each other; Agama-s can be considered as the applied side of the Veda-s and have been passed down through the traditional guru-shishya parampara. They have been incorrectly translated as 'rituals'.

The Agama-s provide specific procedures for the consecration or sanctification of a building, an image or an item to make it effective for the purpose of worship.[179] They also describe presentation of music, dance, drama and other performances in the presence of a deity. These procedures cannot be labeled as rituals because these are the ways, according to Hindu thinking, to realize the transcendent, omnipresent and immanent absolute reality. The procedures specified in the Agama-s facilitate the visualization of that absolute reality to offer worship.

The ceremonies and procedures in the Agama-s are intended to affect the workings of the cosmos, although the effects may not be immediately perceptible in every case. The Agama-s describe the protocols performed for invoking the deity's personal presence in the temple in the form of the vigraha. The processes explained in the Agama-s are practical ways to develop a personal relationship and receive direct experience of the divine. The Agama-s are broadly classified into three groups: Vaishnava Agama-s, Shaiva Agama-s and Shakta Agama-s, according to their affiliation with a particular deity.

The Agama-s, similar to the Dharmashastra-s, provide procedures for carrying out all the samskara-s; thus, Agama-s are a complete knowledge system dealing with the entire gamut of events in a person's life from birth to death.

The procedures provided in the Agama-s are karma-s to be performed to produce certain outcomes. They are designed as per the principles of causation. They eventually lead a person to uplift their consciousness and discard their conditioned existence in this physical body and attain liberation - which, according to Hinduism, is the ultimate purpose of human birth. Agama-s, like science, are not based on mere speculation but on the actual experience of the yogi-s and seers who investigated the subtle inner workings of this nature.

Naga is not Naked

The *Naga-s* form a very ancient sect of Hindu ascetics known for their martial arts and extremely strenuous sadhana-s.[180] They traditionally remain without clothes and besmear their body with specially prepared *vibhuti* or *bhasma* which can be loosely translated as 'sacred ash'. The Western world is greatly fascinated by them because they keep their bodies unclad, leading to the misportrayal of the Naga-s as 'naked' sadhu-s. Such a portrayal undermines the underlying philosophy behind this practice followed by the Naga-s, while also giving undue importance to just one aspect of their spiritual life, overshadowing other significant ones. It is important to distinguish the Naga-s from Western nudists, with whom they are unfortunately compared.

The Naga sadhu-s are fiercely independent, dignified, confident and austere in their behavior unlike Western nudists who practise sensual self-indulgence. In contrast to the Western nudists, the Naga sadhu-s remain unclothed to detach from all worldly feelings and desires. The Naga-s have risen above all bodily identity and do not care about worldly opinion. Their unclad bodies (*digambara*) covered with bhasma signifies their freedom and renunciation of all materialistic and worldly concerns.

According to Hindu philosophy, the physical body is not the true identity of an individual and misplaced focus upon it leads to a further entanglement with the material world. The bhasma covering a Naga sadhu is a reminder of the transitory nature of the physical body, which eventually turns into ash on cremation. This is a part of their sadhana for spiritual realization and not meant for any hedonistic enjoyment like the Western nudists.

A person is ordained as a Naga only after undergoing rigorous tests and tapasya spanning several years. The initiates obey many strict vows which include sleeping on the bare ground, not having more than one meal a day, not indulging in flattering or abusing anyone and, of course, not covering themselves with any cloth. Thus, an initiate has to earn the title of a Naga by proving his worth and it cannot be gained just by discarding clothes.

The Naga-s are organized into formal groups called *akhada*-s and each akhada has its own rules, policies, organization, governance, and lineage traced to ancient times. The Naga-s undergo training in the use of traditional weapons, wrestling and other martial arts for this purpose. Some Naga-s are *shastradhari* sadhu-s (weapon wielding) and others are *shaastradhari* sadhu-s (specializing in the shastra-s). When the Naga-s move in any procession, for example, during the Kumbh mela, they display their martial skills with the various maneuvers of their swords, tridents (*trishula*-s) and spears (*bhala*-s). Thus, the Naga-s are a class of warrior sadhu-s found within many sampradaya-s or traditions of Hinduism. They do their sadhana for spiritual emancipation but are additionally responsible for the protection of non-combatant sadhu-s and can resort to violence for that purpose if necessary.

In historical times, there have been some key battles fought and won by the Naga-s and they do not hesitate to sacrifice their lives for the protection of dharma. In 1757 CE, the Naga sadhu-s fought against the fanatical Afghan forces of Ahmad Shah Abdali at Gokul near Mathura. Ahmad Shah Abdali's decree led to an indiscriminate slaughter of people including sadhu-s and the burning of the region around Agra and Mathura for seven days. Four thousand Naga sadhu-s offered stiff resistance to the Afghans at this crucial moment. Around two thousand Naga sadhu-s sacrificed their lives in this battle at Gokul.[181]

Given this incredible history and background of the highly dignified Naga sadhu-s, it is derisive to compare them with nudists as the two are the very antithesis of each other.

Dasa is not Slave

A Sanskrit word is often deliberately mistranslated into English by Western scholars with an ulterior motive to denigrate the Hindu tradition. A case of spiteful mistranslation can be found in the Sanskrit word *dasa*. The word dasa is mistranslated as 'slave' so frequently that almost everyone accepts this as the correct meaning. Thus, the word *devadasi* comes to mean 'female slaves of the temple'. People see dasa as equivalent to the shameful and inhumane system of slavery followed by the Westerners until just a few generations ago.

The word slave denotes one who is under the forced authority of another person. A slave is completely controlled by his owner and is forced to obey the owner's commands and a slave could be beaten or even killed by his master with impunity. The Europeans were involved in brisk slave trade and captured and forcefully transported them from the African countries to the Americas and Caribbean islands. Similarly, Islamic invaders forcefully took skilled artisans and craftsmen from erstwhile India to Central Asia as slaves to construct various monuments for them. Slaves were disposable property of their masters and in medieval and modern times, were bought and sold in markets.

In Hindu dharma, dasa is nowhere near a derogatory word like 'slave' but carries a sublime philosophical meaning. It is considered to be the true nature (*svarupa*) of a jiva to be a dasa of Bhagavan. One is not a dasa to another human being but only to Bhagavan, through complete surrender to Him. Dasa is one who feels blessed by offering seva to Bhagavan and derives ananda from it. Hanuman is an ideal example of a dasa and is worshipped for the same. Being a dasa of Bhagavan is the highest honor for a person and to attain a continuous *dasya bhava* towards Bhagavan is the culmination of all spiritual sadhana-s. If dasa meant a slave, then such a high regard for it would not have been possible. The slave-masters in Western history did not treat their slaves as human beings and the question of worshipping the slaves would be ridiculous.

A dasa realizes oneself to be an amsha of Bhagavan and as belonging to Him; he feels delighted to do seva for Bhagavan out of prema and his own volition. There is no compulsion or coercion from anyone on him to behave in this manner. Thus, the word dasa has no similarity with the word slave. Slave is a disrespectful term, whereas in India, dasa is a venerated term and this can be seen from the names of many great bhakta-s such as Tulsidasa, Surdasa, Ramdasa and Krishnadasa who proudly called themselves as dasa.

Seva is not Service

Seva is a Sanskrit word commonly used to denote selfless activities done for realization of Bhagavan by the Hindus. It has become commonplace to equate seva with 'service', even though service refers to work done by one for another person or an organization, often in expectation of some material benefit.

The word seva does not refer to work done by someone in an office, shopping center, hotel or other customer service for monetary benefit. Seva refers to the activities done by an individual for the pleasure of Bhagavan without any trace of egoism and is rendered through one's body, mind and wealth.[182] Thus, seva is a devotional act and the highest form of worship of Bhagavan. It is defined as the unbroken flow of mental activities towards Bhagavan.[183] Even a penurious person has the capacity to offer the finest items to Bhagavan during his manasika seva with an unswerving emotion of love. Seva is motivated purely out of love and reverence for its recipient.

In Hinduism, the whole world of insentient and sentient entities is regarded as an amsha or a part of Bhagavan and He exists within all of them as their inner controller; thus, the concept of seva includes all the jiva-s. This is reflected in the emphasis given to offer seva to one's guru, parents, the elderly, guests or any suffering jiva. Seva and Bhakti are closely related and synonymous.[184]

Seva can be offered to Bhagavan directly or indirectly through one's obligations towards family and society or by helping someone in distress. The realization of the underlying presence of Bhagavan in every jiva along with a complete lack of self-interest is essential for one's actions to qualify as seva. It is not only a means to spiritual upliftment, but an end in itself. Service without this principle to help out fellow humans is not seva because such service does not perceive them as manifestations of Bhagavan.

Seva demands a purity of mind and a *sevaka*'s (performer of seva) mind should be free from anger, greed, lust, pride and other negative emotions. Such a pure mental orientation is denoted by the term *seva-bhava* and a person doing seva has to cultivate this seva-bhava within her/him. The concept of seva is a very important element of the Sikh dharma and the Sikhs lay great stress on *kar seva*. Kar means 'hand' and kar seva thus refers to seva done with hands. The Sikhs consider it meritorious and an act of piety to offer seva in gurdwara-s. They do it willingly for the pleasure and happiness of their guru-s and the Supreme Being.

In Christianity, missionaries are motivated to help the poor or needy non-Christian people with the purpose of converting them. Such charitable actions are based on vested interests and cannot be called seva. All the seemingly good work done by them only masks their true agenda of conversion.

Guru is not Teacher

Guru is one of the several words of Sanskrit that has officially been recognized as part of the English lexicon and used in two ways - as an expert, such as management guru or investment guru and as a teacher of any subject, ranging from cooking, sports to science or any other vocation. Teacher is defined as 'a person who teaches or instructs as a profession' and therefore expects remuneration. The Sanskrit word guru is, however, very different in its original meaning and has been distorted and trivialized in its adoption.

The word guru is formed by *gu,* meaning 'ignorance' and *ru,* referring to 'the remover', to denote one who removes ignorance. Guru helps his shishya-s overcome the bondage of the material world by showering them with wisdom.[185] Bhagavan appears in the form of a guru as a *tattva-darshi* to help comprehend the Veda-s and elevate people's consciousness for moksha.[186] A guru is thus an abode of all virtues and serving him is tantamount to the worship of all the devata-s.[187]

A person must exhibit an immaculate moral rectitude to be called a *guru,* besides possessing profound knowledge of the shastra-s. The word *teacher* does not demand so many essential qualifications; anyone with a requisite college degree or other academic qualifications is entitled to become a teacher. Guru, no doubt, is an expert in his subject and also acts as a teacher, but these are necessary, and not sufficient, characteristics of a guru.

In the Indian tradition, no part of human life and activity is devoid of spirituality. The secular and mundane subjects such as military warfare, taught by the guru-s, were also based in spirituality. The various weapons such as *Brahmastra, Varunastra, Indrastra* required the knowledge and application of a higher science of mantra-s, as seen in the spiritual instruction of guru Dronacharya in the *Mahabharata*. This ancient Indian military science (*Dhanur-vidya*), along with others such as engineering (*Sthapatya*) and Ayurveda, are all part of the Veda-s called the Upaveda-s. The guru who teaches these is no doubt dealing with something practical (*vyavaharika*) but this knowledge is always inseparably linked to the transcendental knowledge (*paramarthika*). Being pragmatic in vyavaharika life does not make the activity secular in the modern sense; it is always to be performed as part of one's *sva-dharma*.

As mentioned earlier, a guru must also be a role model of exemplary moral character for his/her students. A guru will not be involved in any act of moral turpitude. However, a teacher in the modern sense is not bound by any such moral code. A teacher can be brilliant in his subject with a plethora of accolades but that cannot be a measure of his character. In fact, in modern Western society a distinction is made between the academic and personal life of a teacher and the flaws of personal life are overlooked as private matter. However, for a guru, personal life is far more significant than academic life. The reverential attitude which the personality of a guru evokes in his students is the very foundation of a *guru-shishya* relationship. This would not be possible if the guru happens to be morally corrupt, notwithstanding his mastery over his subject. This is the reason that the unflinching veneration accorded to Dronacharya by Ekalavya in the *Mahabharata* would not be normally possible for a modern teacher to receive from one's student.[188]

A guru is one who has mastered his senses and behaves with dignity and equanimity. The purity of his inner being is manifested in scrupulous outer behavior and propriety. A guru sets himself as an example for his students to emulate by practicing the virtues that he preaches. The education imparted by a guru is not merely within the classroom, but also shows the disciples the art of leading a dharmic life. In the gurukula system of traditional education, a person lived with the family of his guru and learnt from his behavior towards his children, wife, parents and friends.

Another point of distinction between a guru and a teacher is that the latter imparts knowledge to students for regular monetary benefit, whereas this was considered anathema in the gurukula system. It was only after the completion of education that a student was expected to offer something in return to the guru as *guru-dakshina*. The continuance of the tradition of knowledge inherited was paramount for the guru and not monetary benefit. This is still in practice by some guru-s of classical Indian music.

The Sanskrit word guru cannot just be added as another synonym for the word 'teacher' to enhance the English language. It should come into English on its own terms and without any trivialization of its original meaning.

Shraddha is not Faith

Shraddha is commonly mistranslated as 'faith'. Faith is described as confidence or trust in a person or thing based on casual conviction or blind belief. For example, faith could be directed towards an airline known for its punctuality or a person considered to be honorable. Faith can also be belief in the commandments of a particular religion or confidence of an individual in one's government or society. Faith is also used in the sense of loyalty or commitment towards a promise, or an organization based on character or as a part of a contract.

The word *shraddha* etymologically derives from a combination of two words, *srat* and *dha*. Srat is a Vedic term for truth (*sat*) and *dha* means 'to hold' or 'to nourish'; shraddha thus means 'to hold or align your mind with the truth or reality'. Shraddha in its original and primary sense denotes feelings of reverence towards the divine or a spiritually evolved being; in the secondary sense, shraddha can also be used in the context of mundane things. Having shraddha for the shastra-s is not the same as having faith in an airline; the latter is a transaction based on reputation and business prospects.

There are four types of shraddha: the first is the transcendental shraddha directed only towards Bhagavan and the other three are material shraddha-s affected by the sattva, rajas and tamas guna of prakriti.[189]

One's shraddha in Bhagavan is the result of karma carried over from previous lives and accompanies a jivatman after death. Shraddha purifies the antahkarana and augments the efficacy of sadhana.[190] Shraddha cannot be used in the context of negative and profane matters. Hindus have shraddha in the rivers Ganga or Yamuna because they are the manifestations of the divine Mother. Similarly, Hindus have shraddha in Veda-s because they are the very speech and prana of Bhagavan.[191]

The Sanskrit word closest to faith would be *vishvasa*. Shraddha contains the sense of vishvasa in it but goes much beyond; it is associated with reverential feelings. One can have vishvasa in a business transaction for instance, without having shraddha associated with it.

Shraddha also refers to the absence of 'ill-will', 'spite' and 'judgment' (*asuya*) while doing charity (*dana*). The *Danasagara* places great importance on shraddha and refers to it as an essential character of the donor, i.e., dana must be done happily, unconditionally and without judgment of the recipient.[192] Faith does not have such specific significance and study associated with it in various contexts, as the term shraddha.

Summary of Hindu Dharma Non-Translatables

Hindu Dharma Non-Translatables			
Samskara	≠	Ritual/ Ceremony	**Samskara** refers to acts done to purify the existence of a person and make one's body worthy for the atma. **Rituals** are acts done for the sake of continuing a past tradition and have no higher inner significance.
Hanuman	≠	Monkey God	**Hanuman** is considered to be an avatara of Bhagavan Shiva who appeared on earth to assist Bhagavan Shri Rama. **Monkey-God** is a translation that derides the Hindus as primitives who mindlessly worship monkeys, snakes and elephants.
Sanskriti	≠	Culture	**Sanskriti** aims at spiritual evolution of mankind and the collective society, across lifetimes. Sanskriti refers to not only material upliftment, but also spiritual. **Culture** is usually associated with the pursuit of excellence in the material world. It is for purely aesthetic or entertainment purposes.

Hindu Dharma Non-Translatables			
Agama	≠	Ritual	**Agama** refers to a vast body of Hindu literature which discusses customs and methodology on a range of topics, including temple worship, architecture, fine arts, administration etc. Veda-s are known as nigama-s and agama-s are seen as complementary to them. Translating agama-s as **rituals** is totally misleading.
Naga	≠	Naked	**Naga-s** remain naked because they are free from bodily egotism, worldly feelings and desires. **Naked** and sensual pleasure seekers are the antithesis of this as they believe in materiality.
Dasa	≠	Slave	**Dasa** is a respectful term and refers to one who abandons one's self-centeredness and surrenders completely to the Divine. **Slave** is a derogatory term denoting one who is under the forced authority of another person. Slaves were kept by the Islamic invaders and Europeans and slavery continues in places to this day.

Hindu Dharma Non-Translatables			
Seva	≠	Service	**Seva** refers to selfless acts done for God-realization as a part of sadhana. **Service** refers to work done in return for some material benefit, as in the case of service-industry.
Guru	≠	Teacher	**Guru** is one who helps a person in overcoming the bondage of the material world. Guru is regarded as the embodiment of deva-s and has a strong moral and ethical character. **Teacher** is just an expert in mundane knowledge and no prerequisites of moral faultlessness are required to be a teacher.
Shraddha	≠	Faith	**Shraddha** is associated with feelings of awe and reverence towards its object and is used in the context of Bhagavan. **Faith** refers to confidence or trust one has in another person or entity which may not necessarily be due to any reverential feelings.

11

Kavya

The success of any civilization is measured not only by the levels of perfection achieved in material well-being and science but also in fine arts. Kavya can be considered as an indicator of the richness of a culture and India has been the foremost among world civilizations in producing kavya masterpieces. Ancient seers have declared kavya to be the source of highest ananda and it can even lead a person to moksha. Veda-s, the most ancient texts available to the world, exhibit fine specimens of kavya and abound in the use of various figures of speech. *Ramayana* is regarded as the first ideal kavya in the Indian tradition. *Mahabharata*, another important work of the Itihasa genre, abounds in the various figures of speech such as similes (*upama*), metaphors (*rupaka*), hyperbole (*atishyokti*) used commonly in Indian kavya works. Rajashekhara, an eminent Indian tenth century kavi, states that in certain Indian traditions, *kavya-shastra* was regarded as the seventh Vedanga. Today, Bharata's *Natyashastra* is the oldest extant work on kavya-shastra.

Indian kavya-shastra laid great stress on the qualities required in a person to be called a *kavi*. Any person composing a few catchy lines at leisure did not qualify for this important title. A kavi was expected to know grammar, prosody, lexicons, legends, worldly affairs, logic and the sixty-four fine arts, be proficient (*nipuna*) in the sciences and the shastra-s such as Purana-s and Itihasa-s to create a good kavya.[193] Rajashekhara says that a kavi should always be pure in speech, mind and body. Indian kavya-shastra-s say that a kavi should abound with bhakti, have vast and varied learning, and be free from depression, as Indian tradition believes that *pratibha* or the power to create a good kavya has divine inspiration behind it.

According to kavya-shastra-s, the form of a kavya is not its true essence. Thus, a kavya need not necessarily be in verse but can be both in prose (*gadya*) and in metre (*padya*). Kavya must be grammatically faultless and thus, knowledge of vyakarana is a must for a kavi.[194]

The delight that one gets on reading a kavya is due to the rasa that runs through it. A kavya should be able to bring out different rasa-s through the manner of its description in order to make it full of charm and merit.

Kavya-shastra is intimately connected with the pursuit of dharma and is not meant only for the sake of worldly pleasure as is the case with poetics. This chapter considers seven terms related to the kavya-shastra which have been mistranslated: *kama, bhava, rasa, prema, leela* and *ananda*.

Kavya is not Poetics

The word kavya is not only a part of the vocabulary of Sanskrit language but is used very commonly in other regional languages of India. Kavya is often translated into English as 'poetry' and kavya-shastra as 'poetics' by even important scholars of Sanskrit.

According to Indian texts, the essential function of kavya is ethical and not aesthetic, decorative or recreational. The string of words used in a kavya is just its physical body or outer garb while its atman is dhvani or rasa.[195] Acharya-s of Indian kavya generally reject the Western doctrine of 'art for art's sake'. There is a statement very often found in the Indian kavya texts regarding the purpose of kavya: *ramadivat vartitavyam na tu ravanadivat*.[196] This means that a person should learn from any kavya to emulate the moral principles and ideals depicted in the character and behavior of Bhagavan Shri Rama and not Ravana or his associates. Maharishi Valmiki, revered as the *adi-kavi* in the Indian tradition says that a kavya should be inspired by noble vision and should take all the human values of life into account.[197]

Mahimabhatta, a prominent twelfth century acharya of kavya-shastra from Kashmir, writes in *Vyaktiviveka* that the primary purpose of a kavya is similar to that of shastra-s – kavya imparts instructions regarding the prohibitions and the injunctions to lead an ethical life similar to the shastra-s but it uses the medium of attractive stories.[198] Similarly, Bharata Muni, Acharya Dandin, King Bhojadeva and other writers also believe that imparting wisdom on how to live according to dharma is one of the purposes of kavya.[199] Mammata, another great eleventh century acharya of kavya-shastra from Kashmir, lays down six purposes of kavya in his work *Kavyaprakash*a: acquisition of fame, wealth, imparting knowledge of social living, destruction of evil, attainment of highest ananda and giving moral advice to a person. There are two types of kavya: that which is enacted on the stage (*drishya*) and that which is heard (*shravya*).[200] Both these means were utilized to transmit knowledge to the people.

Kavya provides the wisdom of the Vedic shastra-s through a more delightful and easier medium to those more temperamentally inclined. Poetics can be secular, atheistic or anti-religious; a poet can ridicule the fundamental principles of a religion, be driven by material profit and is not bound by truthfulness in his poems. However, kavya has none of these blemishes and is meant to provide the essence of all the shastra-s and the knowledge contained in Veda-s, Vedanga-s, Itihasa-s and Purana-s to the common masses.

Kama is not Lust

This section discusses the word *kama* which is often translated as 'lust' or 'sex'. Lust is defined as a strong emotion or feeling that manifests in the form of an intense yearning for sex, expensive objects, power, even food; lust is a powerful psychological force and produces an overwhelming desire for its object.

Kama derives from the Sanskrit root *kamu* which primarily means 'desire'. The dharmic point of view considers kama as one of the four purushartha-s or goals of human life along with dharma, artha and moksha. The original and primary kama of every sentient being is happiness which can be fulfilled through various means; thus, kama is a more fundamental and broader concept and not simply lust.

The pursuit of kama is the result of the disconnect between a jivatma and the ananda of the Brahman (Sachidananda), due to the jiva identifying itself only with material reality. It is this pursuit which manifests in yearning for various objects, furthered by misidentifying oneself with physical, emotional and mental entities. Hinduism recognizes this entanglement and provides a structure to legitimately pursue kama without letting it degenerate into mere lust. According to Hindu dharma, kama should not be satisfied in a way that becomes self-perpetuating and an obstacle to dharma or artha.

In Hinduism there are four types of shastra-s corresponding to the four aims of human life: Kamashastra, Arthashastra, Dharmashastra and Mokshashastra. All these shastra-s provide guidance to lead a balanced life by satisfying the legitimate needs of a human. The ancient Indian treatise of *Kamasutra* written by Vatsyayana says that indulgence in kama, which means 'sexual enjoyment' in this treatise, should not be at the expense of dharma and artha. Similarly, in the *Arthashastra,* written by Kautilya, it is said that a person should not make money in a way that goes against the dharma. Thus, the word *kama* used in the shastra-s denotes a concept which is regulated by the scriptural injunctions and is not an unbridled pursuit like lust. The process of karma-yoga as well as the concept of varnashrama dharma in Hinduism is meant to gradually bring a person out of this lower nature towards the higher principles of life.

One of the names of Shri Krishna is Kamadeva and in the *Bhagavad Gita,* he says that He is kama which is not against the dharma.[201] Several scholars with a superficial knowledge of Hinduism, such as Wendy Doniger, desacralize the word kama in Hindu texts and uses this mistranslation to distort the divine relationship between the gopi-s and Bhagavan Shri Krishna, for instance.[202] Doniger's misinterpretations neither have any resonance with the commentarial tradition of the domain nor are they based in any practices of the land.[203] There is a saying in Sanskrit, *atmavan manyate jagat,* which means that a person sees the world according to one's own conditioning.

Bhava is not Mood

Bhava is sometimes translated as 'mood' and this section considers its inappropriateness. The word mood denotes a temporary state of mind of a person, liable to change at any time. Bhava is not a state of mind but refers to a state of consciousness of an individual.

Etymologically, bhava derives from the root *bhu* which means 'to be' or 'to exist' and hence it signifies the natural and persistent state of consciousness of a person, which colors and influences all interactions and functions. In Indian shastra-s on kavya and natya, this dominant bhava is referred to as *sthayi bhava*. Bhava-s form the basis for classifying rasa-s and for each primary rasa, there is a corresponding sthayi bhava.[204]

Bhava is related to the character of a person, is more consistent and permanent than mood and guides a person in all his spiritual and social interactions. The bhava of spiritual people is stable but in the material world, the mood of a person always changes. Although bhava is a consistent state, the same person may have different bhava-s towards different people. According to *Natyashastra,* there are eight sthayi bhava-s, while Rupa Gosvami has discussed five major bhava-s associated with bhakti in his magnum opus *Bhakti-rasamrita-sindhu*.[205]

Anything which is in accordance with the sthayi bhava of a person brings a positive feeling, and anything contrary to it produces a negative feeling. Modern psychology's developments have been based on the study of the abnormal mind more than the normal mind, while being devoid of any understanding of a yogic or meditative mind, not attached to material pleasure. Studying the dominant bhava of a person can give deep insights into the reasons behind the particular way in which they act or behave, while helping predict the response of a person to different situations. Ancient Indian texts on natya, kavya and rasa consist of exhaustive and unique studies and analysis of human psychology. The concept of bhava can be used as a system for developing a new psychology, based entirely on rasashastra-s.

Rasa is not Mellow or Taste

Rasa in the Vaisheshika darshana denotes taste and is of six kinds: sweet, sour, saline, bitter, pungent and astringent. The liquid extracted from any fruit or flower is also commonly denoted by *rasa*. These two commonplace meanings have led to the translation of rasa as 'taste' or 'mellow' even in highly technical subjects such as Kavya and Natya, leading to a trivialization of the profound concept.

In the Sanskrit treatises on Kavya and Natya, the word *rasa* has a highly technical meaning.[206] Rasa manifests through the combination of *vibhava, anubhava* and *vyabhichari* or *sanchari bhava*-s. When these three *bhava*-s come together and combine with any of the eight sthayi bhava-s, it leads to the emergence and realization of rasa by a qualified person.[207] Bharata Muni excludes the senses of touch, taste and smell from contributing to the rasa experience.[208]

An audience for a drama, musical performance or a kavya, must have certain qualifications to realize rasa; such a qualified person is called a *Sahridaya* or a *Rasika* and this quality is called *Rasikatva* or *Sahridayatva*. Bharata Muni lists some of these qualifications as good character, knowledge of the various fine arts in general and Natya in particular.

Bharata Muni's meticulous study of the human mind is reflected in the theory of rasa. When a rasika witnesses a drama, the various bhava-s represented by an artist through words, gestures, music excite the sthayi bhava within a rasika and make him experience a particular rasa. The vibhava-s, anubhava-s and sanchari bhava-s expressed by a performer heightens the sthayi bhava within a rasika, through cognition of the performer's expressions, and consequently culminates into rasa. The theory of rasa thus provides a deep insight into the mechanism of arousal of human emotions and sentiments.

The Upanishads regard Brahman to be rasa and the experience of rasa as similar to Brahman realization.[209] Thus, rasa is a complex and sublime psychological concept and not an ordinary material concept such as taste. Rasa cannot be similarly considered as a description of some physical quality or form of an object and its psychological impact on the human mind. The experience of rasa is transcendental, rooted in the spiritual plane and it is not equivalent to the experience of taste or mellowness of some fruit or of some aesthetically designed physical object.

Prema is not Love

Love is associated with tender, passionate affection of a person for another; it also refers to sexual passion or desire between two people. *Prema* only partially encompasses the first meaning and is completely different from the second. The word *prema* and its cognate *priti* are both derived from the Sanskrit verbal root *prin* which means to give satisfaction or pleasure (*tarpane*). In prema there are two entities: the first is the subject of prema (*ashraya*) and the other is the object of prema (*vishaya*); the ashraya always acts to please the vishaya.

Prema, in the Gaudiya Vaishnava sampradaya, refers to the essence of *Hladini Shakti* or bliss potency of Bhagavan. In Bhakti literature, prema refers to unalloyed and selfless devotion towards Bhagavan and is a very potent element in the human-divine relationship.

Prema is unconditional, self-fulfilling, without the expectation of any return and without undue physical attachment. Prema is its own reward and an end in itself. A better equivalent for love in Sanskrit would be the word *moha* which means fondness or attachment out of self-interest. Although the words *prema* and love may exhibit some overlap in their meanings, they are very different concepts: Prema is uplifting and leads to the dissolution of egotism and material attachment, whereas love may intensify one's attachment to the physical body.

Leela is not Pastime

The Sanskrit word *leela* is often translated into English as 'pastime', 'play' or 'sport'.

Typically, pastime refers to activities of enjoyment or hobby. Leela is totally different as it is connected with the divine activities of Bhagavan and is not used for the mundane recreational activities of humans. Leela is effortless and spontaneous, revealing the inherent Shakti of Bhagavan. Leela springs from the exuberance of the ananda of Bhagavan and has no mundane purpose or any material aim and is thus beyond the law of karma, unlike human pastimes.

Leela-s are eternal and beyond the limitations of space and time. Leela of Bhagavan appears in two-fold ways due to the limitations of jiva and may be manifest (*prakata*) or unmanifest (*aprakata*). When Bhagavan withdraws the effect of Maya-Shakti or descends in this mortal world, then the same aprakata leela becomes prakata. The aprakata leela can also be realized in a limited way through meditation on sacred mantra-s (*upasana*) but the full realization occurs only in moksha. The creation of the world with different types of jiva-s is also an aspect of Bhagavan's leela.[210]

One would not attain liberation by listening to the pastime activities of another; however, listening to the leela-s of Shri Krishna leads to liberation. Bhagavan out of prema for His devotees takes an avatara in this phenomenal world to guide humanity by His leela-s, towards dharma.[211] Thus, leela, besides being a spontaneous, self-conscious activity and an expression of unlimited ananda, is also educative for the conditioned human beings.

India has a long tradition of enacting Bhagavan's leela-s in many traditional art forms and on stage, as seen in the various Rama leela-s or Krishna leela-s performed every year across the country. The enactment of these divine leela-s is a form of sadhana and incurs spiritual benefit for performers as well as the audience. In contrast, the pastime activities of any person may not serve such elevated purposes and may even promote moral degeneracy. Sadly, the Indian tradition of performing leela is being distorted and degraded by reducing it to a secular performance and removing any transcendental and sacred associations. This further highlights the need to retain leela as a non-translatable.

Ananda is not Bliss

Ananda is a fundamental and profound concept in Indian philosophy which is often inappropriately translated as 'bliss' or 'happiness'. While bliss is a mundane concept connected with ordinary life, ananda is a deeper and multidimensional concept with gradation in its meanings.

The original sense of the word ananda signifies an essential characteristic of Brahman or Bhagavan. When a jivatman attains union with Brahman, it loses its individual identity and attains kaivalya mukti. This state, free from all suffering and devoid of all activity, is called *brahmananda*. When a jivatman enters the leela of Bhagavan and performs seva it attains a state called *bhaktyananda*. The limited joy experienced by a human being in this world is called *martyananda*. Thus, there are three levels of ananda, and the highest is when a jivatman attains bhaktyananda.

The supreme reality in its undifferentiated, indeterminate and attribute-less aspect is called Brahman, whereas It is called

Bhagavan when determinate and qualified with infinite auspicious attributes. Bhagavan is called *sacchidananda vigraha* in a verse from *Brahma-Samhita* which means that His vigraha is constituted of ananda.[212]

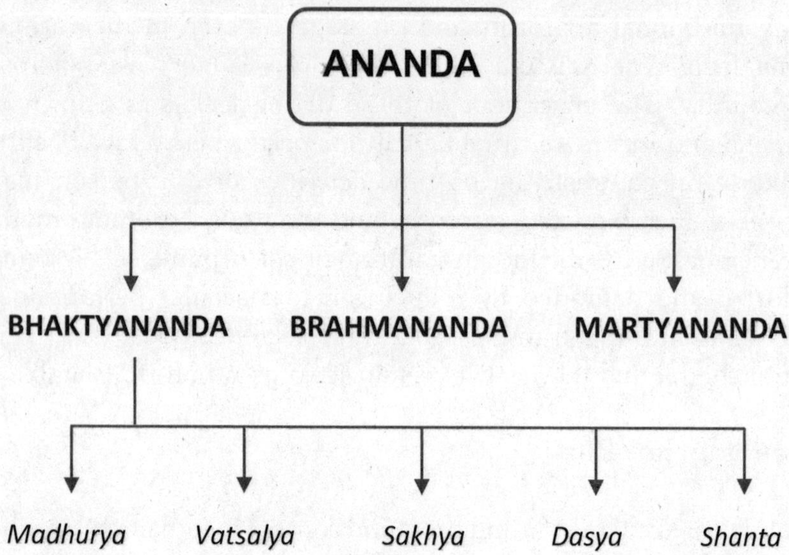

Figure 22: Ananda

A bhakta when doing seva of Bhagavan with prema experiences ananda, which has no equivalent in English. Such ananda by nature is eternal and unlimited unlike bliss or happiness pursued in this world, which is a transient phenomenon and a temporary absence of suffering or pain. There is, thus, an internal gradation in the concept of ananda with a whole spectrum of meanings.[213] When we collapse all the different varieties of meanings denoted by the word *ananda* into words such as bliss, joy, happiness which do not have gradational structure and profundity, then the very essence of the word *ananda* is lost in such translation.

Summary of Kavya Non-Translatables

Kavya Non-Translatables			
Kavya	≠	Poetics	**Kavya** is meant to provide the essence of all shastra-s to the common man. The essential function of kavya is ethical and not merely aesthetic, decorative or recreational. Art for art's sake is not the general view in kavya. **Poetics** can be secular, with a poet even free to ridicule the fundamental principles of a religion.
Kama	≠	Lust	**Kama** is one of the four purushartha-s (goals) of human life according to Hindu dharma. Kama should not be satisfied in a way that it becomes an obstacle to dharma, artha and moksha. **Lust** is a powerful psychological force which manifests in the form of an intense pursuit of sex, expensive objects or power.
Bhava	≠	Mood	**Bhava** refers to the persistent state of consciousness of an individual. **Mood** refers to a temporary state of mind of a person which is liable to change.

Kavya Non-Translatables			
Rasa	≠	Mellow/Taste	**Rasa** is the technical term used in the *Natyashastra*. When a qualified person hears a kavya or witnesses a drama then it leads to the emergence and realization of rasa. **Taste,** unlike rasa, refers to an ordinary material concept.
Prema	≠	Love	**Prema** has no connection with carnal desires and is completely selfless. Prema is not used while referring to insentient things. **Love**, among other associations, has sexual connotations. It could be selfish and directed towards insentient things.
Leela	≠	Pastime	**Leela** is connected with the divine activities of Bhagavan and is not used for mundane recreational activities of humans. Leela reveals the inherent Shakti and springs from ananda of Bhagavan. **Pastime** is an activity that a person indulges in for enjoyment and is synonymous with hobby.
Ananda	≠	Bliss	**Ananda** is gradational, with the highest level called bhaktyananda enjoyed by a bhakta and the lowest level referring to material happiness. **Bliss** refers only to material happiness and has no gradations in it.

Acknowledgments

This book is the result of important support from several individuals throughout its development. The original plan was merely to produce a series of educational videos on the subject in which both the authors would be in conversation. Jessica Richmond of Jiva Institute was immensely helpful in coordinating all the logistics for video recordings over a period of three years, including locations at the studios of Infinity Foundation in Princeton (USA) as well as Jiva Institute in UP (India).

It was then decided to turn the videos into a book and bring out both the book and the videos as multimedia products.

Subhodeep Mukhopadhyay, Seema Mishra and Anurag Sharma turned the video recordings between the authors into a transcript and this became the first rough draft for the book. Manogna Sastry, Shalini Puthiyedam and Anurag worked hard through multiple iterations to edit it both internally as well as with the external editor. T.N. Sudarshan helped with important research on specific topics. Divya Sharma was the in-house graphics expert who polished up the figures while Anurag ensured the accuracy was not lost in the process. Manogna took overall ownership for the quality of the manuscript till it was turned over to the publisher. Shalini coordinated the overall administrative process. Sanjana Roy Choudhury did the final editing making excellent inputs on a tight time schedule.

It is thanks to the combined efforts of this team that the book became possible after many years of work. We are thankful to Nityananda Misra for writing the Foreword and Dr. Korada Subrahmanyam for providing inputs to the book.

Authors

Selected Bibliography

Aurobindo, Sri. 1997. *Collected Works of Sri Aurobindo: The Future Poetry* Pondicherry. Sri Aurobindo Ashram Press.

Aurobindo, Sri. 1998. *Hymns to the Mystic Fire*. Pondicherry. Sri Aurobindo Ashram Press.

Aurobindo, Sri. 1998. *The Secret of the Veda*. Pondicherry. Sri Aurobindo Ashram Press.

Aurobindo, Sri. 1999. *Collected Works of Sri Aurobindo: The Synthesis of Yoga*. Pondicherry. Sri Aurobindo Ashram Press.

Avalon, Arthur. 1953. *The Great Liberation*. Madras. Ganesh & Co.

Avalon, Arthur. 1960. *Principles of Tantra*. Madras. Ganesh & Co.

Bagchee, Prabodh Chandra. 1950. *India and China: A Thousand Years of Cultural Relations*. Bombay. Hind Kitabs Limited.

Balasubramanian, R. 2003. *Theistic Vedānta: History of Science, Philosophy and Culture in Indian Civilization, Vol 2, Part 3*. Delhi. Munshiram Manoharlal Publishers.

Basu, Manoranjan. 1986. *Fundamentals of the Philosophy of Tantras*. Calcutta. Mira Basu Publishers.

Bhanu Swami, HH. 2014. Translation of *Ujjvala-Nīlamaṇi*. Chennai. Sri Vaikuntha Enterprises.

Bhattacharjee, Arun. 1981. *Greater India*. New Delhi. Munshiram Manoharlal Publishers.

Bhattacharya, Rama Shankar. 1976. *Sankhya Tattvakaumudi*. Varanasi. Motilal Banarasidass.

Bhishagratna, Kaviraj Kunjalal. 1911. *An English Translation of the Sushruta Samhita*. Calcutta.

Billimoria, Purushottama. 2007. *Indian Ethics: Classical Traditions and Contemporary Challenges.* England. Ashgate.

Burgess, Ebenezer, Tr. 1935. *Sūrya-Siddhānta.* Gangooly, Phanindralal, Ed. Calcutta. University of Calcutta.

Carman, John Braisted. 1981. *The Theology of Ramanuja.* Bombay. Ananthacharya Indological Research Institute.

Chaitanya, Krishna. 1965. *Sanskrit Poetics: A Critical and Comparative Study.* Bombay. Asia Publishing House.

Chari, S.M.S. 2000. *Vaiṣṇavism: Its Philosophy, Theology and Religious Discipline.* Delhi. Motilal Banarasidass.

Chari, S.M.S. 2004. *Fundamentals of Viśiṣtadvaita Vedānta.* Delhi. Motilal Banarasidass.

Chatterji, Kshitish Chandra. 2003. *Technical Terms and Technique of Sanskrit Grammar.* Kolkata. Sanskrit Pustak Bhandar.

Das, Sudhendu Kumar. 1934. *Sakti or Divine Power.* Calcutta. University of Calcutta.

Doniger, Wendy. 2009. *The Hindus: An Alternative History.* New York. Penguin.

Dwivedi, Rewaprasad. 1936. *Vyaktiviveka.* Varanasi. Chowkhamba.

Dyczkowski, Mark. 1989. *The Doctrine of Vibration.* New Delhi. Motilal Banarasidass.

Eck, Diana. 1982. *Banaras: City of Light.* New York. Knopf.

Eliot, T.S. 1964. *The Use of Poetry and the Use of Criticism: Studies in the Relation of Criticism to Poetry in England.* London. Faber & Faber.

Friedman, Thomas L. 2005. *The World is Flat: A Brief History of the Twenty-first Century.* New York. Farrar, Straus and Giroux.

Gajendragadkar, A.B. 1959. *The Kāvyaprakāśa of Mammaṭa.* Bombay. Popular Book Depot.

Hiltebeitel, Alf. 2001. *Rethinking the Mahābharata.* Chicago. University of Chicago Press.

Jones, William. 1795. 'Botanical Observation of Select Indian Plants'. *Asiatic Researches,* Vol 4: pp. 237-312.

Joshi, Kireet. 2011. *Synthesis of Yoga (History of Science, Philosophy and Culture in Indian Civilization),* Vol XVI, Part 4. New Delhi. Munshiram Manoharlal Publishers.

Kak, Subhash. 2002. *The Gods Within Mind, Consciousness and the Vedic Tradition.* New Delhi. Munshiram Manoharlal Publishers.

Karpatri Maharaja, Sri. 2001. *Ramayana Mīmāṁsa.* Vrindavan. Radhakrishna Dhanuka Prakashan.

Kearns, Cleo. 1987. *T.S. Eliot and Indian Traditions.* Cambridge. Cambridge University Press.

Lamb, Alastair. 1975. 'Indian Influence in Ancient South-East Asia'. In *A Cultural History of India.* Ed. A.L. Basham. London. Oxford University Press.

Lannoy, R. 1971. *The Speaking Tree: A Study of Indian Culture and Society.* London. Oxford University Press.

Malhotra, Rajiv. 2011. *Being Different: An Indian Challenge to Western Universalism.* New Delhi. HarperCollins Publishers with India Today Group.

Malhotra, Rajiv. 2013. 'Vivekananda's Ideas and the Two Revolutions in Western Thought'. in *Vivekananda as the Turning Point: The Rise of a New Spiritual Wave.* Ed. Swami Shuddhidananda. Kolkata. Advaita Ashrama Press.

Mandlik, Vishvanath Narayan. 1886. *Mānava-Dharma Śāstra.* Bombay. Ganpat Krishnaji's Press.

Mishra, Kamalakar. 1999. *Kashmir Śaivism: The Central Philosophy of Tantrism.* New Delhi. Sri Satguru Publications.

Mishra, Sampadananda. 2005. *Sanskrit: And the Evolution of Human Speech (Based on Sri Aurobindo's Linguistic Theory).* Pondicherry. Sri Aurobindo Society.

Nath, Vijay. 2001. *Purānas and Acculturation.* New Delhi. Munshiram Manoharlal Publishers.

Pandey, Kanti Chandra. 1950. *Comparative Aesthetics : Indian Aesthetics.* Vol 1. Banaras. The Chowkhamba Sanskrit Series Office.

Parmeshwaranand, Swami. 2000. *Encyclopaedic Dictionary of Vedic Terms.* New Delhi. Sarup & Sons.

Potter, Karl. 2015. *Encyclopedia of Indian Philosophies Volume XIX.* New Delhi. Motilal Banarasidass.

Rajavade, V.K. 1940. *Yaska's Nirukta.* Poona. Bhandarkar Oriental Research Institute.

Ramanujan, A. 1990. 'Is there an Indian way of thinking? An informal essay'. In *India through Hindu Categories*. Ed. M. Marriott. New Delhi. Sage Publications.

Ramaswamy, K., Nicolas de, Antonio, and Banerjee, Aditi. 2007. *Invading the Sacred: An Analysis of Hinduism Studies in America*. New Delhi. Rupa & Co.

Ryle, Gilbert. 1949. *The Concept of Mind*. Chicago. University of Chicago Press.

Sandal, Mohan Lal. 1923. *The Mimamsa Sutras of Jaimini*. Allahabad. Union Press.

Santideva, Sadhu. 1999. *Encyclopaedia of Tantra*. Vol. 1. New Delhi. Cosmo Publications.

Sarkar, Jadunath. *A History of Dasnami Naga Sanyasis*. Allahabad. Sri Panchayati Akhara Mahanirvan.

Sen Sharma, Deba Brata. 1990. *The Philosophy of Sadhana*. New York. State University of New York Press.

Sharma, Pandit Kedarnath. 1965. *Kavyamimamsa*. Patna. Bihar Rashtrabhasha Parishad.

Singh, Jaideva. 2007. *Spanda-Kārikās: The Divine Creative Pulsation*. New Delhi. Motilal Banarasidass.

Sullivan, Bruce M. 1994. 'The Religious Authority in the Mahābhārata: Vyāsa and Brahmā in the Hindu Scriptural Tradition'. *Journal of the American Academy of Religion*, 62: pp. 377-401.

Tagare, G.V. 2002. *The Praytabhijñā Philosophy*. New Delhi. Motilal Banarasidass.

Travis F., Olson, T., Egenes, T., Gupta, H.K. 2001. 'Physiological patterns during practice of the Transcendental Meditation technique compared with patterns while reading Sanskrit and a modern language'. International Journal of Neuroscience. 109 (1-2): pp. 71-80.

Tripathi, Ramsagar, ed. 1987. *Dhvanyāloka of Ānandavardhana: with the Commentary Locana and the Tārāvalī*. New Delhi. Motilal Banarsidass.

Vasu, Srisa Chandra. 1897. *The Ashtadhyayi of Panini*. Benares. Panini Office.

Whitney, William Dwight. 1905. *Atharva-Veda Samhitā*. Cambridge Massachusetts. Harvard University.

Notes

1 The HIST series refers to the multi-volume History of Indian Science and Technology books. Refer http://www.indianscience.org. The Indian Mind Sciences initiative is another example of work pursued by Infinity Foundation.

2 See Friedman, *The World is Flat: A Brief History of the Twenty-first Century,* 2005.

3 As an example, popular writers like Devdutt Pattanaik (author of more than fifty books in the 'mythology' genre) produce content to feed this market. Infinity Foundation has critiqued his work: *Demolishing Devdutt Pattanaik Point by Point in Detail* https://www.youtube.com/watch?v=vtkMFLuOa3M

4 See Lannoy, 1971:166.

5 See Nath, *Purāṇas and Acculturation,* 2001.

6 See Eck, *Banaras: City of Light,* 1982:69.

7 According to *Skanda Purāṇa* (II.8.6.81-84), by bathing in the place where Sarayu and Ghaghra meet, the pilgrim receives puṇya (merit) equivalent to a thousand Aśvamedha yajña.

8 For example, the *Liṅga Purāṇa* (I.77.8-25) refers to different styles of temple architecture.

9 For example, in the *Mārkaṇḍeya Purāṇa* (XIX.10), drinking liquor is not disapproved of, and meat and liquor are mentioned as acceptable offerings to Bhagavan Dattātreya.

10 As quoted in Lamb, 1975:442-43.

11 As quoted in Bhattacharjee, 1981:199-200.

12 There is synergy between Sanskrit and Prakrit. A tinge of Prakrit

added to Sanskrit brought Sanskrit closer to the language of the home, while a judicious Sanskritization made Prakrit into a language of a higher cultural status. Both processes were simultaneous and worked at conscious, as well as subconscious, levels. As an example of this symbiosis, one may point to various Sanskrit texts in medieval India which were instruction manuals for spoken or conversational Sanskrit by the general public.

13 See Prabodh Chandra Bagchi, 1950:79.

14 See Prabodh Chandra Bagchi, 1950:169.

15 There can certainly be abusive practices in pull marketing; the mere fact that the buyer takes the initiative does not preclude unethical conduct on the part of the seller. Likewise, not all push marketing is unethical but can easily be co-opted by the aggressive ego.

16 See Lamb, 'Indian Influence in Ancient South-East Asia' in *A Cultural History of India,* 1975.

17 Richard Lannoy points out that Indians were structuralists several thousand years before Claude Lévi-Strauss lost all sense of time and became totally absorbed in tracing the labyrinthine geological strata of the Cévennes and long before structuralist physics was developed with the aid of non-numerical, computerised pattern-recognition. Lannoy, 1971:280.

18 See Eliot, 1964:118-19. Kearns explains that Eliot's use of 'shantih shantih shantih' to end *The Waste Land* showed his deep appreciation of the sound and breath effects involved, and that the closest Christian equivalent, 'the peace that passeth understanding', would be a feeble translation. Yet Eliot omits aum at the end. This was the final threshold dividing Indic and Western tradition which Eliot did not want to cross. Kearns, 1987:228-29.

19 See *Totally Unofficial: Rahael Lemkin and the Genocide Convention* of *The Making History Series.* Ed. by Adam Strom et al., 2007:20.

20 https://www.un.org/en/genocideprevention/documents/atrocity-crimes/Doc.1_Convention%20on%20the%20Prevention%20and%20Punishment%20of%20the%20Crime%20of%20Genocide.pdf. Accessed on 8 August 2020.

21 Having equal vision, samadarśana, should not be misunderstood

as samavartana or treating everything or everybody equally. Samadarśana means to see one Reality beneath the variety but consider the variety and multiplicity for action. Kṛṣṇa says that a wise person has samadarśana and sees a brāhmaṇa, a cow, an elephant, a dog and an outcaste equally (*Bhagavad Gīta* 5.18). But the wise person does not treat them equally. He would not treat a brāhmaṇa and a dog in the same manner.

22 See Malhotra, *Being Different,* 2011.

23 Article in the volume published by the Ramakrishna Mission to commemorate the 150th anniversary of Vivekananda's birth gives an overview of his major influences that became digested over time. Malhotra, Rajiv, 'Vivekananda's Ideas and the Two Revolutions in Western Thought', in *Vivekananda as the Turning Point: The Rise of a New Spiritual Wave.* Ed. Swami Shuddhidananda, 2013:559-583.

24 The opposite, i.e., the pursuit of artificial and synthetic unities promoted by modern Western science, the theories of liberalism and progress emanating from Western thought are leading us to planetary scale implosion. It suffices to point out that the modern annihilation of nature is proof that such unities have basis in adharma.

25 See Kak, 2002:151.

26 Patañjali's *Yoga Sūtra* (I.48-51). Such enlightenment/understanding is saturated with harmony, order and righteousness. Whatever one has learned or heard from external sources is outside of the consciousness, but this special realization is of a different category. This spontaneous self-awareness completely transmutes the entire being and there is total change. All other habits and tendencies are overcome by it. When even this special realization (with the seed of fragmentation still present in it) gets transcended, everything is transcended, and the seeker has, as it were, come full circle. The Reality realizes itself, without the need for the separate individual even in his subtlest state. This indeed is the enlightenment in which there is no seed at all for the manifestation of duality.

27 Pure, ecstatic contemplation of phonetic sounds reverberating on the ether in the sacred chant is comparable to the contemplation of geometrical forms and mathematical laws by the Pythagoreans.

"Only the Pythagorean master can hear the music of the spheres: only the perfect Hindu sage can hear the primordial sound – nada. One system exalted numbers, and the other, words." Lannoy, 1971:276.

28 An example of such a study was reported in the article titled 'Physiological patterns during practice of the Transcendental Meditation technique compared with patterns while reading Sanskrit and a modern language', published by the Psychology Dept., Maharishi University of Management, Fairfield, Iowa. It claims: 'This study tested the prediction that reading Vedic Sanskrit texts without knowledge of their meaning produces a distinct physiological state. We measured EEG, breath rate, heart rate, and skin conductance during: (1) 15-min Transcendental Meditation (TM) practice; (2) 15-min reading verses of the *Bhagavad Gītā* in Sanskrit; and (3) 15-min reading the same verses translated in German, Spanish, or French. The two reading conditions were randomly counterbalanced, and subjects filled out experience forms between each block to reduce carry-over effects. Skin conductance levels significantly decreased during both reading Sanskrit and TM practice, and increased slightly during reading a modern language. Alpha power and coherence were significantly higher when reading Sanskrit and during TM practice, compared to reading modern languages. Similar physiological patterns when reading Sanskrit and during practice of the TM technique suggests that the state gained during TM practice may be integrated with active mental processes by reading Sanskrit'. Travis, et al., 2001.

29 Also see Anjali Jaipuria, 'Mantric Poetry', presented at National Seminar on Philosophy of Indian Poetics & Value-Oriented Education, 24-26 January 2003, Sriperumbudur, India.

30 In texts such as *Śṛṅgāra Prakāśa* of Bhoja (Chapter 7) and *Durghaṭavṛitti* of Śaraṇadeva, the authors declare that intonation has an important role to play in revealing the intention of the speaker, and it helps in the interpretation of texts in the right manner. Bhoja has given several divisions and subdivisions of intonation and their importance. In *Śṛṅgāra Prakāśa,* each category of intonation has been illustrated with examples from Sanskrit literature.

31 See Sri Aurobindo, 1999:11-12.

32 For example, the word *ushas* in the Veda-s has both 'light' and 'darkness' as its meanings. The experience of light is not complete without the experience of darkness, and so the word meaning 'light' also expresses the sense of 'darkness'.

33 See Rajiv Malhotra, 2011:231.

34 The correct method is prescribed by the Vedāṅga, called *śikṣā*, which covers enunciation (uchāraṇa), tone (svara), duration (mātra), pitch (balam), evenness (samam) and compounding (santānam). These rules, designed to ensure clear, lucid and effective pronunciation of mantra-s, require that the sounds be properly audible and not mumbled or overemphasized; nor should they be uttered in a casual manner or in a staccato fashion, nor delivered too fast or too slow or with a shaking of the head. The sounds should have been orally learnt from a teacher and should be orally chanted with concentration and understanding and never read from a written script.

35 In his *Mahābhāṣya* (1.1.1), Patañjali gives a beautiful example to illustrate this point. Indra killed Triśira, the son of Tvaṣṭā. This enraged Tvaṣṭā, who, to avenge his son's death, conducted a sacrifice to bring into life a powerful being that could kill Indra. He had recited repeatedly 'indraśatrurvardhasva', meaning 'may the killer of Indra grow stronger'. But unfortunately, Tvaṣṭā recited the mantra with the wrong accentuation. As a result, the word *indraśatru,* meaning 'the killer of Indra' (*indrasya śatruḥ*) gave the sense 'he whose killer is Indra' (*indrahyasya śatruḥ*) and ultimately the being that came out of the sacrificial urn was killed by Indra. Tvaṣṭā could not get the desired result, and all his efforts proved futile because he accented incorrectly. Erroneous intonation or accentuation, then, can bring harmful results or no result at all.

36 See Ramaswamy, Nicolas and Banerjee, 2007, for details on this example and the controversy surrounding it.

37 See Sullivan, 1994:377-401.

38 Epistemologically, there are many theories in Indian philosophy which emphasize the contextual nature of subject-object relationships. One sophisticated theory is propounded in the Vijñaptimātratā

philosophy of the Yogācāra school of Buddhism, according to which all erroneous cognitions are said to arise in the form of bifurcation of subject and object (*grāhyagrāhaka-vikalpa*) in what is more fundamentally a non-dual experience (*advayavijñaptimātratā*) in which duality discrimination (*dvaya-vikalpa*) is introduced as an inveterate tendency to dichotomize. The general Buddhist theory of 'dependent arising' (*pratītyasamutpāda*) also emphasizes the mutually dependent nature of the subject-object (*nāma-rūpa*) relation.

39 The *Bṛhadāraṇyaka Upaniṣad* (5.2) provides an illustration of this interdependence of subjective and objective context. The DA DA DA sound of three-part thunder is Lord Prajāpati speaking three times to three entirely different kinds of listeners: the devatā-s, given to pleasure, hear the first syllable, which to them means *damyatā* (control). The asura-s, given to cruelty, hear *dayādhvam* (be compassionate). Humans, prone to greed, hear *datta* (give to others). Thus, the same utterance is heard entirely differently, depending on the change Prajāpati wishes to bring about in each listener. These three *da-s* comprise a model conversation policy, an intense desire to preserve the equilibrium, and a subsistence ethic designed not to upset the social ecology. This institutional framework is rooted in the exchange of services and social reciprocity called the 'jajmāni' system wherein the law of karma operates as the ethical correlative. See Lannoy, 1971:194-95.

40 janmādyasya yataḥ (*Brahma Sūtra*-s 1.1.2).

41 For example, the *Taittirīya Upaniṣad* defines Brahman as *satyam jñānam anantam Brahma* (2.1.1): satyam (not subject to any kind of modification), jñānam (possessing infinite, eternal knowledge) and anantam (not conditioned by space, time or any object).

42 vadanti tat tattva-vidas tattvaṁ yaj jñānam advayam
brahmeti paramātmeti bhagavān iti śabdyate (*Śrīmad-Bhāgavatam* 1.2.11).

43 acintyāḥ khalu ye bhāvā na tāṁs tarkeṇa yojayet (*Mahābhārata*, Bhīṣma Parva 5.12).

44 Yāska says in *Nirukta* (3.15) that the word *ātman* is derived from the root *at* meaning constant motion or the root *ap* standing for

permeation or pervasion. The second derivation signifies that ātmā permeates or pervades the body.

45 See for example, *Śvetāśvatara Upaniṣad* 5.10.

46 yāvat sạñjāyate kiñcit sattvaṁ sthāvara-jaṅgamam
kṣetra-kṣetrajña-sanyogāt tad viddhi bharatarṣabha (*Bhagavad Gītā* 13.27).

47 na jāyate mṛiyate vā kadācin (*Bhagavad Gītā* 2.20).

48 *Brahma Sūtra* (2.3.43) very clearly states that jīvātmā is an aṃśa or a part of Paramātmā. Similarly, Bhagavān Śrī Kṛṣṇa says in the *Bhagavad Gītā* that the jīvātmā-s in this material world are a part of Bhagavān - mamaivānśo jīva-loke jīva-bhūtaḥ sanātanaḥ (*Bhagavad Gītā* 15.7).

49 The functions of avidya-māya, again, are two-fold and further classified as āvaraṇa Śakti and vikṣepa Śakti according to the two functions. Āvaraṇa Śakti conceals the true nature of a jīva and makes them forget that they are an eternally self-conscious dāsa of Bhagavān and totally dependent on Him. Vikṣepa Śakti, on the other hand, bewilders a jīva by creating distortion in the form of limited empirical consciousness of the material body and also by projecting the material sense objects.

50 ajñānenāvṛitaṁjñānaṁ tena muhyanti jantavaḥ (*Bhagavad Gītā* 5.15).

51 daivī hyeṣā guṇa-mayī mama māyā duratyayā
mām eva ye prapadyante māyām etāṁ taranti te (*Bhagavad Gītā* 7.14).

52 yogasthaḥ kuru karmāṇi saṅgaṁ tyaktvā dhanañjaya
siddhy-asiddhyoḥ samo bhūtvā samatvaṁ yoga ucyate (*Bhagavad Gītā* 2.48).

53 According to *Amarakośa*, a thesaurus in Sanskrit written by Amarasiṁha, the terms mukti, mōkṣa, apavarga and nirvāṇa are among the synonyms given for the word kaivalya, thus indicating the general sense of liberation denoted by the word.

54 Acharya Śrīla Jīva Gosvāmi of the Gauḍīya Vaiṣṇava Sampradāya has given the meaning of kaivalya as prīti or prema. *Śrīmad-Bhāgavatam* gives *vedanta-sāra* or the essence of Vedanta and its *prayojana* or purpose is to help a bonded jīva to attain kaivalya (sarva-vedānta-

sāraṁ hi śrī-bhāgavatam iṣyate (*Śrīmad-Bhāgavatam* 12.13.15). This text too defines kaivalya as priti with Bhagavān Śrī Kṛṣṇa.

55 This is reflected in the invocatory verse of the *Īśopaniṣad*:
Pūrṇam adah, pūrṇam idam, pūrṇāt pūrṇam udachyate
Pūrṇasya pūrṇam ādāya pūrṇam evāvaśiṣyate.

56 See for further references: Bhagavān Śrī Kṛṣṇa says in the *Bhagavad Gītā*, that He is the sacred syllable Om among all the Vedic mantra-s [praṇavaḥ sarva-vedeṣu (*Bhagavad Gītā* 7.8)]. Again, Patañjali says in the *Yoga Sūtra*-s that Īśvara is the referent of the sacred syllable Om [tasya vācakaḥ praṇavaḥ (*Yoga Sūtra*-s 1.27)]. Similarly, *Śvetāśvatara Upaniṣad* says that through meditation on Om, one can experience God (1.14) and *Taittirīya Upaniṣad* says that Om is Brahman and everything in this world (1.8.1). All these illustrations from the Hindu śāstra-s imply that Om is the sound form of Supreme Reality and expresses the totality of all cosmos. *Chāndogya Upaniṣad* says that just as leaves are held together by a stalk, so is all speech held together by Om (2.23.3).

57 Oṁ ityekākṣaraṁ brahma vyāharan mām anusmaran
yaḥ prayāti tyajan dehaṁ sa yāti paramāṁ gatim (*Bhagavad Gītā* 8.13).

58 See Commentary on śloka 19 of *Vijñāna Bhairava*. Refer to Sudhendu Kumar Das, 1934:76-77.

59 This word is derived from the root *mṛś* which means 'to feel', 'discriminate', 'understand', 'examine' or 'reflect'.

60 See Mark Dyczkowski, 1989:69.

61 In Śrīvaiṣṇava Sampradāya, Śakti acts as the mediatrix between jīva-s and Bhagavān and intercedes on behalf of humanity with Bhagavān.

62 In Sanskrit Vyākaraṇa the roots or stems, from which various words are produced by adding suffixes and prefixes, are called prakṛti.

63 This is one of the four kinds of pralaya described in the Purāṇa-s and is called Prakṛita Pralaya. The others are Naimittika Pralaya when Bhagavān Brahmā sleeps, Ātyantika Pralaya and Nitya Pralaya.

64 In the *Mīmāṃsā Sūtra*-s of Jaimini, the two terms prakṛti and vikṛiti are used very frequently. The paradigmatic original sacrifice is called

prakṛti. Prakṛti are sacrifices whose processes are related in full in the Veda-s. Thus, prakṛti-s are model sacrifices or archetypes from which innumerable modified sacrifices are derived. These modified or derived sacrifices are called vikṛiti-s. Refer English translation of *Mīmāṃsā Sūtra*-s by M.L. Sandal, the sūtra-s IX.3.1, III.3.23, I.1.10, XII.2.20.

In Ayurveda texts prakṛti means 'the normal healthy condition of an individual' and vikṛiti means 'an abnormal state of illness or disease'.

In phonetics or śikṣā the sound that remains unchanged in euphonic combination during recitation is called prakṛti whereas the altered sound is called vikṛiti.

65 See Sarva-bhūtāni kaunteya prakṛtiṃ yānti māmikām
Kalpa-kṣaye punastāni kalpādau visṛjāmyaham (9.7),
prakṛtiṁ svām avaṣṭabhya visṛjāmi punaḥ punaḥ
bhuta-grāmamimaṁ kṛtsnam avaśaṁ pkṛter vaśāt (*Bhagavad Gītā* 9.8),
sadṛiśam cheṣṭate svasyāḥ prakṛiter jñānavān api
prakṛtiṁ yānti bhūtāni nigrahaḥ kiṁ kariṣyati (*Bhagavad Gītā* 3.33).

66 Another meaning denoted by the word prakṛti in the *Bhagavad Gītā* (4.6) is the Māyā or Śakti of Bhagavān. This is not the material māyā which is extrinsic to His inner personality but His intrinsic Śakti. Bhagavān Śrī Kṛṣṇa says that although He is the unborn lord of all beings, He comes into being by His own Māyā or intrinsic Śakti. Again, Bhagavān (7.4) says that earth, water, fire, air, space, mind, intellect and ego are the eight components of His lower insentient eight-fold prakṛti. In the next śloka Bhagavān says that besides this eight-fold insentient lower prakṛti, He has another higher sentient prakṛti in the form of various jīva-s. It is very clear that prakṛti carries very profound technical meanings which cannot even remotely be suggested by the English word 'nature'.

67 āsamantāt kāśte iti ākāśaḥ.

68 For example, in Sāṅkhya philosophy two kinds of ākāśa are described by Ācārya Vijñānabhikṣu, namely *kāraṇa* ākāśa and *kārya* ākāśa. Kāraṇa ākāśa is undifferentiated tamas and very subtle. It is kāraṇa

ākāśa which evolves into kārya ākāśa. Kārya ākāśa is the one which has the quality of sound.

69 See *Bhāgavata Purāṇa* (3.26.34).

70 The modern notion of space is closer to the Nyāya-Vaiśeṣika concept of *dik,* which is a separate substance in this system and different from ākāśa. Dik is regarded as the cause of the notion of distance. However, many schools of Indian philosophy like Sāṅkhya, Viśiṣṭādvaita do not recognize dik and ākāśa as separate entities. In Dvaita Vedanta two types of ākāśa are postulated, namely *avyākṛtākāśa* and *bhūtākāśa.* Bhūtākāśa posseses the property of dark color and is perceptible just like the space. Nyāya-Vaiśeṣika also regard ākāśa as a substratum of movement and consider its postulation as a necessity for explaining the motion of objects.

71 In *Agni sūkta,* Agni devatā is called *purohita* which means 'the one who is first to bring welfare to living beings'. Agni miḷe purohitam (1.1).

72 In Vedanta, and more specifically in Vaiṣṇava schools of Vedanta, reality has three levels (forms) of existence: *ādhidaivika* (divine), *ādhyātmika* (spiritual) and *ādhibhautika* (material). The same Sanskrit word is used to denote all three forms. For example, *kāla* (time) has material form in Sun, planets and stars which we use to measure time and also a divine form.

Similar logic applies to the word *Sūrya* which is not just the physical Sun but also a Deva and similarly for the names of various rivers.

73 See Sri Aurobindo, 1998:65-66.

74 Nyāya texts mention three kinds of Tejas/Agni or fire (i.e., Śarīra Tejas, Indriya Tejas and Viṣaya Tejas) with further divisions in these types. The *Nyāya-Śrī* Śaṅkara Miśra classifies fire into four kinds depending on whether its color and/or hot touch are manifested or not. Sun's rays manifest both color and touch, in hot oil only touch is manifested, in eyes both are unmanifest while in a shiny metal like gold only color is manifest.

75 aham vaiśvānaro bhūtvā prāṇinām deham āśritah prāṇāpāna samāyuktah pacāmy annam caturvidham (*Bhagavad Gītā*_15.14).

76 In Yajur Veda, Vāyu is described as the swiftest devatā.

Yajur Veda Taittirīya Saṃhitā (2.1.1) says
Vāyurvai kṣepiṣṭhā devatā
Vāyu is called the messenger of devatā-s because of his swiftness.

77 According to the *Puruṣasūkta* of the *Rig Veda* (10.90), Vāyu is said to be born from the prāṇa of the Supreme cosmic being called *Puruṣa*. Also see *Śatapata Brāhmaṇa* 8.4.1.26.

78 The *Śiva Purāṇa* 7.1.4.5 says that Vāyu devatā sustains the bodies of all living beings with the help of his own functionaries, like prāṇa.

79 This is reflected in a hymn of *Rig Veda* (5.78.7-8) where Vāyu devatā or Vāta is invoked for good childbirth.

80 Śabda pramāṇa is free of defects such as: *bhrama* (delusion), *pramāda* (carelessness), *vipralipsā* (cheating) and *kāraṇapāṭava* (inaccuracy of the senses).

81 In the *Mahābhāṣya,* Patañjali describes Śabda with the following epithets: *nitya* (eternal), *kūṭastha* (subtle), *avicali* (motionless), *avikāri* (without modification), *anupajana* (without origin) and *anapāya* (indestructible).

82 Pronounced sounds or written alphabets at the phenomenal level only manifest or reveal an already-existent Śabda. When the sound of a Śabda is no longer heard after it is spoken, it is only the destruction of the vaikhari level but Śabda at subtler levels always exist non-perceived. Śabda can be articulate (expressed through language) or inarticulate (produced from an instrument, chirping of birds, a baby gurgling, etc.). The essence of Śabda does not lie in its sonority and is seen from the fact that Śabda can be expressed in written form or through gestures.

83 In Sāṅkhya metaphysics, Śabda is one of the five tanmātra-s from which the concrete element ākāśa evolves.

84 In a hymn from the *Rig Veda* (10.125) Vāk identifies Herself with everything in the universe and according to a śloka from the *Maitrī Upaniṣad* (6.22), there are two types of Brahman: Śabdabrahman and Parabrahman. One who gets to know the Śabdabrahman also reaches Parabrahman. Śabdabrahman is also called Parā Vāk. The *Brahma Sūtra*-s also say that the world originates from Śabda.

85 Anādinidhanam Brahma Shabdatattvam yadaksharam |

Vivartate arthabhāvena prakrīyā jagato yatah || (*Vākyapadīya* 1.1)

86 The grammarian Pāṇini defines indriya in his work *Aṣṭādhyāyī* as the liṅga (sign) by which we can infer the existence of a jīvātmā (i.e., wherever there is an indriya, there is also Indra or ātmā). Indrasya jīvasya liṅgam indriyam (V.2.93). See V.2.93 in English translation of *Aṣṭādhyāyī* by Srisa Chandra Vasu.

87 See *Yukti-Dīpikā* on *Sāṅkhya Kārikā* 28 and *Sāṅkhya Tattva Kaumudi* on *Sāṅkhya Kārikā* 26. Similarly, according to Advaita Vedanta, indriya-s evolve from sāttvika portion of sūkṣma bhūta-s or tanmātra-s. Tanmātra-s are not gross matter but kind of subtle matter from which physical matter evolves.

88 According to Western science, sense-organs are identical with their locations in the body, whereas in the Indian tradition, the organs are only the seats or physiological locations of indriya-s and not the indriya-s themselves. *Caraka Saṃhitā* (Ayurvedic text) very clearly states that the eyes, ears, nostrils, tongue and skin are the five locations (*adhiṣṭhāna*) of indriya-s. All darśana-s agree that indriya-s are different from golaka-s.

The indriya of vision (cakṣus) is not the eyeball or the pupil of the eye. The pupil or the eyeball is the seat of vision but cakṣus is subtler and of the nature of tejas. Cakṣus, as an indriya, is one but golaka-s or eyes are two in number and hence, they are different. The Indriya of vision is cured when medicines are applied to eye golaka-s because the treatment of adhiṣṭhāna (golaka) also purifies the subtle indriya (ādheya). Suśruta in *Suśruta Saṃhitā* says, *śirasindriyaṇi* meaning that the indriya-s are located in the head area, the brain. Manas, which is also an indriya in the Indian tradition, is located in the heart.

According to Nyāya philosophers, all indriya-s have different magnitudes (*ākṛiti*) which may or may not coincide with the magnitude of their seats in physical body (i.e., sense-organs). Thus, indriya-s for tactile, gustatory and olfactory perceptions, called *tvak*, *rasanā* and *ghrāṇa* in Sanskrit respectively, are co-extensive with their seats and have the magnitude of their sites. Cakṣus, though, located in the pupil, is co-extensive with the field of vision and śrotra, concerned with auditory perception, is all pervading like ākaśa.

89 'atīndrayāṇi indriyāṇi'

90 In that case there would be no difference between indriya-*s* and sense organs. It would be absurd to regard indriya-s of vision and hearing as prāpyākāri if they were products of concrete matter and identical with eyes or ears. We do not see our eyes or ears moving out of our body to the objects before us in order to see or hear them. Thus, modern science explains the phenomena of vision and hearing from purely an objective angle.

91 In the Indian theory of perception, indriya-s reach out to distant objects in the form of vṛitti-s and it is vṛitti-s that connect indriya-s with their objects. Vṛitti-s are a modification of the antaḥakaraṇa, which due to the preponderance of the sattva guṇa, expand and emerge out of the gates of indriya-s and transform them into the form of the object of perception, thus establishing a relation between the inner psychical and the outer physical world. The presence and mediation of vṛitti in the operation of perceptual cognition is not just confined to ocular perception but is a necessary condition for all other kinds of perceptual cognitions. It should be noted that external objects are not regarded as completely unreal. Vṛitti-s require external physical objects in order to assume their form. However, perceptual cognition of each person also has a unique subjective side to it. This means that the external world perceived by a person has commonalities that are perceived by all other persons, but at the same time it is not completely identical to the perception of other persons.

92 *Bhagavad Gītā* indriyāṇi daśaikaṁ ca (13.6) clearly says that there are eleven indriya-s and similarly the Veda-s and *Upaniṣad*-s, along with most darśana-s. Only the schools of Nyāya and Prabhākara Mīmāṃsā-s regard six indriya-s as they do not believe in karmendriya-s. *Bhagavad Gītā* also at one instance (15.7) takes the count of indriya-s to be six. However, none of them says that indriya-s are five in number like the sense-organs.

93 The five buddhīndriya-s are cakṣu, śrotra, *ghṛāṇa*, rasanā and tvak responsible respectively for ocular, auditory, olfactory, gustatory

and tactual perception. Similarly, the five karmendriya-s are called *vāk, pāṇi, pāda, pāyu* and *upasthā* – responsible respectively for: vocalization, gripping, movement of the body, excretion and reproduction. Manas is called *antarīndriya* and is responsible for the perception of pleasure, pain, desire, feeling. Manas is unique in the sense that it can apprehend not just what is in the present, like other indriya-s, but also what was in the past and what will be in the future.

94 Certain interpretations of Christianity believe in Purgatory as a place where souls get tormented to make them eligible to proceed to heaven permanently.

95 Yāna, again, does not just mean a spacecraft. It also means a spiritual vehicle through which one can reach a spiritual realm. Some of these yāna-s are actually conscious beings.

96 The word loka is explained as *lokyate anena iti lokaḥ*, which translates to 'that by which everything is observed or perceived is loka' and so the word refers to the witness subjective human consciousness; alternatively, it can mean *lokyate iti lokaḥ*, or 'that which is perceived is lokaḥ'.

97 In Kashmir Shaivism there are concepts of *kalā* and *bhuvana*-s/*loka*-s or states of being. One hundred and eighteen different bhuvana-s/loka-s or worlds are described (with different combinations of tattva-s) varying from most concrete level of manifestation to the subtlest, and yogī-s can experience these bhuvana-s in samādhi. This physical world which we see around is just one bhuvana. Different sādhana-s lead a spiritual aspirant to different bhuvana-s (e.g., karma-yoga leads to a bhuvana named Kṛita). These bhuvana-s are discussed in *Tantrasāra* and *Tantrāloka* by Ācārya Śrī Abhinavagupta.

98 Again, Bhagavān Śrī Kṛṣṇa says
te taṁ bhuktvā svarga-lokaṁ viśālaṁ
kṣīṇe puṇye martya-lokaṁ viśanti (*Bhagavad Gītā* 9.21)
which means that after a person has exhausted the stock of merits by enjoying pleasures in svarga they are sent back to the mortal world.

99 There is a famous incident narrated in *Rāmāyaṇa* where king Triśanku was made to enter svarga in his physical body by Maharṣi Viśvāmitra

through his ascetic power. Maharṣi Viśvāmitra even created a new parallel svarga for the king when Indra deva refused to let him stay in the original svarga. There are also those such as Mucukunḍa, Khaṭavāṅga, and Arjuna who travelled to svarga to help Indra. Similarly, king Nahuṣa took the post of Indra for some time.

100 Jīvatma-s acquire a subtle body in naraka called the *yātnā śarīra* through which they cleanse their pāpa.

101 Surprisingly, the word demon is derived from the Greek word daímōn which meant 'a benevolent spirit or god'. Perhaps the influx of Christianity changed the meaning to a negative sense.

102 There is an interesting story narrated in the *Chāndogya Upaniṣad* (8.7-12) concerning Indra and the king of asura-s Virocana describing the difference in nature of asura-s and devatā-s.

103 The etymology of the word asura is explained as *asuṣu ramate iti asuraḥ*. The word is also derived from the verbal root *as* which means to throw something; and vitality. Asura means 'one who is with vitality' or 'a mighty one' or 'one capable enough to throw down his opponent'. This is the reason that in *Bṛhadāraṇyaka Upaniṣad* (V.2.3) when Bhagavān Brahmā instructs the asura-s by the letter *da*, He tells them to show dayā (mercy) towards the weak. For Deva-s, the letter *da* meant *damana* or 'self-restraint in enjoying pleasures' and for humans it meant dāna or 'charity'.

The word *asu* means an animal life or a sensuous life devoid of spiritual pursuit. Thus, one who takes pleasure only in enjoying the material pleasures of life is called an asura. In the sixteenth chapter of the *Bhagavad Gītā*, Bhagavān Śrī Kṛṣṇa says that there are two types of created beings in this world with opposite types of prakṛti or innate characteristics: *āsurika* and *daivika*. He then elucidates the attributes of a person who behaves like a deva and also of a person who is an asura. He says for the asura-s:

dambho darpo abhimānaś ca krodhaḥ pāruṣyam eva ca
ajñānaṁ cābhijātasya pārtha sampadam āsurīm (*Bhagavad Gītā* 16.4)

which means that hypocrisy, arrogance, pride, anger, rudeness and ignorance are the qualities of an asurika person. Thus, somebody who is addicted to sensual pleasures and enjoys hurting and exploiting others is called an asura. Thus, one way of understanding the meaning of asura is in terms of innate features of a person.

104 In fact, Bhagavān Śrī Kṛṣṇa says
daityānam prahlādoh asmi (*Bhagavad Gītā* 10.30).
which means that "..among the daitya-s, I am Prahlāda".

105 See *Sūrya Siddhānta* Chapter 1, verses 2-7. English translation by Ebenezer Burgess, edited by Phanindralal Gangooly, 1935.

106 Yajña is a process of transformation of the concrete into subtle through the medium of agni. It can also be considered as symbolic of a daivika process of withdrawing the consciousness inwards and away from the concrete towards the realization of true subtle self, which is ātmā. Contrary to this, the āsurika process or an anti-yajña would be to externalize consciousness and direct it towards the enjoyment of material objects. Movements which promote a hedonistic lifestyle are examples of anti-yajña.

107 For example, Devdutt Pattanaik contends that Bhagavān Śrī Kṛṣṇa was not a good father because his son Sāmba committed many improper acts which ultimately led to the downfall of his own Yādava clan. (See: *Children of the Great*, 7 August 2015, in the *Economic Times* http://devdutt.com/articles/applied-mythology/leadership/children-of-the-great.html) However, this is furthest from the truth. According to *Bhāgavata Purāṇa* (10.61.1), Kṛṣṇa's sons were like Him in character. Nārada personally witnessed Kṛṣṇa taking care of His children (10.69.23, 32, 33). Description of Kṛṣṇa teaching moral values to His sons, including Sāmba, is found in the sixty-fourth chapter of tenth canto. As far as Sāmba's misbehavior is concerned, it is clear from the description found in the first chapter of eleventh canto of *Bhāgavata Purāṇa* that it happened by the will of Kṛṣṇa Himself. He wanted his family to be annihilated before He left the earth. Thus, He made Sāmba act in a disrespectful manner towards the sages who cursed the Yadu dynasty. The sages also understood it to be will of Kṛṣṇa, otherwise they would not have dared to curse.

108 There is some difference of opinion regarding the number of tattva-s in sūkṣma śarīra. According to *Pañcadaśī* (1.23) and *Vedānta-paribhāṣā*, sūkṣma śarīra has seventeen tattva-s as listed here. However,

according to *Sāṅkhya Tattvakaumudi* (Kārika 40) written by Vācaspati Miśra, sūkṣma śarīra has eighteen constituents: *buddhi* (Mahān), ahaṅkāra, eleven indriya-s and five tanmātra-s. See Hindi translation of *Sāṅkhya Tattvakaumudi* of Rama Shankar Bhattacharya, 1976: 250.

109 According to Advaita Vedanta, sūkṣma śarīra consists of three sheaths or kośa-s called the prāṇamaya kośa, manomaya kośa and vijñānamaya kośa.

110 4.2.11 - Asyaiva copapattereṣa ūṣmā.

111 See *Mana* eva manuṣyānām kāraṇam bandhe mokshayoh (*Amritabindu Upaniṣad* 2nd śloka).
And rāga-dveṣa-viyuktais tu viṣayān indriyaiścaraṇ ātma-vaśyair-vidheyātmā prasādam adhigachchhati (*Bhagavad Gītā* 2.64).

112 See *The Concept of Mind* by the British philosopher Gilbert Ryle.

113 The modified condition of the buddhi wherein it makes the choice is technically called *adhyavsāya* in Sāṅkhya psychology. See 23rd kārikā in the text of *Sāṅkhya kārikā*.

114 Bhagavān Śrī Kṛṣṇa makes a very important statement in the *Bhagavad Gītā*, "Oh Arjuna! When you work with buddhi you can be freed from the bondage of karma": buddhyā yukto yayā pārtha. Also see buddhir buddhimatām asmi (Bhagavad Gita 7.10) and karma-bandhaṁ prahāsyasi (*Bhagavad Gītā* 2.39).

115 In the Purāṇa-s, one comes across a personality named Citragupta. He is considered to be the secretary of Yamarāja, the devatā of death. It is Citragupta who maintains a record of the karma-s done by all the jīva-s in this world and provides it to Yamarāja so that he can punish or reward them accordingly in the interval between their deaths and rebirths. The word *citra* means 'a photo' in Sanskrit and *gupta* means 'secret'. Thus, Citragupta can be regarded as the hidden camera of Yamarāja by which he keeps a watch on the karma-s done by every individual. Similarly, citta can also be regarded as the hidden camera which records all our activities.

116 Yogaś citta vṛtti nirodhaḥ (*Yoga Sūtra* 1.2).
tadā draṣṭuḥ svarūpe avasthānam (*Yoga Sūtra* 1.3).

117 This superimposition of spiritual 'I' over material ahaṅkāra is also

called *hṛdaya-granthi* or *chit-jaḍa granthi* in the Indian tradition.

118 sukha-saṅgena badhnāti jñāna-saṅgena cānagha (*Bhagavad Gītā* 14.6).

119 Bhagavān Śrī Kṛṣṇa says, aham sarvasya prabhavo mattaḥ sarvaṁ pravartate (*Bhagavad Gītā* 10.8), which means, "I am the source of everything, and everything proceeds from Me."

120 See Ahastāni sahastānām apadāni catuṣpadām
Phalgūni tatra mahatāṁ jīvo jīvasya jīvanam (*Śrīmad-Bhāgavatam* 1.13.47). We thank Dr. Korada Subrahmanyam for this additional line: Ahimsa is defined as cessation of hostility by two naturally hostile entities, like cat and rat, in one's presence (अहिंसा प्रतिष्ठायां वैरत्याग:-योगसूत्रम्).

121 According to *Suśruta Saṃhitā,* prāṇa is not vital air, air or breath but the energy that activates all these and other elements in the body. See Introduction, Volume 2 of English translation by K.L. Bhishagratna, 1911.

122 According to *Chāndogya Upaniṣad* (1.3.3) Yadvai prāṇiti sa prāṇaḥ Which means that prāṇa is not 'breath' but 'that which breathes'. The Veda-s compare the body of a being to a house and prāṇa to the central support on which the other minor supports such as senses, mind and speech rest; see *Aitareya Āraṇyaka* 3.2.1.

123 According to *Yoga Vaśiṣṭha* (Book 5, Chapter 78, verse 14) even the movement of thought in mind arises from prāṇa.

124 The number of total cakra-s are fourteen, but in our human body six or seven are of prime importance. Beginning from the Mūlādhāra cakra, there are seven cakra-s below and six above.

125 Tatra pratyayaika-tānatā dhyānam (*Yoga Sūtra* 3.2).

126 Four kinds of sabīja samādhi are mentioned in the *Yoga Sūtra*-s 1.42, 1.43 and 1.44: savitarka, nirvitarka, savicāra and nirvicāra.

127 In the *Yoga Sūtra,* nirbīja samādhi is considered as the highest. However, there is some difference of opinion on this among the different sampradāya-s of Hinduism and according to the Vaiṣṇava traditions it is sabīja samādhi which is considered as the highest. According to the yoga of Kashmir Shaivism, there are two types of samādhi: *unmīlana* and *nimīlana*. Unmīlana samādhi is a state of citta in which even when the eyes are wide open, the external

world appears as Universal Consciousness.

128 See *Yoga Sūtra*-s 3.4.

129 Bhuvana jñānaṁ sūrye saṁyamāt (*Yoga Sūtra* 3.26).

130 In the *Gītā* Bhagavān says that śāstra-s should be the authority in determining what should be done (*kārya*) and what should not be done (*akārya*). tasmāt śāstraṁ pramāṇaṁ te kārya-akārya vyavasthitau. jñātvā śāstra-vidhānoktaṁ karma kartum ihārhasi (*Bhagavad Gītā* 16.24).

131 yogaḥ karmasu kauśalam (*Bhagavad Gītā* 2.50).

132 In the *Bhagavad Gītā,* Bhagavān says to Arjuna that whatever deeds he (Arjuna) performs, he should do them as an offering to Him.
yat karoṣi yad aśnāsi yaj juhoṣi dadāsi yat
yat tapasyasi kaunteya tat kuruṣva mad-arpaṇam (*Bhagavad Gītā* 9.27).

133 In the *Bhagavad Gītā,* Bhagavān says that one should perform one's karma for the sake of duty and not become attached to the fruits of those karma-s: karmaṇyevādhikāraste mā phaleṣu kadācana (*Bhagavad Gītā* 2.47).

134 prakṛteḥ kriyamāṇāni guṇaiḥ karmāṇi sarvaśaḥ
ahaṅkāra-vimūḍhātmā kartāham iti manyate (*Bhagavad Gītā* 3.27).

135 This distinction is found in Kashmir Shaivism as *bauddha jñāna* and *Pauruṣa jñāna*. Similarly, in the Śaiva Siddhānta philosophy, *jñāna* is three-fold, namely *pāśa jñāna* (knowledge of the material objects), *paśu jñāna* (knowledge of the atma or self) and *pati jñāna* (knowledge of Universal Consciousness or Bhagavān Śiva).

136 The six virtues are: control of the mind (*śama*), control of the senses (*dama*), non-dependence on anything external (*uparati*), endurance of all worldly afflictions without lamenting (*titīkṣā*), conviction in the teachings of the śāstra-s (*śraddhā*) and constant establishment of buddhi in Brahman (*samādhāna*); *mumukṣatva* means 'an intense desire for liberation'. See verses 20 to 28 of *Vivekacūḍāmaṇi*.

137 Bhagavān Śrī Kṛṣṇa says in the *Bhagavad Gītā,* "Arjuna while you speak words of knowledge like a pandit or a jñāni, you are mourning for that which is not worthy of grief. This is contradictory because the wise lament neither for the living nor for the dead": aśocyān-

anvaśocas-tvaṁ prajñā-vādānśa ca bhāṣase gatāsūn-agatāsūnśa-ca nānuśocanti paṇḍitāḥ (*Bhagavad Gītā* 2.11).

138 According to *Nighaṇṭu*, which is a glossary of Vedic terms, the words bhakti and sevā convey the same meaning. See *Vaisnavism: Its Philosophy, Theology and Religious Discipline* by S.M.S Chari, 2000:117. Also, *Śrutaprakāśikā*, commentary on *Rāmānuja Bhāṣya* on VS 1-1-1 which says 'sevā bhaktir upāsti iti naighaṇṭukaḥ'.

139 According to *Śrīmad-Bhāgavatam* (3.29.12-14) the characteristics of bhakti-yoga are that it is beyond the three guṇa-s of prakṛti and unadulterated by any material desires to the point that a bhakta does not accept the five kinds of mokṣa if they are devoid of bhakti. Also see Śrīla Rūpa Gosvāmī's magnum opus *Bhakti-rasāmṛita-sindhu*: Anyābhilāṣitā śūnyaṁ jñāna-karmādi anāvṛtam ānūkūlyena Kṛṣṇa-anūśilanaṁ bhaktir uttamā (*Bhakti-rasāmṛta-sindhu* 1.1.11).

140 This seven-fold discipline comprises *viveka* (purification of the body), *vimoka* (purification of the mind), *abhyāsa* (repeated contemplation of Bhagavān), *kriya* (performance of five-fold duties to sub-human species, fellow beings, teachers, forefathers and gods), *kalyāṇa* (truthfulness), non-violence, *anavasāda* (freedom from any worry) and *anuddharṣa* (absence of exultation). See *Synthesis of Yoga* by Kireet Joshi 2011:452 and *Theistic Vedanta* by R. Balasubramanian, 2003:iv.

141 This is the view of the Sāṅkhya, Mīmāṁsa and all the Vedanta schools of Hindu philosophy. Only the Nyāya-Vaiśeṣika school regards Veda-s as created by Bhagavān. Thus, for them, *apauruṣeya* means 'not created by a human being, puruṣa'.

Many of the Tamil Vaiṣṇava saints called Āḻvār-s are traditionally regarded to have been born much before the avatāra of Bhagavān Śrī Kṛṣṇa but their compositions are filled with descriptions of Bhagavān Śrī Kṛṣṇa's Līlā-s.

142 In Purāṇa-s, the Veda-s are frequently presented as personified beings residing in *vaikuṇṭha* along with Bhagavān. See, for example, *Śrīmad-Bhāgavatam* 10.87.12-13, 5.1.7.

143 It is important to note that it was by conscious choice that the

Veda-s were not written down. Hindus traditionally regard oral transmission as the only appropriate vehicle for correctly learning the Veda-s. The *Mahābhārata* (13.23.72) explicitly condemns the writing down of the Veda-s. This is due to two reasons: firstly, the powerful Vedic mantra-s are required to be reproduced accurately with not just correct pronunciation but also correct intonation of sound for effecting the desired results on an individual and the environment, and preserving the sacred order of this universe. The auxiliary Vedic disciplines or Vedāṅga-s like phonetics (śikṣā) and prosody (chandas) are studied specifically for this purpose. Secondly, the exclusive oral transmission of the Veda-s acted as a safeguard against their possible misuse and profanation through disclosure to an unqualified person. The same Vedic text is memorized with eleven different modes of recitation called the *pāṭha*-s. Each pāṭha requires a complex grammatical and recitative manipulation of the base text.

144 Scripture is derived from the Latin word *scriptura* which means 'writing'. At the same time, the Vedic tradition, while focusing on oral transmission, does not preclude writing – *Atharva Veda* has references to words indicating written text.

145 The Hindu śāstra-s recognize *sāmanya dharma* and *āpad dharma* which deal, respectively, with normal and emergency situations in a person's life. During adverse circumstances, a person is given more leeway to function by the śāstra-s and their dharma is not violated by such acts of omission or commission in that period which under normal circumstances would have been against the dharma. Thus, abandonment of rigidity in the observance of certain rules and regulations during adverse times is allowed in the śāstra-s. This adjustable nature of Dharmaśāstra-s helps Hinduism to regularly reinvent itself and stay abreast of modern times.

146 Smṛti-s, also included among the śāstra-s, are composed by the enlightened ṛṣi-s on the basis of Vedic knowledge. Smṛti-s are derived from the Veda-s and they elucidate dharmic principles in various kinds of practical ways to help lead a constructive life based on the Vedic dharma. Smṛti-s also allow the freedom for

their reinterpretation according to the changing spirit of the times, provided this does not lead to any contradiction with the Veda-s. Dharmaśāstra-s such as *Manusmṛti* and *Yajñavalkyasmṛti* are pliant enough for reinterpretation according to the changing context and times. This reinterpretation, however, should be consistent with certain eternal unchanging Vedic truths. Thus, the complete body of Hindu śāstra-s, which includes the Śruti-s and the Smṛti-s, have this built-in static-dynamic duality.

147 Originally Śruti (the Veda) was revealed to Brahmā at the dawn of creation when He sat in meditation and performed tapas for a long time. After intense meditation, Brahmā became receptive and attuned to the eternal cosmic vibrations of the Śruti-s. He heard the eternal Śabda of the Śruti-s within Himself in a spontaneous flash of intuition without the aid of any external ears.

148 This sound is emitted by the anāhata cakra within the subtle body of a person.

149 See: Itihāsa Purāṇaṁ ca pancamaṁ Veda uccyate (*Śrīmad-Bhāgavatam* 1.4.20); and *Chāndogya Upaniṣad* (7.1.2).
The *Mahābhārata* says in the ādi parva that one should understand the import of the Veda-s with the aid of Itihāsa-s and the Purāṇa-s: Itihāsa Purāṇābhyām Vedam samupabrmhayet (*Mahābhārata* 1.1.204).

150 According to *Viṣṇu Purāṇa* (3.6.28-29), the fourteen are counted as: four Veda-s, six Vedāṅga-s and also Mīmāṁsa, Nyāya, Purāṇa and Dharmaśāstra-s. This list increases to eighteen if Āyurveda, Dhanurveda, Gandharvaveda and Arthaśāstra are also included.

151 In Hinduism, kalpa denotes a period of one cycle of cosmos between creation and dissolution.

152 Manu in Hinduism is the first man and progenitor of all humanity who also rules the earth at the beginning of each Manvantara. The ten characteristics of Purāṇa-s given in the *Śrīmad-Bhāgavatam* (12.7.9-10 and 2.10.1-2) are: sarga, visarga, vṛtti, rakṣā, antara, vamśa, vamśānucarītaṁ, saṁsthā, hetu and apāśrayaḥ.

153 See Yāska's *Nirukta,* 2.10 and V.K. Rajavade, 1940:343.

154 See *Śrī Tattva Sandarbha* 12.2.

155 This discrepancy is explained by Kalpa-bheda or by difference in the

kalpa to which these similar stories belong. See *Ramayana Mīmāṁsa* by Swami Sri Karpatri Maharaja, 2001:67 and 2001:49 for quote by Śrī Gosvāmi Tulsidāsa who says in *Śrī Rāmacaritamānas* Kalpabheda Haricarita Suhāe, bhānti aneka munisanha gāe (1.32.4) which also clearly points to this fact.

156 It is believed in Hinduism that the same events are repeated in every kalpa but with slight variations depending on the predominance of a guṇa of prakṛti in that kalpa, which can make a whole kalpa to be sāttvika, rājasika or tāmasika. These variations in the narration of the same incident are due to the different kalpa-s to which they correspond and not because the author of the Purāṇa-s has concocted something on his own. See *Tattva Sandarbha Anuccheda* 17.

157 Although Tantra-s and Āgama-s are used synonymously, Tantra-s are broader in scope than Āgama-s. Tantra-s deal with as many as twenty-five subjects whereas Āgama-s cover only seven. See Manoranjan Basu, 1986:1.

Kullūka Bhaṭṭa, the famous commentator on *Manusmṛti*, states that Śruti-s are two-fold, namely, Vaidika and Tāntrika. He says in the commentary on *Manusmṛti* 2.1: Śrutiśca dvividhā vaidikī tāntrikī ca. See *Mānava-Dharma-Shastra* by Vishvanath Narayan Mandlik, 1886:88.

158 See *Encyclopaedia of Tantra* Volume 1 by Sadhu Santideva, 1999:3-4. The word Tantra is made up of two roots *tan* and *tra*. The root tra means 'protection' and so Tantra-s protect a person from various distresses.

159 The *Kulārṇava Tantra* discusses the four yuga-s and their corresponding śastra-s: Śruti-s for Satyuga, Smṛti-s for Tretā Yuga, Purāṇa-s for Dvāpara Yuga and Tantra-s for Kali Yuga. See *Synthesis of Yoga* by Kireet Joshi, 2011:304. Also see *The Great Liberation (Mahaānirvāṇa Tantra)* by Arthur Avalon, 1953:11.

160 See Kamalakar Mishra, 1999:5.

161 In India, there have been two divergent ways of life prevalent among people since the beginning of time. One is the way of worldly involvement (*pravṛtti*) followed by a householder (*gṛhasta*) and other is the way of renunciation (*nivṛtti*) followed by a sannyāṣī. The Tantra-s integrate these two ways by incorporating the merits

of both and lead a person from pravritti towards nivṛtti.

162 There are also Saura and Gāṇapatya Tantra-s, as well as Jain and Buddhist Tantra-s.

163 The third chapter of the text *Siddha-siddhānta paddhati* by Ācārya Gorakhnāth describes the presence of Brahmāṇḍa (universe) in the pinḍa (body) in an elaborate manner.

164 See Arthur Avalon, 1960:14.

165 There are two major schools of Tantra called *vāmācāra* (*kaulācāra*) and *dakṣiṇācāra*. The five *pañca-makāra*-s (i.e., *matsya, madya, māṁsa, mudra* and *maithuna*) of Tantra sādhana can be interpreted literally (*mukhya*) or symbolically (*gauṇa*). The literal interpretation (i.e., fish, alcohol, meat, gesture, and copulation) is followed in the vāmācāra (left-hand school), whereas symbolic or metaphorical interpretation (i.e., *Iḍa* and *Piñgaḻa nāḍi*-s, nector, control of speech, *satsanga* or good company and union between Kundalini Śakti with Śiva), is followed in the dakṣiṇācāra (right-hand school). Adherents of the vāmācāra school are not hedonists but believe in the dictum *viṣam viṣasya auṣadham* which means that poison is the remedy of poison. Sage Nārada tells Vyāsa that an object that causes a disease can also cure it if consumed in a prescribed manner (*Bhāgavata Purāṇa* 1.5.33). Unfulfilled or repressed desires which lie latent in the unconscious mind of a person can lead to aberrations in their behavior. Thus, adherents of vāmācāra school try to get rid of this poison in the form of desires by resorting to their natural satisfaction during sādhana which acts like a remedial poison. It should be noted that casual enjoyment of these pañca-makāra-s in everyday life is strictly prohibited even in the vāmācāra school and is considered a sin. See *Kulārṇava Tantra* 2.123. Also 2.124 which states that an ignorant person (paśu) should not even smell, see or touch wine.

The pañca-makāra sādhana in the vāmācāra school is always done under the guidance of a qualified guru. *Kulārṇava Tantra*, an authoritative work on pañca-makāra sādhana, expressly cautions everyone against the use of it as an excuse to indulge in unrestrained hedonism.

In vāmācāra sadhana, a woman is not regarded as an object of enjoyment but as a manifestation of Śakti. In his magnum opus, *Tantraloka,* Ācārya Abhinavagupta states that the Śakti of the whole cosmos (Kuṇḍalinī Śakti) resides in the human body in the form of Kāma Śakti (29.68). Therefore, vāmācāra school considers sex as an important channel for reaching Bhagavān Śiva. The dakṣiṇācāra school performs the same symbolically as the actual physical use of pañca-makāra-s is not absolutely essential.

166 The *Bhagavad Gītā*, Bhagavān Śrī Kṛṣṇa describes the various qualities of the three guṇa-s: sattva, rajas and tamas: sattvāt saṁjāyate jñānaṃ rajaso lobha eva ca pramādamohau tamaso bhavatojñānam eva ca (*Bhagavad Gītā* 14.17)

167 The *Bhagavad Gītā* (18.40) says that there is nothing in this mundane world which is not made up of the three guṇa-s.

168 Yāska in his *Nirukta* (VI.36) derives the word guṇa from the root *gaṇa* which means 'to count'. Thus, in Sanskrit grammar a, e and o are called 'guṇa -vowels'. Patañjali, in his vyākaraṇa text *Mahābhāṣya,* mentions different meanings of the word guṇa, including 'strand', 'secondary' or 'subordinate refinement and property of a thing'. See Kshitish Chandra Chatterji, 2003:19.

169 The six forms of state policy are: peace, war, observance of neutrality, marching, alliance and making peace with one and waging war against another.

170 Every ātmā has its store of accumulated good and bad karma-s from previous lives, called *sañcita karma,* waiting to be fructified. The purpose of garbhādhāna saṁskāra is to prepare for the entry of a suitable ātmā into the womb of a woman and realize the desire of a couple for begetting a child with a particular set of good qualities. In farming, before sowing begins, the field (*kṣetra*) has to be prepared at a proper time of the year by removing weeds, ploughing and the seed has to be purified to ensure a good crop. Similarly, garbhādhāna saṁskāra is done through the chanting of sacred hymns so that they ensure the birth of a good child.

171 In *Manusmṛti* 2.26 it is mentioned that the performance of saṁskāra-s sanctifies the body of a person and purifies him in the life beyond.

172 They came in this peculiar form because Rāvaṇa, in his arrogance,

regarded human beings and other living species in this mortal world as too weak to challenge his authority in any manner and he did not include them among the beings who could kill him when he asked for a boon from Brahma Deva.

173 Hanumān was a disciple of Sūrya Devatā and gained knowledge from him. In the *Hanumān Cālisā* section of the *Rama-Carita-Mānasa*, Hanumān is eulogized in the very beginning as jñāna guṇa sāgara which means 'an ocean of knowledge and auspicious qualities'. In the *Kiṣkindhā kāṇḍa* of Vālmiki *Ramāyāṇa*, on listening to Hanumān's eloquent speech in Sanskrit, Bhagavān Śri Rāma says that only a person learned in the Veda-s and Vyākaraṇa can speak in this fluent manner.

174 According to Hindu scriptures, Rāvaṇa had received a boon from Bhagavān Brahma that he could not be killed by any devatā. Rāvaṇa, in his arrogance, regarded human beings and other living species in this mortal world as too weak to challenge his authority in any manner. He, thus, did not include them in his request for a boon. The devatā-s took advantage of this and incarnated in the form of vānara-s to fight against him along with Bhagavān Śrī Rāma. Thus, according to Hindu scriptures, vānara-s were just the avatāra-s of various devatā-s who disappeared after completing the mission of eliminating Rāvaṇa.

175 In *Śrīmad-Bhāgavatam*, it is stated that among the devotees of Viṣṇu, Śiva is a great Vaiṣṇava. Thus, He appeared in the form of Hanumān to serve Bhagavān Śri Rāma.

176 Hanumān appears in the Vana Parva of the *Mahābhārata* and meets Bhīma. See: The *Mahābhārata* of Kṛṣṇa-Dvaipāyana Vyasa, Vol. 3 (Vana Parva), pp. 310-319.

177 Western sociologists like Max Weber and Robert MacIver consider civilization as concerned with human endeavors in the field of science and technology, whereas culture is concerned with human pursuits in the field of philosophy, arts and religion. Philosophy and religion here refer to Western philosophy and Christianity, respectively. Thus, there is no scope for culture to represent any Indian Hindu concept.

178 See Integral Unity v/s Synthetic Unity, *Being Different*.

179 One of the popular Āgama-s is the *Hayaśīrśa-pāñcarātra Āgama*. This text is called the *pratiṣṭātantra* (1.1.28) and gives us the process for construction and consecration of sacred images and the offering of worship to the Vigraha.

180 It is believed that the naked philosophers whom the Greek king Alexander met in India were none other than the Nāgā Sādhu-s. The Greeks called them Gymnosophists. See for reference pp. 1 of *A History of Dasnami Naga Sanyasis* by Jadunath Sarkar.

181 See pp. 154 of *A History of Dasnami Naga Sanyasis* by Jadunath Sarkar.

182 Śrī Vallabhācārya, of the Puśṭi Sampradāya or Śuddhādvaita school, calls them Tanujā seva, Manujā seva and Vittajā seva. Of the three, Manujā seva is the highest and the seva in its real form whereas the other two types of seva are resorted to in the preliminary stages to purify the mind.

183 This is the definition of seva provided by Śrī Vallabhācārya in the second śloka of his work, *Siddhānta Muktāvali*.

184 Etymologically, the word bhakti is derived from the root *bhaj* by affixing it with *ktin*. The root bhaj is employed here in the sense of seva and ktin is a pratyaya which further qualifies the nature of that seva with the sentiment or emotion of love. Bhakti essentially means *seva* offered to Bhagavān to express one's emotional love towards Him. There is a śloka cited by Jīva Gosvāmī in *Bhakti Sandarbha* (Anuccheda 216), in *Garuḍa Purāṇa* (227.3) which says

"Bhaj iti eṣa vai dhātu sevāyam prakirtitaḥ,
tasmāt sevā buddhaiḥ proktāh sarvo sādhanam bhūyasī" (Pūrva Khaṇḍa 231.3).

185 Guru is called *karṇa-dhāram* (*Śrīmad-Bhāgavatam* 11.20.17) which means that he/she is captain of the boat which successfully takes a person beyond the ocean of this material world.

186 In the *Śrīmad-Bhāgavatam* (11.17.27), Bhagavān explains that guru is *sarva devamaya* (the personification of all the devatā-s). In the *Bhagavad Gītā*, Bhagavān says that one should learn the ultimate truth by approaching a guru with reverence, serving him and then enquiring from him:

tad viddhi praṇipātena paripraśnena sevayā
upadekṣyanti te jñānaṁ jñāninas tattva-darśinaḥ (*Bhagavad Gītā* 4.34).

187 The importance of guru in the Hindu tradition can be appreciated from the fact that the last instruction given to a student after the completion of their education in the *gurukula* was *Mātṛ Devo Bhavaḥ, Pitṛ Devo Bhavaḥ, Atithi Devo Bhavaḥ, Guru Devo Bhavaḥ*. Thus, along with father and mother, the guru, too, is regarded as an embodiment of deva-s.

In the Hindu tradition, the *Gurustotram* is normally recited by a person before beginning any instruction to gain the blessings of one's guru. The third verse from the *Gurustotram* says that the guru dispels the darkness of ignorance by opening our eyes to the light of spiritual wisdom:

Ajñāna timirāndhasya jñānānjana śalākayā
cakṣur unmīlitaṁ yena tasmai śrī-guruve namaḥ

188 Another example of such unflinching faith and devotion to one's guru can be found in the Śrī Vaiṣṇava Sampradāya. Madhurakavi Āḻvār is among the twelve Āḻvār-s but he did not directly worship Bhagavān but surrendered to his guru, or Ācārya Nammāḻvār , who is also among the twelve Āḻvār-s. Madhurakavi Āḻvār's bhakti was directed towards his guru Nammāḻvār and he composed a hymn called *Kanninun Siruthāmbu* in praise of him. *Kanninun Siruthāmbu* is a part of 4000 hymns of *Divya Prabandham* which are the foundation of the Śrī Vaiṣṇava or Viśiṣṭādvaita Sampradāya. In this hymn, Madhurakavi Āḻvār says in the second Pāsuram or śloka that he is totally surrendered to Nammāḻvār's golden feet and that he knows of no other God than Nammāḻvār who is filled with all the auspicious qualities.

189 Bhagavān Śrī Kṛṣṇa says that those who are sāttvika have their śraddhā in the devatā-s, those who are rājasika have it directed towards yakṣa-s and rākṣasa-s, while those who are tāmasika have their śraddhā for bhūta-s and preta-s:

yajante sāttvikā devān yakṣarakṣāṁsi rājasāḥ
pretān bhūtagaṇāñś cānye yajante tāmasā janāḥ (*Bhagavad Gītā* 17.4)

190 See *Chāndogya Upaniṣad* (7.19.1, 1.1.10), Rig Veda (9.113.2).

191 See *Chāndogya Upaniṣad* 1.1.5, which says that Rik is the speech and Sāma is the prāṇa.

192 See Purusottama Bilimoria 2007:196.

193 See Bhāmaha in his text *Kāvyālaṅkāra* 1.9.

194 Rājaśekhara, in his work *Kavyamīmāṁsa*, is of the opinion that śāstra-s are not only connected with kāvya but even form its basis. He says that a person who believes that the two are unconnected is like a fool who wants to have the knowledge of things lying in darkness without lighting a lamp. See Pandit Kedarnath Sharma, 1965:6.

In the eighth chapter of *Kavyamīmāṁsa*, Rājaśekhara mentions the sources of themes of a kāvya. The sixteen sources listed by him are Śruti-s, Smṛti-s, Itihasa-s, Purāṇa-s, *Pramāṇa-vidya* (science of logic, interpretation and valid knowledge), *samayavidya* (systems of philosophy), *Arthaśāstra* and *Nāṭyaśāstra*. See Pandit Kedarnath Sharma, 1965:87-9. Rājaśekhara regards Śruti-s as equivalent to the divine cow which is milked to the capacity of their intelligence by a seer, philosopher and kavi.

195 See, for example, *Kāvyādarśa* 1.10 and *Vṛtti* on Ācārya Ānandavardhana's *Dhvanyāloka* 1.1 which says 'Śabdārtha Śarīram Tāvatkāvyam'. See Dr. Ramsagar Tripathi, 1987:30, for the second reference.

196 See *Kāvya-prakāśa* 1-2 of Ācārya Mammaṭa; English translation by A.B. Gajendragadkar, 1959:2.

197 See Krishna Chaitanya, 1965:276.

198 See Rewaprasad Dwivedi. 1936:95-97.

199 See *Nāṭyaśāstra* chapter 1 sloka-s 109 to 115 and *Kāvyādarśa* 1.3b 'vācāmeva prasādena lokayātrā pravartate'.

200 Krīḍanīyakamicchhāmo dṛśyaṁ śravyaṁ ca yadbhavet (*Nāṭyaśāstra* 1.11).

201 dharmāviruddho bhūteṣu kāmo asmi bharatarṣabha (*Bhagavad Gītā* 7.11)

202 Wendy Doniger translates kāma as 'erotic heat' and 'lust' at several places, including the Index. See Chapters 7 and 8 of her book, *The Hindus: An Alternative History*.

203 For a counter view from the tradition, see *Ujjvala-nīlamaṇi* of Śrī Rūpa Gosvāmī 3.26 and 3.27 (English translation by HH Bhanu

Swami, 2014:126-127). Also see Potter, 2015:34.

204 See *Nāṭyaśāstra* 7.1-3

205 The first bhāva is *śānta-bhāva* found among the jñāna yogī-s and it is characterized by detachment and indifference towards everything in this material world. The second bhāva is that of being a dāsa of Bhagavān and is called *dāsya-bhāva*. This is exemplified by the behavior of Hanumān towards Bhagavān Śrī Rāma. The third is *sakhya-bhāva* shown by the cowherd friends and Arjuna towards Bhagavān Śrī Kṛṣṇa. The fourth is the *vātsalya-bhāva,* manifested in the parental feelings of Yaśodā and Nanda Mahārāja for Bhagavān Śrī Kṛṣṇa. Finally, there is the *madhura-bhāva,* which has two expressions in the form of a wife and a lover. The first expression of madhura-bhāva is displayed by Devi Rukmiṇī for Bhagavān Śrī Kṛṣṇa and second by the gopī-s.

206 Bharata Muni in his *Nāṭyaśāstra* provides the following definition for the origin of rasa: vibhāva-anubhāva-vyabhicāri-saṁyogādrasaniṣpattiḥ (*Nāṭyaśāstra* 6.32).

207 The eight sthāyi bhāva-s mentioned by Bharata Muni are: rati (love), hasaḥ (mirth), śokaḥ (sorrow), kṛodaḥ (anger), utsāḥ (excitement), bhayam (fear), jugupsā (disgust) and vismayaḥ (wonder). It is not said that the sthāyi bhāva-s are restricted to these eight only.

208 See K.C. Pandey, 1950:7.

209 See the sloka 2.7.1 of the *Taittirīya Upaniṣad*: "Raso vai saḥ Rasaṁ hi evāyaṁ labdhvānandī bhavati".

210 According to *Śrīmad-Bhāgavatam* there are ten kinds of līlā: sarga, visarga, sthāna, pośaṇa, uti, manvantara, īśānukathā, nirodha, mukti and āśraya.

211 bhajate tādṛśīḥ krīḍa yāḥ śrutvā tat-paro bhavet (*Śrīmad-Bhāgavatam* 10.33.36)

212 īśvaraḥ paramaḥ Kṛṣṇaḥ, saccidānanda vigrahaḥ (*Brahmasaṃhitā* 5.1)

213 In *Taittirīya Upaniṣad* there is an entire section called *Ānandavalli* which deals with the gradation in ānanda experienced by different beings of this universe such as the ānanda of gandharva-s, pitṛ-s, devata-s up to Brahmā by increasing the ānanda one hundred times at each higher level (see 2.8.1 in *Taittirīya Upaniṣad*). Beyond all

these different kinds of ānanda is Brahmānanda which the Upaniṣad says is inexpressible in words [*yato vāco nivartante aprāpye manasā saha* (*Taittirīya Upaniṣad,* Brahmānanda Valli, 2.4.1)]. Beyond even Brahmānanda is Bhaktyānanda which *Taittirīya Upaniṣad* describes in a verse where Bhagavān is called Rasa tattva and a bhakta who realizes or attains Bhagavān experiences bhaktyānanda [*Raso vai saḥ. Rasaṁhyevāyaṁlabdhvānandi bhavati.* (*Taittirīya Upaṇiṣad, Brahmānanda Valli,* 2.7.1)].

Index